# School Choice: Separating Fact from Fiction



School choice is a hot topic in the United States. Private school vouchers, public charter schools, open enrollment, and homeschooling all regularly appear on the policy agenda as ways to improve the educational experience and outcomes for students, parents, and the broader society. Pundits often make claims about the various ways in which parents select schools and thus customize their child's education. What claims about school choice are grounded in actual evidence?

This book presents systematic reviews of the social science research regarding critical aspects of parental school choice. How do parents choose schools and what do they seek? What effects do their choices have on the racial integration of schools and the performance of the schools that serve non-choosing students? What features of public charter schools are related to higher student test scores? What effects does school choice have on important non-cognitive outcomes including parent satisfaction, student character traits, and how far students go in school? What do we know about homeschooling as a school choice?

This book, originally published as a special issue of the *Journal of School Choice*, provides evidence-based answers to those vital questions.

**Patrick J. Wolf** is Distinguished Professor of Education Policy and 21st Century Endowed Chair in School Choice in the Department of Education Reform, University of Arkansas College of Education and Health Professions.

# School Choice: Separating Fact from Fiction

*Edited by*
**Patrick J. Wolf**

Routledge
Taylor & Francis Group
LONDON AND NEW YORK

First published 2019
by Routledge
2 Park Square, Milton Park, Abingdon, Oxon, OX14 4RN, UK

and by Routledge
52 Vanderbilt Avenue, New York, NY 10017, USA

First issued in paperback 2020

*Routledge is an imprint of the Taylor & Francis Group, an informa business*



*British Library Cataloguing in Publication Data*
A catalogue record for this book is available from the British Library

ISBN 13: 978-0-367-58329-3 (pbk)
ISBN 13: 978-0-367-03095-7 (hbk)

Typeset in Minion Pro
by RefineCatch Limited, Bungay, Suffolk

**Publisher's Note**
The publisher accepts responsibility for any inconsistencies that may have arisen during the conversion of this book from journal articles to book chapters, namely the possible inclusion of journal terminology.

**Disclaimer**
Every effort has been made to contact copyright holders for their permission to reprint material in this book. The publishers would be grateful to hear from any copyright holder who is not here acknowledged and will undertake to rectify any errors or omissions in future editions of this book.

# Contents

# Citation Information

The chapters in this book were originally published in the *Journal of School Choice*, volume 11, issue 4 (December 2017). When citing this material, please use the original page numbering for each article, as follows:

**Introduction**
*Introduction to the Special Issue—School choice: Separating fact from fiction*
Patrick J. Wolf
*Journal of School Choice*, volume 11, issue 4 (December 2017), pp. 487–490

**Chapter 1**
*How do parents choose schools, and what schools do they choose? A literature review of private school choice programs in the United States*
Heidi Holmes Erickson
*Journal of School Choice*, volume 11, issue 4 (December 2017), pp. 491–506

**Chapter 2**
*Can we have it all? A review of the impacts of school choice on racial integration*
Elise Swanson
*Journal of School Choice*, volume 11, issue 4 (December 2017), pp. 507–526

**Chapter 3**
*Evidence on charter school practices related to student enrollment and retention*
Kaitlin P. Anderson
*Journal of School Choice*, volume 11, issue 4 (December 2017), pp. 527–545

**Chapter 4**
*Do self-interested schooling selections improve society? A review of the evidence*
Corey A. DeAngelis
*Journal of School Choice*, volume 11, issue 4 (December 2017), pp. 546–558

**Chapter 5**
*What's the secret ingredient? Searching for policies and practices that make charter schools successful*
Philip M. Gleason
*Journal of School Choice*, volume 11, issue 4 (December 2017), pp. 559–584

**Chapter 6**

*A review of the research on parent satisfaction in private school choice programs*
Evan Rhinesmith
*Journal of School Choice*, volume 11, issue 4 (December 2017), pp. 585–603

**Chapter 7**

*A systematic review of the empirical research on selected aspects of homeschooling as a school choice*
Brian D. Ray
*Journal of School Choice*, volume 11, issue 4 (December 2017), pp. 604–621

**Chapter 8**

*Can I choose to have grit? Non-cognitive skills, behavior, and school choice*
Malachi Nichols
*Journal of School Choice*, volume 11, issue 4 (December 2017), pp. 622–641

**Chapter 9**

*Educational attainment effects of public and private school choice*
Leesa M. Foreman
*Journal of School Choice*, volume 11, issue 4 (December 2017), pp. 642–654

# Notes on Contributors

**Kaitlin P. Anderson** is a Postdoctoral Research Associate at Michigan State University, whose research interests include school choice, teacher labour markets, and student discipline, all with a focus on improving access to high quality educational opportunities for all students regardless of socioeconomic background, with an emphasis on educational policy in Arkansas. Her work has been published in peer-reviewed journals, and she has contributed to policy briefs and reports providing timely, relevant research to Arkansas policymakers. Dr. Anderson has presented her findings to the Arkansas State Board of Education and other state educational organizations, making an impact on education policy in Arkansas.

**Corey A. DeAngelis** is a Policy Analyst for the Center for Educational Freedom, Cato Institute, Washington D.C, and received his Ph.D. in Education Policy from the University of Arkansas. His research interests include school choice and school choice law. He has presented papers to the Annual Meeting of the Southern Political Science Association and the Association for Public Policy Analysis and Management, and has received grants from the Foundation for Economic Education and the Arkansas Center for Research in Economics.

**Heidi Holmes Erickson** graduated from Brigham Young University, UT, with a B.A. in Political Science. During school she worked for an education policy reform group focusing on private school vouchers and charter schools in Utah. Following school, she worked as a research analyst and lobbyist for a non-profit tax policy group in Salt Lake City, UT. She is now a Ph.D. student and research assistant in the Department of Education Reform at the University of Arkansas.

**Leesa M. Foreman** is a doctoral candidate and Distinguished Doctoral Fellow in the Department of Education Reform, and a Research Assistant in the Office for Education Policy at the University of Arkansas. With over 15 years of classroom experience in grades 1–12 in both the general and special education settings in private, public, and public charter schools, she also has experience as an administrator and curriculum coach. Leesa served as Secretary on a charter school governing board and as Chairperson/President of a charter school foundation board. She has presented at several national conferences and some of her research interests include school choice, teacher preparation, and teacher quality.

**Philip M. Gleason** is an expert in evaluation design with extensive experience directing studies of education initiatives and federal nutrition programs. He currently directs a study for the Institute of Education Sciences at the U.S. Department of Education that examines a school reform effort centred on implementing data-driven instruction to improve teacher effectiveness. Other recent work includes a large-scale evaluation of Knowledge Is Power Program (KIPP) schools that examined the impacts of KIPP elementary, middle, and high schools and tracked the performance of the charter school network over time, and a study that examined the distribution of highly effective teachers in school districts around the country.

**Malachi Nichols** is a Ph.D. student and a Research Assistant in the Department of Education Reform at the University of Arkansas. He graduated with a B.S. in Mechanical Engineering and a minor in African and African-American Studies from the University of Arkansas in 2015. During his time as an undergraduate, he served in various positions, including Robotics Teacher and a Director's Assistant to an AmeriCorps Service Member at Prism Education Center in Fayetteville, AR., which fuelled his interest and desire for education reform. His research interests include higher education, values-based education, and non-cognitive skills.

**Brian D. Ray** was awarded his Ph.D. in Science Education from Oregon State University, his M.S. in Zoology from Ohio University, and his B.S. in Biology from the University of Puget Sound, Washington. Dr. Ray has been a middle school and high school classroom teacher in both public and private schools, an undergraduate college professor, and a university professor at the graduate level. He is a leading international expert regarding home schooling and home education research. Dr. Ray executes and publishes research, speaks to the public, testifies before legislators, and serves as an expert witness in courts and legislatures.

**Evan Rhinesmith** is a Postdoctoral Fellow at Saint Louis University, MO. He earned his Ph.D. in Education Policy from the University of Arkansas, where he analyzed parent satisfaction in school choice settings and higher education policy. Evan's dissertation was the first evaluation of Arkansas' mandatory postsecondary remediation policy and the impacts on students at all thirty-two of the state's public colleges and universities. Prior to his doctoral studies, Evan taught 3rd and 4th grade at Sacred Heart School in Washington, DC and as a Teaching Fellow in the Alliance for Catholic Education at the University of Notre Dame, Indiana.

**Elise Swanson** is a Distinguished Doctoral Fellow in the Department of Education Reform and a Research Assistant in the Office for Education Policy at the University of Arkansas. Elise graduated from the University of Wisconsin with a B.A. in Political Science and English Language and Linguistics in 2013. For two years after graduation, Elise taught 11th grade English and AP Language and Composition in Pine Bluff, AR through Teach for America. While there, Elise also served as Department Chair and trained incoming Teach for America teachers in the Mississippi Delta. Her research focuses on educational equity, including racial and socioeconomic integration in schools, teacher quality in disadvantaged districts, and improving college access for first-generation students.

**Patrick J. Wolf** is Distinguished Professor of Education Policy and 21st Century Endowed Chair in School Choice in the Department of Education Reform at the University of Arkansas College of Education and Health Professions. He previously taught at Columbia University, NY, and Georgetown University, WA. As principal investigator of the School Choice Demonstration Project, he has led or is leading major studies of school choice initiatives including longitudinal evaluations of school voucher programs in Washington, DC; Milwaukee, WI; and the state of Louisiana. He has authored, co-authored, or co-edited four books and over 150 journal articles, book chapters, and policy reports on school choice, civic values, special education, public management, and campaign finance.

INTRODUCTION

# School choice: Separating fact from fiction

Patrick J. Wolf

Parental school choice is a hot topic. This development likely comes as no surprise to readers of the *Journal of School Choice* but it has caught many journalists, pundits, and policymakers off guard and poorly informed about what school choice is and does. Lacking a solid grounding in the research literature and facts about choice, school choice dilettantes are vulnerable to mistaken claims and misleading observations.

This project germinated with a graduate seminar at the University of Arkansas on the entire research field of school choice. My advanced doctoral students and I found there was much to discuss and debate yet few evidence-based reviews of certain key aspects of parental school choice. We also noticed that our classroom discussions, grounded in the research literature on choice, were decidedly different from the choice debates occurring in the public square, which were untethered from research at best, unhinged at worst.

I decided to remedy that situation by requiring that my students write systematic reviews as seminar papers. My only rule was that the papers could not be summaries of the test score effects of school vouchers or charter schools, since thorough compilations of the evidence regarding those questions already exist (e.g., Betts & Tang, 2014; Egalite & Wolf, 2016; Shakeel, Anderson, & Wolf, 2016).

The quality and originality of the papers led me to propose this special issue. To avoid insularity, I reached out to school choice researchers outside of the University of Arkansas to submit manuscripts on important topics not covered by the seminar papers or to serve as scientific peer-reviewers of the manuscripts. The peer-review process identified a cohesive set of nine high-quality articles to publish in this special issue.

These reviews are not intended to teach the reader everything there is to know about the burgeoning field of school choice. My graduate seminar on choice assigned 109 different readings and even that expansive set required some painful cuts. For an encyclopedic review of the field of school choice, I recommend *The Wiley Handbook of School Choice* (Fox & Buchanan, 2017). I am confident, however, that even school choice experts will learn from reading these brief, up-to-date review essays. I know that I did.

The article order is linked to the logic of parental school choice. The first piece, by Heidi Holmes Erickson, examines how parents choose schools and what school features are important to them, focusing on private school choice. Erickson finds that parents consistently say that academic considerations influence their choice of schools, though academics often are not the single most important aspect of a school for them. Test scores do not regularly define the academic quality of a school for parents, she reports.

The second article, by Elise Swanson, scrutinizes the evidence surrounding the effects of public and private school choice programs on school-level racial integration. The claim that school choice segregates has been central to the current policy debate regarding vouchers and charters. Swanson demonstrates the fallacy of sweeping claims that expanded choice necessarily worsens or improves the integration of U.S. schools. The effect of choice on integration depends crucially on the kind of choice program, key elements of its design, and the context in which it takes place as well as the definition of integration used in the study.

Kaitlin P. Anderson provides a natural extension to the Swanson article by examining the extent to which school choice enrollments appear to be influenced by student ability in ways that suggest school "cream-skimming" or selective "push-out." Although the charter sector as a whole educates slightly lower proportions of students with disabilities and English learners than traditional public schools, the rates differ substantially within the sector, with some charter schools serving students with special needs exclusively. Anderson points out that no studies to date have determined if lower enrollments of students with special needs in charter schools is because of actual cream-skimming or due to a strong "attraction-bias" of such students to the extensive special programs in traditional public schools. Once enrolled in charter schools, there is no evidence that students with special needs are systematically pushed out of their schools of choice.

The effects of school choice on civic values is another topic central to the current choice debate. Corey A. DeAngelis examines the results from 11 statistical studies of how attending a private school through a choice program affects student political tolerance, civic engagement, and social order. He finds that, in all cases, private school choice has either a positive effect on civic outcomes or no clear effect. He reports no findings of private school choice harming civic outcomes.

Phillip M. Gleason provides a much-needed systematic review of the empirical evidence regarding charter school best practices. Gleason reports that an urban location, extended learning time, consistent behavioral policies, and an achievement mission are the charter school features most consistently associated with higher student test scores. Characteristics of charter schools with no evidence yet supporting their test-score efficacy include class size, school size, teacher qualifications, status as a networked or independent school, and school age.

The effects of private school choice on parent satisfaction with schools are summarized by Evan Rhinesmith. Experimental evaluations of this question, which rely on scholarship lotteries, are guaranteed to be free from self-selection bias but could suffer from other biases because private school lottery winners know that they won and families that lost the lottery might feel "sour grapes" from the loss that affect their subsequent evaluations of schools. Conversely, observational studies that compare private school choosers with public school choosers are not vulnerable to the "sour grapes" threat but could be biased by self-selection. Fortunately, the results of the research are remarkably consistent, regardless of methodology. Allowing parents to choose a private school for their child increases parent satisfaction with schools.

Brian D. Ray provides the first systematic review of the peer-reviewed scientific literature addressing several crucial questions surrounding homeschooling. Ray reports that homeschooled children generally reflect the diversity of the school-age population regarding race, ethnicity, and income. The most distinctive feature of most homeschooled families is married parents. Empirical studies indicate that homeschooling has a positive effect on a variety of outcomes including educational achievement, educational attainment, and social development.

Malachi Nichols examines the effect of various forms of public and private school choice on noncognitive attitudes, such as grit and conscientiousness, and behaviors, such as school attendance and crime. He reports many null effects from the research base but concludes that the findings tilt negative regarding noncognitive attitudes but positive regarding noncognitive behaviors. Students in schools of choice may be holding themselves to higher standards than their comparison group peers when self-reporting their noncognitive attitudes, a phenomenon known as "reference group bias."

Leesa M. Foreman concludes the set of articles with a review of the attainment effects of public and private school choice. Foreman finds that both forms of school choice tend to increase the likelihood of students graduating from high school and enrolling and persisting in college but cautions that generalizing from only 13 studies of these effects would be premature.

Please dive into these articles. They provide a cornucopia of evidence regarding what happens to students, families, schools, and communities when parents have more educational choices.

## References

Betts, J. R., & Tang, Y. E. (2014). *A meta-analysis of the literature on the effect of charter schools on student achievement.* Bothell, WA: Center on Reinventing Public Education. Retrieved from http://www.crpe.org/sites/default/files/CRPE_meta-analysis_charter-schools-effect-student-achievement_workingpaper.pdf

Egalite, A. J., & Wolf, P. J. (2016). A review of the empirical research on private school choice. *Peabody Journal of Education, 91*(4), 441–454. doi:10.1080/0161956X.2016.1207436

Fox, R. A., & Buchanan, N. K. (Eds.). (2017). *School choice: A handbook for researchers, practitioners, policy-makers and journalists.* West Sussex, UK: John Wiley & Sons.

Shakeel, M. D., Anderson, K. P., & Wolf, P. J. (2016). *The participant effects of private school vouchers across the globe: A meta-analytic and systematic review* (Working Paper 2016-07). Economics Research Network, Department of Education Reform, College of Education and Health Professions, University of Arkansas, Fayetteville, AR. Retrieved from https://papers.ssrn.com/sol3/papers.cfm?abstract_id=2777633

# How do parents choose schools, and what schools do they choose? A literature review of private school choice programs in the United States

Heidi Holmes Erickson

**ABSTRACT**

I review the literature on how parents select schools when participating in private choice programs in the United States. I address two sub-questions. First, do parents have the incentives and motivation needed to participate in a schooling market? Second, when selecting a school, what school characteristics do parents consider? I find three general patterns in the literature: (1) There is great consistency in parents' stated preferences of school characteristics across choice programs; (2) Parents value academic quality, but it is not always their most prized school feature; (3) Parents make trade-offs among their preferences when selecting a school.

School choice programs are expanding in scope and size throughout the United States. The majority of private school choice programs are limited to low-income families or families who have children with disabilities. As of 2016, just under 400,000 students were using a private school choice option in 59 programs; whereas, in 2000, 10 years after the Milwaukee Parental Choice Program (MPCP) was passed in 1990, less than 50,000 students were participating in just 10 programs (Friedman Foundation for Educational Choice, 2016). Private school choice programs include vouchers, which provide a set amount of money for families to attend a private school of their choice; tax credit scholarships, which allow taxpayers to donate tax-free money to nonprofit organizations that offer scholarships for private schools; and, educational savings accounts, which provide parents an account with a set amount of money for purchasing a wide variety of educational services including private school tuition, tutoring services, and even later college expenses. Voucher and tax credit scholarships are the most common private school choice programs.

Many questions regarding school choice focus on whether parents are rational decision-makers and select quality schools. There is particular concern that disadvantaged parents have a difficult time selecting schools given resource constraints. School choice theory assumes that parents are rational actors that can gather and consume information to find a school that matches their child's needs. Parents' desires and ability to choose quality schools is crucial for school choice to be effective. If parents neither wish to nor have the incentives to choose, then school choice holds little to no legitimacy as an effective alternative to traditional public schooling. Questions also surround what information parents use and what school characteristics they consider when choosing a school. The answers to these questions are informative in two ways. One, they shed light on what parents want from schools, and two, they provide insight into whether parents are rational decision-makers and select quality schools.

I review the literature on how parents select schools within school choice systems, specifically focusing on private school choice. I address two subquestions. First, do parents have the incentives and motivation needed to participate in a schooling market? For this question I focus on parents' desire and ability to engage in the school choice process, specifically examining how parents gather information and make decisions, based on the relevant theoretical and empirical literature. Second, when selecting a school, what school characteristics do parents consider? Here I focus on research that evaluates parents' experience with actual private choice programs to understand what they value and the type of schools they choose. I find three primary patterns in the literature. First, parents report similar and consistent school preferences across many choice programs. Second, depending on their circumstances, parents vary in how much they consider a school's academic quality when selecting a school. Third, parents make trade-offs among their preferences when selecting schools.

The article proceeds as follows. First, I describe my search strategy. Then, I address parents' motivation and incentives to choose schools. Third, I present the literature on what school characteristics parents consider when shopping for a school. Finally, I discuss broadly how the literature can be applied to school choice policy as well as gaps in the literature.

## Search criteria

I focus this review on parents' experiences with private school choice. Questions of how parents select schools are more salient in private school choice than other choice programs because private schools do not fall under the traditional public school institutions. Private schools, while subject to regulations that vary across choice programs, are not governed by a public bureaucracy and have less requirements regarding curriculum and performance measures than public schools. The public school system, including open enrollment districts and charter schools, have formal institutions and mechanism that help parents make decisions. If parents are able to successfully navigate private school choice, then they are surely equipped to handle other forms of choice. While focusing on private school choice, I included literature that covered a combination of private, charter, and open enrollment public school choice. I excluded works that focused only on forms of public school choice without reference to private school choice.[1] I prioritized recent literature that focused on parents' actual experience with specific private choice programs, but I included literature dating back from the early theoretical discussions of school choice in the 1960s to works published in 2016.

I conducted a combined network and computer search.[2] I started with a couple recent (Kelly & Scafidi, 2013; Lincove, Cowen, & Imbrogno, 2016) and classic (Friedman, 2002; Moe, 1995) studies, searched their sources, and continued to snowball until there was overlap of similar sources continually cited. I gave additional attention to sources that focused on specific private choice programs because they provided the most detailed information on parents' school preferences. I also searched online databases for any additional sources that were not included in my network search. I included peer-reviewed journal articles, published books, and organizational reports.

I included two general types of literature. First, I incorporated theoretical literature on parental participation in school choice; specifically, how parents function as consumers in the market. Second, I included empirical literature on how parents who have participated in specific school choice programs gathered information and what information they valued when selecting a school. I included both rigorous qualitative and quantitative research. Most studies were descriptive in nature and used data primarily from parent surveys, focus groups, and school applications. Experiments and other rigorous econometric methods designed to understand causality are rare in this literature given that the topic is descriptive. The most common reason for excluding sources was that they addressed parents' experiences with public school choice but not with private. Other sources were excluded because they focused on the type of families that participate in choice or parent satisfaction. This literature review is not intended to be a comprehensive review of all theoretical and empirical research on how parents choose schools, but to provide readers with an analysis of some of the most recent and prominent literature in the field. Table 1 is a list of specific private choice programs and studies that evaluated parents' participation in the given programs. This is not a comprehensive list of all studies included in the review, but it provides specific program details that are relevant when discussing the literature.

## Question 1: Do parents have the incentives and motivation needed to participate in a schooling market?

School choice as a reform developed in the hope that by giving parents options, schools would compete and education for all students would improve. Accordingly, school choice requires effort from parents; it assumes that parents are rational actors, have preferences, influence local schools (Fuller, Elmore, & Orfield, 1996), and make trade-offs among their preferences (Schneider, Teske, &

**Table 1.** School choice program details and respective studies.

| Program | School choice type | Program requirements | Citations | Data | Other program information |
|---|---|---|---|---|---|
| D.C. Opportunity Scholarship Program (D. C. OSP) | Private school voucher | Family incomes 185% of the poverty line | Stewart and Wolf (2014); Kisida and Wolf (2010); Stewart et al. (2009); Teske et al. (2007)** | Focus group, surveys | Program operated by Washington Scholarship Fund (WSF) |
| Signature Scholarship Program (SSP) | Private school voucher | Family income at or below 270% poverty | Trivitt and Wolf (2011) | Survey, enrollment data | Predates the D.C. Opportunity Scholarship and since 2004, the SSP serves families that do not receive the D.C. OSP |
| Milwaukee Parental Choice Program | Private school voucher | Family incomes 300% of the poverty line* | Stewart et al. (2010); Teske et al. (2007)** | Focus group | |
| Georgia's Education Expense Credit: GOAL Scholarship Program | Tax-credit scholarship | GOAL voluntarily created guidelines on household income; average household income around $52,000 | Kelly and Scafidi (2013) | Survey | Georgia's Educational Expense Credit Program allows people to donate to Student Scholarship Organizations (SSO) which awards scholarships to attend a private school. GOAL is the largest of the 36 SSOs |
| Indiana's Choice Scholarship Program and School Scholarship Tax Credit | Private school voucher and tax-credit scholarship | Voucher requirements: family incomes up to 150% of the federal FRL rate<br>Tax-credit requirements: family income up to 200% federal FRL rate | Catt and Rhinesmith (2016) | Survey | Voucher amount it determined by family income: families that qualify for FRL receive 90% of state per-student spending, families at 150% FRL receive up to 50% of state funding |
| New Orleans School District | Portfolio model: traditional public choice, charters, and private school voucher | Voucher requirements: family incomes 250% of the federal poverty line and students in a "C" or lower school | Lincove et al. (2016); Harris & Larsen (2015) | OneApp Applications | New Orleans has a complete choice district. Students must select a traditional public or charter school. Students who qualify for the voucher can select a private school |

All program details were taken from respective paper. This table is not a comprehensive list of all literature included in the review. Works covering theoretical discussions on school choice were not included. Studies that covered specific locations but not specific choice programs, such as Wolf and Stewart's (2012) study on Detroit parents, and studies that focused on national samples of choice families, such as Zeehandelaar and Winkler (2013), were not included in this table. Descriptions of these studies are included in the body of the article.

*Information taken from Friedman Foundation (2016) because it was not included in referenced paper.

**Teske et al. (2007) interviewed parents in Washington, D.C., Milwaukee, WI, and Denver, CO. They did not focus on one program specifically, but included parents who participated in private school choice.

Marschall, 2000). School choice theory also assumes that parents know their children and have greater interest in their well-being than anyone else (Friedman, 2002; Walberg, 2007). Milton Friedman, largely credited with the idea of private school vouchers, asserts that given the freedom to choose, parents would operate in a market of schools and even low-income parents would choose schools that fit their children's needs (Friedman, 2002; Friedman & Friedman, 1980). Parents would navigate a schooling market in similar ways that they navigate other complicated and expensive markets such as houses, doctors and hospital, and automobiles. Information is essential for markets to work well and imperfect and asymmetric information is likely to exist in schooling markets; however, perfect information is the exception more than the rule in markets (Bast & Walberg, 2004). For a robust schooling market, all parents do not have to be fully informed. A group of marginal consumers or "market mavens" who are well informed can help create a competitive market from which all consumers benefit (Buckley & Schneider, 2003; Schneider et al., 2000). Commenting on parents' ability to choose, Rose and Milton Friedman (1980, 160) said: "No doubt, some parents lack interest in their children's schooling or the capacity and desire to choose wisely. However, they are in a small minority. In any event, our present system unfortunately does little to help their children."

Critics of school choice disagree on the assumptions made about parent's incentives and abilities to participate in a market for schooling. One main critique is that choice theory assumes too much of parents; it "assumes that all parents are fully informed of their choices and fully capable of acting in their child's best interests" (Saltman, 2000, 24) and believe few parents gather the needed information. There is specific concern that low-income parents would be particularly disadvantaged in gathering information and selecting a school for their children (Berliner & Biddle, 1995; Carnegie Foundation for the Advancement of Teaching, 1992; Moe, 1995; Schneider et al., 2000). Due to resource constraints or a lack of desire, low-income parents would select schools based primarily on convenience instead of educational quality. School choice could then widen gaps between middle- and low-income families as middle- and high-income parents use school choice more fully (Berliner & Biddle, 1995).

Another critique is that society would be harmed from school choice because parents' incentives are not aligned with their children's or society's needs. Public education is a democratic institution designed to teach students civic values and introduce children to a diversity of thought. In a school choice system, parents are able to select their own vision of the "good life" without consideration of societal goals. This could lead to a loss of diverse and educationally sound public schools and democratic values (Gutmann, 2003).

There is a large empirical literature on how parents actually operate in the market given that school choice programs are expanding and more families are participating. However, it can be difficult to empirically answer this question because it requires defining what quality is and determining what information is important for parents to have. Defining a quality school is immensely difficult and highly debated in school choice. School choice is designed to facilitate a better school match for students' unique needs, so what might be a quality school for some families will not be for others. Some school choice researchers equate school test scores with school quality (e.g., Gross & Denice, 2017). While this should be part of a school's overall quality, it would be inappropriate to assume that parents who choose a lower performing academic school or consider safety or religious instruction in their choice are incapable of identifying quality. In this article, I do not use a specific definition of quality but focus on what information parents use and how they gather it. There are a couple ways researchers empirically evaluate parents' ability and involvement in selecting schools. One, they ask parents' information about specific schools in their choice set and assess the accuracy of the information parents have. This approach demonstrates if parents are gathering correct information about the schools they select. This method, however, does not capture what parents actually value; it only tells us if parents gather and recall the specific information asked. Two, researchers interview parents to see how parents actually accumulate information. This approach provides insight into how active parents are in gathering information about schools.

Research that looked at what information parents gather has found that most parents who participate in choice have better information about the school they selected than other parents who did not participate. Kisida and Wolf (2010) tested whether or not choice parents had greater incentives to gather school information than nonchoice parents. Using experimental data from the Washington Scholarship Fund (WSF), they found that parents of students who were offered a voucher were 12% more likely to have reported accurate information on school and class sizes than parents of students who were not offered a voucher.

In several studies, parents expressed a desire to and confidence in their ability to select schools and gather useful information (Kelly & Scafidi, 2013; Stewart, Wolf, Cornman, McKenzie-Thompson, & Butcher, 2009; Teske, Fitzpatrick, & Kaplan, 2007; Wolf & Stewart, 2012). In Detroit, 71% of parents reported having shopped for an alternative to their assigned school (Wolf & Stewart, 2012). When shopping for a new school, parents said that they relied most heavily on information from other parents and second on information from school fairs. While Detroit did not have a private school choice program, many of the parents who had shopped or expressed interest in shopping for a school reported that they did or would consider private schools.

Research that has interviewed parents on how they gathered information had similar findings. Choice parents accumulated school information from a variety of sources. The most common sources were information fairs or packets provided by the program provider, school visits, and social networks (Kelly & Scafidi, 2013; Stewart et al, 2009; Teske et al., 2007). Parents participating in the D.C. Opportunity Scholarship Program reported primarily using information provided by the program administrator and school visits. As the program progressed, parents said that school visits were the best source of information (Stewart et al., 2009). This was a common pattern in other programs as well; parents consistently said that school visits were increasingly important (Teske et al., 2007).

While most parents in various programs expressed a generally willingness to select schools and gather information, two studies showed differences in how much information lower and higher income parents gathered. Kelly and Scafidi (2013) found that Georgia parents who participated in Georgia's GOAL Scholarship Program were willing to take multiple steps to gather information about private schools and were confident in their ability to get the information needed. Ninety-three percent of parents said they asked for a school tour, and 78% of parents said they asked neighbors, friends, relatives, and other parents for information. High-income, college educated, married, white parents took an average of 5.3 steps to gain information, whereas low-income parents took 4.8 steps. Teske et al. (2007) interviewed 800 moderate-to-low income parents ($50,000 or less in income) in Washington, D.C., Milwaukee, and Denver on how they gathered information and how satisfied they were with their school choice.[3] Parents reported feeling well informed, but lower income parents (less than $20,000 in income) engaged in slightly less information gathering than higher income parents and were also less satisfied with their choice. Lower income parents reported relying less on other parents' input and trusted teacher recommendations more. Differences could be due to smaller social circles or fewer resources available to lower income families. The research does not suggest that low-income families are unable or lack the desire to select schools but that they gather less information and do so in different ways than higher income families. The included choice programs had income requirements, so differences are between moderate- and low-income families. These findings can inform the design and marketing of school choice programs to ensure that lower income families have access to relevant information.

From the literature, it is clear that parents in specific choice programs are active participants and feel confident in their ability to select schools. Most of the included studies interviewed parents who were already participating in a choice program. Aside from Wolf and Stewart (2012), other studies did not address if parents who were ineligible for choice programs shared the desire to actively participate in choice. However, even if there are parents who do not desire to be active choosers, there is clear evidence that there is a group of parents who are active participants.

## Question 2: What school characteristics do parents consider when selecting a school?

Now I turn to what specific school characteristics parents consider in their decisions. Critics of school choice suggest that parents may select schools for reasons of convenience or sport team prowess rather than academic quality (Harris & Larsen, 2015). It is difficult to quantify, let alone define academic quality because it includes test scores, teacher quality, learning environment, and curriculum. It is also incorrect to suppose that parents should value academic quality the most because families' needs vary. However, as academics are a foundational component of education, it is worth summarizing the literature on how families value academic quality and what other school characteristics they consider. I focus on three main themes I find in the literature. One, parents across choice programs report considering similar school characteristics when selecting a school. Two, the extent to which parents value academic quality is dependent on their circumstances. Three, parents make trade-offs among their preferences when selecting a school.

### *Theme 1: Parents have similar school preferences across choice programs*

There is great consistency in parents' preferences across different private choice programs. Earlier research found that parents considered academics along with a wide variety of factors (Teske & Schneider, 2001) including teacher quality, safety, test scores, and values (Schneider et al., 2000). Recent research showed parents considered a similar variety of factors when selecting schools, including academic rigor (Catt & Rhinesmith, 2016; Kelly & Scafidi, 2013; Lincove et al., 2016; Stewart et al., 2010, 2009; Zeehandelaar & Winkler, 2013), safety (Catt & Rhinesmith, 2016; Kelly & Scafidi, 2013; Stewart et al., 2010, 2009), extracurriculars (Catt & Rhinesmith, 2016; Kelly & Scafidi, 2013; Lincove et al., 2016), teacher quality (DiPerna & Catt, 2016; Kelly & Scafidi, 2013; Stewart et al., 2010, 2009; Teske et al., 2007), religious or moral instruction (Catt & Rhinesmith, 2016; DiPerna & Catt, 2016; Kelly & Scafidi, 2013; Stewart et al., 2009; Trivitt & Wolf, 2011), class size (Catt & Rhinesmith, 2016; DiPerna & Catt, 2016; Kelly & Scafidi, 2013; Stewart et al., 2009), and overall fit to their child (Catt & Rhinesmith, 2016; Kelly & Scafidi, 2013; Stewart et al., 2009, 2010; Teske et al., 2007).

#### *Stated versus revealed preferences*

Parents' preferences are generally measured by self-reports, referred to as parents' stated preferences. The recent research looking at stated preferences uses primarily two methods: surveys (Catt & Rhinesmith, 2016; DiPerna & Catt, 2016; Kelly & Scafidi, 2013; Teske et al., 2007; Trivitt & Wolf, 2011; Zeehandelaar & Winkler, 2013) and focus groups (Stewart et al. 2009; & Stewart et al., 2010; Teske et al., 2007). Stated preferences are susceptible to social desirability bias as parents may feel that they should care about a given school characteristic when in reality they may not actually consider it in their decision. A smaller body of research considers parents' revealed preferences (Lincove et al., 2016; Trivitt & Wolf, 2011) by looking at characteristics of schools where parents actually enroll their children. Revealed preferences overcome some issues with self-reports, but parents exact reason for selecting a school remains unclear. Revealed preferences are also only a reflection of school options available to parents. Findings on both stated and revealed preferences should be considered together to better understand parents' true preferences. There seems to be small but relatively insignificant differences in the private choice literature on stated and revealed preferences.[4]

Trivitt and Wolf (2011) found differences between parents' stated and revealed preferences. Using data from the WSF, Trivitt and Wolf compared parents' preferences on questionnaires prior to receiving a voucher with the characteristics of schools parents actually selected. Parents who stated they preferred Catholic schools were likely to select a Catholic school; however, 55% of parents reported that they most preferred a Catholic school but 71% actually enrolled in a Catholic school. Parents that stated they preferred a nonreligious school were more likely to select a Catholic school than any other. The reason for the disconnect between stated and revealed preferences was unclear, but Trivitt and Wolf suggested that parents could have received additional information following the survey that changed their preferences or that Catholic schools had a "well-known brand identity" (2011, 204) that was helpful for parents.

Lincove et al. (2016) also looked at parents' revealed preferences using students' school applications through the New Orleans OneApp, a centralized lottery and enrollment process for all schools. New Orleans had an extremely robust choice program; students were able to select traditional public, charter, and private schools.[5] They found that parents generally preferred private schools over public schools, but parents were likely to have listed both private and public schools on their application. Parents' preference of private over public schools remained constant when distance to the school was considered. Kindergarten parents or parents of new students were willing to travel further to attend a private school. Parents also appeared to value schools with extracurricular activities and sports, but these characteristics did not have an effect on the specific parent rankings.

Research on revealed preferences gives a fuller picture of what parents consider when selecting a school. It highlights potential trade-offs parents make as well as information shortcuts parents may use while shopping for schools. Further research on revealed preferences will help in better understanding what parents value and what type of schools they actually select.

### *Theme 2: Parents value academic quality, but it is not always the most important*

General patterns in the literature show parents value academic quality along with school conveniences and extracurricular activities. Table 2 lists school characteristics that parents report as very important in their school selection. Parents across five different private choice programs heavily consider a school's academic quality when shopping for a school. Academic quality can include specific academic features such as curriculum (Stewart et al., 2010, 2009), better academics than previous schools (Catt & Rhinesmith, 2016; Kelly & Scafidi, 2013), test scores (Lincove, Cowen, & Imrogno, 2016), class size (Catt & Rhinesmith, 2016; Stewart et al., 2009), and individual attention/better learning environment (Catt & Rhinesmith, 2016; Kelly & Scafidi, 2013). School safety (Kelly & Scafidi, 2013; Stewart et al., 2009) and

**Table 2.** Parents' reported top school preferences when selecting a school in specific private school choice programs.

| School characteristics | Program | Reference |
|---|---|---|
| Academic quality | | |
| Curriculum | D.C. OSP, MPCP | Stewart et al. (2009); Stewart et al. (2010) |
| Better academics | Georgia GOAL, Indiana voucher and tax credit scholarship | Kelly and Scafidi (2013); Catt and Rhinesmith (2016) |
| Test scores | New Orleans | Lincove et al. (2016) |
| Class size | D.C. OSP, Indiana voucher and tax credit scholarship | Stewart et al. (2009), Catt and Rhinesmith (2016) |
| Individual attention/better learning environment | Georgia GOAL, Indiana voucher, and tax credit scholarship | Kelly and Scafidi (2013); Catt and Rhinesmith (2016) |
| Safety | D.C. OSP, Georgia GOAL | Stewart et al. (2009); Kelly and Scafidi (2013) |
| Religious/moral environment | D.C. OSP, Georgia GOAL, Indiana voucher and tax credit scholarship | Stewart et al. (2009); Kelly and Scafidi (2013); Catt and Rhinesmith (2016) |
| Catholic schools | SSP | Trivitt and Wolf (2011) |
| Extracurriculars | | |
| Sport programs | MPCP, New Orleans | Stewart et al. (2010); Lincove et al. (2016) |
| Conveniences | | |
| Location | MPCP | Stewart et al. (2010) |
| Prior attendance of family member | MPCP | Stewart et al. (2010) |
| School reputation | MPCP | Stewart et al. (2010) |
| Prefer private over public | New Orleans | Lincove et al. (2016) |
| Child's preference | MPCP | Stewart et al. (2010) |

This table does not contain a complete list of reviewed sources that address parents' school preferences. It only includes the six studies that included specific private choice programs. The specific school characteristics noted here are some of parents' top preferences when considering a school. These do not represent a comprehensive list of all characteristics parents considered when selecting a school. These specific characteristics were included in the table because (1) parents mentioned them in their top considerations when surveyed (Catt & Rhinesmith, 2016; Kelly & Scafidi, 2013; Trivitt & Wolf, 2011), (2) researchers reported that parents frequently discussed the characteristics in focus groups (Stewart et al., 2009, 2010), or (3) they were characteristics that were most predicative of actual schools parents selected (Lincove et al., 2016).

religious or moral instruction (Catt & Rhinesmith, 2016; Kelly & Scafidi, 2013; Stewart et al., 2009) were also frequently cited parent preferences. While cited across fewer programs, parents highly consider other factors such as sports programs (Lincove et al., 2016; Stewart et al., 2010), school convenience (Stewart et al., 2010), school reputation (Stewart et al., 2010), as well as the child's preference (Stewart et al., 2010). In two nationwide surveys, parents report that they strongly prefer schools with better education quality and strong curriculum along with a focus on study habits, communication skills, and critical thinking (DiPerna & Catt, 2016; Zeehandelaar & Winkler, 2013). National surveys do not specifically focus on parents who participated in private school choice programs but show that all parents, regardless of having school choice, value academic quality.

Parents did not consider academics as purely test scores. In Georgia's GOAL scholarship program, 34% of parents stated they considered test scores in their school decision (Kelly & Scafidi, 2013). When asked to rank their top two reasons for selecting a private school, parents' most common responses were better education and better learning environment; less than 1% of parents said standardized test scores were one of their top two reasons. Lincove et al. (2016) found that parents in New Orleans were more likely to rank schools with higher test scores on their applications. It is unclear if parents considered test scores or other academic qualities that are associated with test scores when developing their rankings.

While parents across multiple programs consistently valued academic quality, parents varied in how they ranked academics; it was not always their first priority. Indiana parents valued academics, but many ranked it second to religious or moral instruction (Catt & Rhinesmith, 2016). Washington D.C. parents considered academic quality, but many were primarily concerned about safety. Parents considered academic quality more once their children were in a safe school. Families followed Maslow's hierarchy of needs when selecting schools. Families were concerned first with health and safety in schools, but once basic needs were satisfied, parents could focus on higher-order student needs, such as academics (Stewart & Wolf, 2014, 52).

### *Theme 3: Parents make trade-offs between their preferences when selecting schools*

The literature also showed that parents made trade-offs among their preferences. Stewart et al. (2010) recounted that parents in focus groups mentioned specific trade-offs they made between religious schools and a more diverse environment. Other parents recalled trade-offs between a school's reputation and their overall satisfaction with the school. Survey research captured trade-offs by asking parents to list all the reasons they chose a private school and then asking them to rank their preferences in different orders (Catt & Rhinesmith, 2016; Kelly & Scafidi, 2013). Trade-offs were clearly seen among Georgia GOAL parents' rankings of extracurricular activities and safety. Twenty-one percent of parents said that more extracurricular offerings were a reason they selected a private school. However, when asked their top two reasons, less than 1% of parents listed more extracurricular activities. Fifty-two percent of parents listed increased safety as a reason they selected a private school, where only 7% percent listed it as their top reason, and 4% percent listed it as their second-highest reason.

New Orleans was an ideal place to look at trade-offs among school preferences because parents had to order their preferred schools on an application. Lincove et al. (2016) found that parents were making clear trade-offs between school sectors: traditional public, charter, and private. While the exact school characteristics parents considered were unclear, parents tended to favor high-performing schools that were close to where they lived, but were willing to list a higher performing school above a school that was closer to them.

## Discussion

There is clear evidence that parents desire to and feel confident in their ability to participate in choice. Parents consider a variety of factors that are specific to their circumstances when participating in private school choice, and they make trade-offs among their preferences based on their experiences and needs. There is a general consensus in the literature that parents value a school's academic quality and consider it when selecting a school in a private choice program. I found no study that showed a majority of parents considered only religious instruction, school location, or extracurricular activities without accounting for academic quality.

There is no consistent pattern in the literature regarding differences between lower and higher income families' experiences with choice. Two studies found that lower income parents took fewer steps when gathering school information (Kelly & Scafidi, 2013; Teske et al., 2007). One study (Kelly & Scafidi, 2013) found that unmarried and disadvantaged parents were more likely to list education quality as the most important reason for choosing a private school. Most private choice programs are means tested, so any comparisons are made between moderate-income and lower income families. Literature on public school choice has also found differences between how lower and higher income families participate in choice. Harris and Larsen (2015) showed that low-income parents selecting charter schools value extracurricular offerings more than academics. Hastings, Kane, and Staiger (2007) showed that lower income parents value academics less than higher income parents. Hastings and Weinstein (2008), however, found that low-income families who have information about academic quality select high-quality schools. More research on differences between how low- and high-income families participate in private and public school choice is needed.

The literature only covers parents' experiences in a handful of private school choice programs. Programs vary greatly in design, eligibility, and regulations, and as such each family will have unique experiences. Parents' motivation and preferences are nuanced and are difficult to categorize or put in a rank order. I do not intend to overstate the trends and apply them to all parents in all choice programs. These questions address the heart of school choice. School choice is designed to give parents the freedom to find schools that fit the needs and preferences of their families. While there are consistent patterns, school choice is about individuals finding particular schools, and this should not be forgotten when discussing how and what type of schools parents choose.

There remain many questions regarding parents' experiences with choice. It is assumed that the school characteristics parents consider will affect their children's outcomes. There is a large and growing body of research on academic and long-term outcomes from school choice (Cowen, Fleming, Witte, Wolf, & Kisida, 2013; Forster, 2016; Mills & Wolf, 2016; Shakeel, Anderson, & Wolf, 2016). There is less known about whether parents' preferences when selecting a school affect student outcomes. Hastings and Weinstein (2008) show that students of parents who seek public school choice for academic reasons experience increased test scores. While the same pattern could remain when parents participate in private school choice, private schools can offer a wider variety of schooling options, such as religious schools, which may influence parents' preferences and student outcomes.

Questions also remain about how parents select schools as school choice increases in size and scope. Education Savings Accounts (ESAs) offer parents the options of selecting multiple educational services from various providers. Parents must make decisions between paying for tuition, tutoring, therapy, homebased materials, and saving money for college. Therefore, ESAs require parents to have greater information on a variety of services and make financial trade-offs among them. While there is early research on the types of services parents purchase (Butcher & Burke, 2016), much remains unknown about how parents gather information and make trade-offs among multiple education providers when their choices are expansive.

## Notes

1. For some relevant works on parents' decision-making in public school choice see (Schneider & Buckley, 2002; Hastings, Kane, & Stanger, 2007; Hastings & Weinstein, 2008; Harris & Larsen, 2015; and Glazerman & Dotter, 2016).
2. ProQuest and Ebsco databases were used for the computer search.

3. Teske et al. (2007) interviewed parents who participated in public open-enrollment districts, charter schools, and private choice programs in those three cities.
4. There is some evidence and further discussion of differences between stated and revealed preferences in the literature on public school choice (Schneider & Buckley, 2002; Stein et al., 2009).
5. Private school vouchers were available only to students with family incomes below 250% of the federal poverty line and who were also in a school with a "C" grade or lower.

## References

Bast, J. L., & Walberg, H. J. (2004). Can parents choose the best school for their children? *Economic of Education Review, 23*, 431–440. doi:10.1016/j.econedurev.2003.08.003

Berliner, D. C., & Biddle, B. J. (1995). Poor ideas for reform. In *The manufactured crisis: Myths, fraud, and the attack on America's public schools* (pp. 173–180). Reading, MA: Addison-Wesley.

Buckley, J., & Schneider, M. (2003). Shopping for schools: How do marginal consumers gather information about schools? *The Policy Studies Journal, 31*(2), 121–145. doi:10.1111/psj.2003.31.issue-2

Butcher, J., & Burke, L. M. (2016). *The education debit card II what Arizona parents purchase with education savings accounts.* Friedman Foundation for Educational Choice. Retrieved from https://www.edchoice.org/wp-content/uploads/2016/02/2016-2-The-Education-Debit-Card-II-WEB-1.pdf

Carnegie Foundation for the Advancement of Teaching. (1992). *School choice: A special report.* Princeton, NJ: Author.

Catt, A. D., & Rhinesmith, E. (2016). *Why parents choose: A survey of private school and school choice parents in Indiana.* The Friedman Foundation for Educational Choice. Retrieved from https://www.edchoice.org/research/why-parents-choose/

Cowen, J. M., Fleming, D. J., Witte, J. F., Wolf, P. J., & Kisida, B. (2013). School vouchers and student attainment: Evidence from a state-mandated study of Milwaukee's parental choice program. *Policy Studies Journal, 41*(1 February), 147–168. doi:10.1111/psj.12006

DiPerna, P. & Catt, A. D. (2016). 2016 Schooling in America survey: Public opinion on K-12 Education and school choice. Edchoice, Polling Paper no. 28. Retrieved from. https://www.edchoice.org/research/2016-schooling-america-survey/

Forster, G. (2016). *A win–win solution: The empirical evidence on school choice* (4th ed.). The Friedman Foundation for Educational Choice. Retrieved from http://www.edchoice.org/wp-content/uploads/2016/05/A-Win-Win-Solution-The-Empirical-Evidence-on-School-Choice.pdf

Friedman Foundation for Educational Choice. (2016). The abcs of school choice: The comprehensive guide to every private school choice program in America. Retrieved from: https://www.edchoice.org/research/the -abcs-of-school-choice/.

Friedman, M. (2002). *Capitalism and freedom* (Fortieth Anniversary ed. ed.). Chicago, IL: The University of Chicago Press.

Friedman, M., & Friedman, R. (1980). *Free to choose: A personal statement.* Orlando, FL: Harcourt Brace & Company.

Fuller, B., Elmore, R. F., & Orfield, G. (1996). Policy-making in the dark: Illuminating the school choice debate. In B. Fuller, R. Elmore, & G. Orfield (Eds.), *Who chooses? Who loses? Cultural, institutions, and the unequal effects of school choice* (pp. 1–24). New York, NY: Teachers College, Columbia University.

Glazerman, S., & Dotter, D. (2016). Market signals: How do DC parents rank schools, and what does it mean for policy? Mathematica policy research, policy brief. Retrieved from:

https://www.mathematica-mpr.com/our-publications-and-findings/publications/market-signals-how-do-dc-parents-rank-schools-and-what-does-it-mean-for-policy

Gross, B., & Denice, P. (2017). *Can public transportation improve students' access to Denver's best schools of choice?* Bothell, WA: Center for Reinventing Public Education. Retrieved from https://www.crpe.org/sites/default/files/crpe-public-transportation-denver.pdf

Gutmann, A. (2003). Assessing arguments for school choice: Pluralism, parental rights, or educational results? In A. Wolfe (Ed.), *School choice: The moral debate* (pp. 126–148). Princeton; Oxford: Princeton University Press.

Harris, D. N., & Larsen, M. (2015). What schools do families what (and why)? *Technical Report.* Education Research Alliance for New Orleans.

Hastings, J. S., Kane, T. J., & Staiger, D. O. (2007). Parental preferences and school competition: Evidence from a public school choice program. *Working paper.* Retrieved from: http://aida.wss.yale.edu/~jh529/papers/HastingsKaneStaiger_Prefs&Competition.pdf.

Hastings, J. S., & Weinstein, J. M. (2008). Information, school choice, and academic achievement: Evidence from two experiments. *Quarterly Journal of Economics, 123*(4 Nov), 1373–1414. doi:10.1162/qjec.2008.123.4.1373

Kelly, J. P., & Scafidi, B. (2013). More than scores: An analysis of why and how parents choose private schools. The Friedman Foundation for Educational Choice. Retrieved from https://www.edchoice.org/research/more-than -scores/

Kisida, B., & Wolf, P. J. (2010). School Governance and information: Does choice lead to better-informed parents? *American Politics Research, 38*(5), 783–805. doi:10.1177/1532673X09350981

Lincove, J. A., Cowen, J. M., & Imbrogno, J. P. (2016). What's in your portfolio?: How parents rank traditional public, private, and charter schools in post-Katrina New Orleans' citywide system of school choice. *Education Finance and Policy*, Accepted for publication.

Mills, J., & Wolf, P. J. (2016). The effects of the Louisiana scholarship program on student achievement after two year. School Choice Demonstration Project, Fayetteville, AR: University of Arkansas. Louisiana Scholarship Program Evolution Report #1. Retrieved from: http://www.uaedreform.org/downloads/2016/02/report-1-the-effects-of-the-louisiana-scholarship-program-on-student-achievement-after-two-years.pdf

Moe, T. (1995). *Private vouchers.* Stanford, CA: Hoover Institution Press.

Saltman, K. (2000). *Collateral damage: Corporatizing public schools—A threat to democracy.* Lanham, Maryland: Rowman & Littlefield Publishers, Inc.

Schneider, M., & Buckley, J. (2002). What do parents want from schools? Evidence from the Internet. *Educational Evaluation and Policy Analysis, 24*(2), 133–144. doi:10.3102/01623737024002133

Schneider, M., Teske, P., & Marschall, M. (2000). *Choosing schools: Consumer choice and quality of American schools.* Princeton, NJ: Princeton University Press.

Shakeel, D. M., Anderson, K. P., & Wolf, P. J. (2016). The participant effects of private school vouchers across the globe: A metaanalytic and systematic review. *SSRN working paper.* Retrieved from: http://www.uaedreform.org/downloads/2016/05/the-participant-effects-of-private-school-vouchers-across-the-globe-a-meta-analytic-and-systematic-review-2.pdf.

Stein, M. L., Goldring, E., & Cravens, X. (2009). Choosing Indianapolis charter schools: espoused versus revealed academic preferences. *National Center of School Choice, working paper.* Retrieved from: http://www.vanderbilt.edu/schoolchoice/conference/papers/Stein%20Goldring%20Cravens_COMPLETE_with%20page%20numbers.pdf.

Stewart, T., Lucas-McLean, J., Jensen, L. I., Fetzko, C., Ho, B., & Segovia, S. (2010). Family voices on parental school choice in Milwaukee: What can we learn from low-income families? *Report #9, School Choice* Demonstration Project, Fayetteville, AR: University of

Arkansas. Retrieved from: http://www.uaedreform.org/family-voices-on-parental-school-choice-in-milwaukee-what-can-we-learn-from-low-income-families/.

Stewart, T., Wolf, P., Cornman, S. Q., McKenzie-Thompson, K., & Butcher, J. (2009). Family reflections on the District of Columbia opportunity scholarship program. Final Summary Report. SCDP Report #0901, School Choice Demonstration Project, Fayetteville, AR: University of Arkansas. Retrieved from: http://www.uaedreform.org/new-family-reflections-on-the-district-of-columbia-opportunity-scholarship-program-final-summary-report/

Stewart, T., & Wolf, P. J. (2014). *The school choice journey: School vouchers and the empowerment of urban families.* New York, NY: Palgrave Macmillan.

Teske, P., Fitzpatrick, J., & Kaplan, G. (2007). Opening door: How low-income parents search for the right school. Center on Reinventing Public Education. Retrieved from http://www.crpe.org/publications/opening-doors-how-low-income-parents-search-right-school

Teske, P., & Schneider, M. (2001). What research can tell policymakers about school choice. *Journal of Policy Analysis and Management, 20*(4), 609–631. doi:10.1002/(ISSN)1520-6688

Trivitt, J. R., & Wolf, P. J. (2011). School choice and the branding of Catholic schools. *Education Finance and Policy, 6*(2), 202–245. doi:10.1162/EDFP_a_00032

Walberg, H. J. (2007). Customer satisfaction. In *School choice the findings* (pp. 91–101). Washington, D.C.: Cato Institute.

Wolf, P. J., & Stewart, T. (2012). Understanding school shoppers in Detroit. Michigan Future Inc. Retrieved from http://www.uaedreform.org/downloads/2016/01/detroit-school-shoppers-report.pdf

Zeehandelaar, D., & Winkler, A. M., Eds. (2013). What parents want: Education preferences and trade-offs. Thomas B. Fordham Institute. Retrieved from: http://edex.s3-us-west-2.amazonaws.com/publication/pdfs/20130827_What_Parents_Want_Education_Preferences_and_Trade_Offs_FINAL.pdf

# Can we have it all? A review of the impacts of school choice on racial integration

Elise Swanson

**ABSTRACT**
This article reviews the literature evaluating the impact of school choice programs on racial integration. Evidence on the impacts of magnet schools, voluntary busing programs, open enrollment practices, charter schools, and voucher programs is reviewed. The literature is mixed on this question, finding that the impacts of choice on racial integration are highly context-specific and varies across regions and type of choice.

## Introduction

Under a school choice system, defined here as a publicly funded route to non-residentially assigned schools, families are free to choose schools for any reason. There are conflicting theories as to whether this will increase or decrease integration. By decoupling the link between residence and school, choice programs could transcend patterns of residential segregation. However, families may choose schools in which the majority of students are racially similar to their child. These choices could result from implicit racial bias, or simply from not wanting their child to be a member of a racial out-group in their school. Given the public's valuation of equity, these competing theories affect the public's level of support for school choice. These two countervailing theories result in an empirical question: how do choice programs impact levels of integration?

In this article, I review evidence of the impacts of school choice on integration in traditional public and choice schools. While systematic, this review is not necessarily comprehensive, as relevant studies may not have been found using the search terms detailed in the next section. However, this review provides extensive documentation of the impacts of school choice on racial integration in schools, and suggestive evidence as to whether choice, and in what form, advances or prevents increased integration. I organize the literature based on the type of choice program, beginning with district-level choice initiatives, then moving to charters, and concluding with voucher programs.

## Search methodology

### *Search process*

This search progressed in two stages. First, I used the University of Arkansas Library's QuickSearch feature to search for "'school choice' AND integration", which simultaneously scanned the library's book collection, open access journals, subscribed journals, and e-books. This search included EbscoHost, ProQuest, JSTOR, and Google Scholar, as well as smaller databases. This streamlined strategy combined all relevant material into one results page, and removed duplicates. I excluded newspaper articles, book reviews, dissertations, magazine articles, newsletters, and transcripts. The search was further restricted to only include results from the disciplines of economics, education, political science, social sciences, and sociology and social history. Subject terms were refined to focus on K-12 racial integration in the United States.

I reviewed the abstracts of the relevant articles for the criteria outlined above, and retained 28 articles for full review. I extracted information on the years of analysis, type of choice program studied, location of choice program, research design, unit of analysis, comparison group, outcome measures, and main findings from these studies. Relevant citations from these 28 reviewed studies were located and read in full. This resulted in an additional 27 articles for review and coding. The next section describes the review process of these 55 studies.

### *Inclusion criteria*

Studies were included if they examined a school choice program, defined as a publicly funded route to a non-residentially assigned school. Studies evaluating the impact of within-school tracking, for example, were excluded, because students did not choose their school. Literature reviews, theoretical papers, reviews of litigation, historical overviews of integration in schools, evaluations of district gerrymandering, and analyses of familial preferences for district characteristics were excluded. One study examining the impact of a privately funded scholarship program was excluded, as the program did not meet the school choice definition of a publicly funded initiative used here. While privately funded voucher programs could have implications for publicly funded voucher programs, there are enough publicly funded voucher programs to directly inform the policy conversation about the impact of vouchers on school racial integration.

The public generally thinks of integration as students interacting with peers who have different backgrounds than their own, but integration is a difficult concept to quantify and measure. To determine the impact choice programs have on integration, authors need an operationalized definition of integration and a comparison group to evaluate whether choice programs serve to increase, decrease, or hold constant levels of integration. Studies of trends over time, case studies, and textual analyses of desegregation plans are excluded. While changes in school composition over time could be of interest to readers, without an external comparison group the significance of those changes may be unknown. For example, consider a school whose racial composition shifts from 80% White in 2000 to 70% White in 2005. We know that the share of White students in that school decreased over time, which could indicate that the school became more racially integrated as the share of students of color increased. However, if that school is located in an area in which 85% of school-aged children were White in 2000, and in 2005 only 50% of school-aged children were White, it could be argued that the school actually became less integrated over those five years, because the student demographics are now less representative of the community. Without a proper reference group, we cannot know if the school became more or less integrated, or if the level of integration held constant. Thus, while time trends can be informative, in this review I focus only on studies that include an external reference group in order to more accurately assess the relationship between a choice program and racial integration.

I do include studies that use an absolute threshold of integration but compare schools in different sectors to that standard. For example, multiple studies define a school as racially isolated if 90% of the student body or more are in the same racial group, and compare the percent of students who attend racially isolated schools in either the "choice" sector--magnet, charter, or private schools--or the traditional sector--district public schools. Because these studies compare sectors, I consider them to have a valid comparison group; however, I consider studies that use the community or surrounding area as the comparison group as methodologically stronger, as the reader is better able to gauge what the schools could look like if they were "integrated"--representative of the community--while studies that compare both sectors to an absolute standard do not provide a larger context in which to understand the results.

Only studies evaluating racial integration in U.S. K-12 schools were included. Studies examining another type of integration, such as socioeconomic integration, were excluded. Studies examining the achievement impacts of integration were also excluded. After reviewing all articles initially deemed relevant, 24 were retained for this review. The next section evaluates the strength of the methods utilized by included studies before discussing their findings.

## Racial integration methodology

Researchers must define integration in a clear, quantifiable manner, and then compare traditional public schools and school choice programs to that metric. In the literature, there are two common ways to operationalize integration: first, set an absolute benchmark of segregation; and, second, compare the racial composition of schools to the composition of the area in which the school is located. Under the first method, schools are generally classified as segregated if 90–95% or more of the student body is of the same race. The second method compares the racial composition of traditional public schools and choice schools to that of the community, but definitions of the community vary greatly between studies. Schools may be compared to national, state, or metro area demographics. Researchers present either the absolute difference between the community's and schools' demographics, or classify schools whose demographics are within a certain range of the community's as integrated. Studies that use the metro area as the point of comparison for school demographics use a more appropriate measure of integration. The metro area is large enough to encompass various neighborhoods that may be segregated because of residential segregation, but small enough to reasonably expect schools to have a student body that reflects the community.

Studies either look at static measures of integration, taking a snapshot of integration in an area with a choice program, or at dynamic measures of integration, examining the impact of student moves between traditional public schools and schools of choice on the level of integration in the area. These studies may use the Gini coefficient, index of dissimilarity, exposure index, or a simple difference between the composition of the choice school and the comparison area to measure how well integrated schools are at that moment in time. Studies that use a dynamic measure of integration are more rigorous, as they identify how levels of integration change in response to the presence of school choice. Further, studies examining the impact of student moves on both the sending schools (traditional public schools) and receiving schools (schools of choice) are the most comprehensive, as the true question is how choice is impacting the share of students who attend integrated schools. Typically, the studies using a dynamic analysis examine how the difference in racial composition between the choice school and the reference area changes as students transfer between schools. Dynamic analyses are the best way of assessing the impact of choice on racial integration, as choice schools may improve integration but still have lower levels of integration than traditional schools—or vice versa—an important finding that would be missed in a static analysis that only captured the final levels. Studies conducting more dynamic analyses thus are given more credence in the discussion below.

## District choice

Seven studies examine the integrative impact of intra-district choice policies. District choice policies allow students to move between schools *within* a district. Although the district allows choice, it generally retains all students within its borders and aggregate district funding is not affected. While district choice may attract families to live in the district, the studies reviewed here do not explicitly disentangle the impact on racial integration of families moving into a district because of choice and the impact of students moving between schools within a district (that they already lived in) on racial integration.

### *Magnet schools*

Started in the 1960s, magnet schools originally had the explicit goal of increasing integration by attracting students through a specific curricular focus, although it is no longer the case that all magnets have an explicit focus on increasing integration. Indeed, many magnets now exist simply to provide students and families with options for rigorous, themed instruction. In theory, magnets increase integration by attracting students with similar interests—performing arts, science, or an International Baccalaureate program, for example—while transcending patterns of residential segregation reflected in residentially assigned traditional public schools (TPSs). Magnet schools with an explicit mission to reduce segregation receive additional federal funding through the Magnet Schools Assistance Program (MSAP), and may use race-conscious admissions policies. Table 1 summarizes the impacts of magnet schools on racial integration.

Six studies included an evaluation of the impact of magnet school choice on racial integration. Although the studies covered multiple states, the findings are generally limited to urban contexts. Cobb and Glass (2009) reviewed the literature on district school choice to determine the impact of choice programs without an explicit integration mission relative to the impact of integration-focused inter-district desegregation plans. They found that choice programs without an explicit focus on integration were associated with decreased racial integration, while "controlled choice" programs were found to increase racial integration. Their review focused on the impacts of regulated versus unregulated school choice, and whether unregulated school choice led to large enough academic gains for students to ameliorate any segregative impacts of choice. As Cobb and Glass (2009) is not a primary study, I do not include it in this review, but point readers to that review if they are interested in the impacts of controlled choice versus choice programs without a specific focus on integration.

Bifulco, Ladd, and Ross (2009), Saporito (2003), and Koedel, Koedel, Betts, Rice, and Zau (2009) all examined magnet programs within a single city.

**Table 1.** Impacts of magnet school choice on racial integration.

| Paper | Year of analysis | Location | Research design | Unit of analysis | Comparison group | Main findings—racial integration |
|---|---|---|---|---|---|---|
| Koedel et al. (2009) | 2000–2001 | San Diego | Racial comp; exposure indices | Student/school | School comp w/o choice | Magnet program increases racial integration |
| Bifulco et al. (2009) | 2002–2003 | Durham | Probit model; exposure index | Student/parent | Projected composition of assigned school (if everyone assigned to it went there) | White and college-educated parents more likely to make non-integrating moves in elem; in middle school, Black students more likely to make integrative moves; integration is lower in choice system than if students attended assigned school |
| Christenson et al. (2003) | 1999–2000 through 2000–2001 | 57 MSAP schools | Matching | School | Matched TPSs | 57% of deseg-focused magnet schools decreased minority isolation; 43% did not. More likely in schools under voluntary than required deseg; elem schools than high schools; whole school than nested school |
| Saporito (2003) | 1990–1992 | Philadelphia | Logistic regression | Student/school | Actual racial comp vs. comp with no (all) magnets | 68% of schools would be segregated with no magnet schools, 59% of schools would be segregated if all first choices were given |
| Rossell and Armor (1996) | 1968–1991 | 600 districts | Multiple regression | District | Districts with no deseg plan | Mandatory plans associated w/a 33% decrease in White enrollment, controlled choice w/29% decrease, voluntary deseg w/2.9% decrease. Racial Imbalance: no sig difference between plans; Racial Exposure: voluntary plans result in a 19 point gain, mandatory in 11 point gain |

While Saporito focused exclusively on Philadelphia's magnet school program, Bifulco, Ladd, and Ross, and Koedel et al., examined the entire choice system within Durham, NC, and San Diego, CA, respectively. However, Koedel et al. separated the effect of the magnet program from the effects of the Voluntary Ethnic Enrollment Program and an open enrollment option. The authors used district records to determine what the racial composition of district schools would have been without choice, and compared that to observed racial composition with choice.

Bifulco et al. (2009) found that segregation was higher under choice than it would have been if all students had attended their residentially assigned school, but observe different patterns between White students and students of color in making integrative or segregative moves. While Saporito (2003) found evidence of White flight—White students were more likely to transfer when students of color are in the majority at their assigned school—he also found that the district would be less segregated if all students were assigned to their first choice magnet school. However, Saporito noted that this effect would be driven by the higher levels of integration in magnet schools, while the students remaining in TPSs would be in more segregated environments. Koedel et al. (2009) found that the magnet program in San Diego, CA increased racial integration.

Christenson et al. (2003) evaluated a national sample of magnet schools receiving federal funds. The evaluation determined the extent to which the magnet schools were preventing, reducing, or eliminating racial isolation within the magnet school. The MSAP program, somewhat arbitrarily, defined a school as racially isolated if more than 50% of enrolled students were students of color. The authors evaluated the change in the percent of schools with minority group isolation relative to the change in the district's percent of minority group isolation. They found that in 5% of MSAP schools minority group isolation was prevented or eliminated, in 17% of MSAP schools minority group isolation was reduced by at least 5 percentage points relative to the district, in 28% of schools minority group isolation was reduced by 1–5 percentage points relative to the district, and in 7% of schools minority group isolation was reduced by less than 1 percentage point. However, 43% of MSAP schools saw no decline or increased minority group isolation relative to the district. Reductions in racial isolation were more likely in elementary schools than upper grades, and whole-school programs had a larger impact on increasing integration than school-within-a-school models. While descriptive, these results suggest a positive relationship between magnet schools and racial integration.

Rossell and Armor (1996) did not disentangle the effects of magnet schools from other integration programs, such as majority-to-minority transfer programs, districtwide enrollment procedures with race-conscious admissions, or catchment rezoning. Using a national probability sample of 600 districts, they found that court-ordered desegregation plans were less effective at preventing White flight and increasing interracial exposure[1] than plans districts adopted without a court order, but mandatory and voluntary desegregation plans had virtually the same impact on lowering racial imbalance.[2]

### Voluntary busing

While mandatory inter-district busing plans were struck down by the Supreme Court in *Milliken v. Bradley* (1974), voluntary inter-district busing is still allowed. The Voluntary Enrollment Exchange Program (VEEP) in San Diego provides transportation for students in specific geographic zones to attend schools in other communities. Koedel et al. (2009) used administrative records to determine what the racial composition of schools would be without VEEP and compared those projections to the actual demographics of schools. They found that VEEP increased racial integration.

### Open enrollment

Open enrollment policies allow students to attend any school in the district. Districts may require parents to rank all district schools, then assign students to schools. Other districts may retain catchment zones, but parents can apply to enroll their student at any school, and they are admitted if there is space. Transportation is not necessarily provided for students in schools outside their catchment zone. Table 2 summarizes the findings on the impact of intra-district transfers and open enrollment policies.

Three studies examined the impact of open enrollment policies in urban settings where other choice options were available. Siegel-Hawley noted the existence of magnet schools in Richmond, VA, although they did not have an explicit integration focus and did not receive federal MSAP funds, and the focus of her study was the open enrollment policy. Koedel et al. (2009) examined San Diego, which boasted magnet schools, a voluntary busing program (VEEP), charters, and open enrollment. Kodel et al. attempted to disentangle the effects of each of these programs, and the results presented in Table 2 refer to the impacts of the open enrollment program. However, these contexts may have impacted the level of integration observed in schools. Specifically, the presence of multiple choice programs creates a specific environment in which these results are observed, and the findings from studies examining a district with multiple choice options may consist of different results than similar districts with only one choice program.

Siegel-Hawley (2014) used publicly sourced data, state administrative data, Census data, and local books, newspaper articles, school board minutes, and other district assignment documents to compare segregation in elementary schools and in Richmond, VA. Siegel-Hawley calculated the Index of Dissimilarity, which indicates the share of one racial group that would have to move to achieve integration. She found that racial segregation in elementary schools was greater than segregation in the city—more students would

**Table 2.** Impacts of open enrollment programs on racial integration.

| Paper | Years of analysis | Location | Research Design | Unit of analysis | Comparison group | Main findings |
|---|---|---|---|---|---|---|
| Siegel-Hawley (2014) | 1990–2012 | Richmond, VA | Index of Dissimilarity | School | Community | Black–White elementary integration lower than residential integration and falling; open enrollment hurts integration |
| Koedel et al. (2009) | 2000–2001 | San Diego, CA | Compare comp; exposure | Student/school | School comp if students attended assigned schools | Open enrollment program decreases integration between White and Black students. |
| Cullen, Jacob, and Levitt (2000) | 1993–1997 | Chicago, IL | Compare racial comp of schools | Student/school | School comp if students attended assigned schools | W/o choice 69.1% in schools w/85%+ minority students; w/ choice 67.5% do. 16.1% of students in integrated school (<70% minority) w/o choice; 20.0% of students in integrated school w/choice. |

have to switch schools to achieve integration than families would have to move for integration—and that segregation increased over the 22 years examined. Siegel-Hawley concluded that the open enrollment policy was associated with greater segregation than if students were only permitted to attend their assigned schools.

Koedel et al. (2009) and Cullen, Jacob, and Levitt (2000) used administrative data to calculate the racial composition of schools if all students attended their residentially assigned school, and compared those projections to the observed racial composition of schools. Koedel et al. examined student records in San Diego in the 2000–01 school year, while Cullen, Jacob, and Levitt examined entering 9th grade cohorts in the Chicago Public Schools (CPS) in 1993, 94, and 95, and followed students through high school. While Koedel et al. found that open enrollment decreased integration between White and Black students, Cullen, Jacob, and Levitt found that choice in CPS decreased the percent of students in hyper-segregated schools and increased the percent of students attending integrated schools (defined in the study as less than 70% students of color).

### *District choice—summary*

The evidence on whether district choice policies increase or decrease racial integration is mixed, with results varying across time, region, and type of program. Three studies (Christenson et al., 2003; Saporito, 2003; and Koedel et al., 2009) find that magnet schools lead to increased racial integration, while one study (Bifulco et al., 2009) finds that magnets lead to decreased racial integration. Rossell and Armor (1996) find varying results based on whether the district desegregation plan was implemented voluntarily or as the result of a court decision. However, they generally find that district desegregation choice plans increase racial integration. The one study on voluntary busing (Koedel et al., 2009) finds evidence of increased racial integration. Two studies (Siegel-Hawley, 2014; Koedel et al., 2009) find that open enrollment programs decrease racial integration, while one study (Cullen, Jacobs, and Levitt, 2000) finds a positive impact.

## Charter schools

Charter students are not drawn exclusively from a traditional public district's boundaries, and open-enrollment charter schools are not governed by a traditional public school district. If a charter is oversubscribed, students are typically admitted through a lottery, although not all states require charters to conduct admissions lotteries. Table 3 summarizes the relationship between charters and integration. Each study compared the racial composition of charter schools to the composition of a relevant community.

**Table 3.** Impacts of charter schools on racial integration.

| Paper | Years of analysis | Location | Unit of analysis | Comparison group | Main findings |
|---|---|---|---|---|---|
| Zimmer et al. (2009) | Varies, 1994–2007 | 5 cities and 2 states[4] | School | Feeder TPSs | Charters demographically similar to feeder TPSs; variation between states (TX, Philadelphia–reduce integration, Chicago–increase integration) |
| Bifulco and Ladd (2007) | 1996–1997 through 2001–2002 | North Carolina | School | TPSs | Students 2.5 times more likely to be in racially unbalanced school if in a charter; charter Black and White students more racially isolated |
| Swanson, McKenzie, and Ritter (2016) | 2008–2009 through 2014–2015 | Little Rock, AR | Student/school | Composition of all charters and TPSs in metro area | 48% of student moves from TPSs to charters increased the level of integration in the exited TPS, 35% had a null impact, and 17% decreased the level of integration. However, student moves from outside the metro area to metro area charters decreased the racial representativeness of charter schools |
| Ritter et al. (2016) | 2004–2005 through 2009–2010 | Little Rock, AR | Student/school | Composition of all charters and TPSs in metro area | Greater share of TPS students in hypersegregated schools; charter school demographics an avg 25 percentage points from area; TPS demographics an average 19 percentage points from area; 72.8% of transfers have positive impact on TPSs |
| Ritter et al. (2010) | 2007–2008 | 39 CBSAs | School | Central city of CBSA | 63% of charter students attend hyper segregated schools, as do 53% of TPS students |
| Booker, Zimmer, and Buddin (2005) | TX: 1997–1998 to 2003–2004; CA: 1997–1998 through 2001–2002 | California and Texas | Student/school | TPSs | Black students more likely to switch than White students. Black students more likely make segregative moves in both states. In CA, White, Hispanic, and Asian students make integrative moves; in TX, White students make segregative moves, Hispanic students make integrative moves. |
| Miron et al. (2010) | 2000–2001, 2003–2004, 2006–2007 | National | School | Sending district | 25% of charters have demographic composition similar to sending district |
| Renzulli and Evans (2005) | 1998–2000 | National | School | District charter is in | Mean percentage of White enrollment in charters is same as district, but bimodal distribution |
| Parker (2012) | | St. Louis, Kansas City | Schools | TPSs | 61% of TPSs have over 90% of students of color; 69% of charters have over 90% of students of color in St. Louis; 56% of KC TPSs have over 90% of students of color, as do 74% of charters |

Two studies looked at integration in charter schools nationally. Miron, Urschel, Mathis, and Tornquist (2010) compared the racial composition of charters to the composition of the districts from which students transferred into charters, while Renzulli and Evans (2005) compared the racial composition of charters to that of the district in which the charter was physically located. Miron et al. found that nationally only 25% of charters are demographically similar to their sending districts, arguing that meant the majority of charters were more segregated than TPSs. However, Renzulli and Evans (2005) found that on average charters were demographically similar to surrounding TPSs, but impacts on racial integration varied greatly between regions. Renzulli and Evans (2005) found that charters either had high or low concentrations of White students, leading to a misleading average finding of similarity between charters and TPSs.

Three studies examined the impact of charter schools on racial integration across multiple states. These papers again found geographic variation in the impacts of charters on racial integration. Ritter, Jensen, Kisida, and McGee (2010) compared the racial composition of charters in 39 Census-defined Core Based Statistical Areas (CBSA) to the composition of the central city in the same CBSA. They measured the percent of students in charters and TPSs who attended hyper segregated schools, defined as schools in which 90% or more of students were the same race. Ritter et al. (2010) found that 63% of charter students attended hyper segregated schools, as did 53% of TPS students, but noted that a better analysis would analyze student movements between sectors.

Zimmer et al. (2009) compared the racial composition of charters to the composition of the districts from which students transferred into charters in five cities and three states, finding that on average charters were demographically similar to surrounding TPSs, but impacts on racial integration varied greatly between cities and states. The authors also reported regional variation, finding that charters in Texas and Philadelphia reduced integration, while charters in Chicago increased integration.

Booker, Zimmer, and Buddin (2005) examined patterns of student movement in charters in six districts in California and in the entire state of Texas, finding that Black students were more likely to move to charters than White students in both states. However, they also found that in California, White, Hispanic, and Asian students moved to schools with a lower concentration of same-race students, while in Texas White students tended to self-segregate but Hispanic students did not.

Finally, Rapp and Eckes (2007) compared charter demographics to state-level demographics of all TPS students, finding that White students were overrepresented among charter students in 11 states, students of color were overrepresented among charter students in 21 states, and in only 2 states were there no significant differences in racial composition between charters and TPSs. While state-level demographics do not serve as an ideal comparison group for assessing whether a school is integrated, as attending any particular charter school may not be feasible for students living in certain parts of the state, the study meets this review's inclusion criteria of providing an external reference group. This situation highlights the need for continued research into the impacts of choice on racial integration, and for the selection of an appropriate reference group in these analyses.

Bifulco and Ladd (2007) compared the racial composition of charters and traditional public schools in North Carolina. They found that students were 2.5 times more likely to be in a racially imbalanced school if they attended a charter instead of a TPS, and that both White and Black students were more racially isolated in charters than TPSs. They found evidence of self-segregation regardless of the level of academic achievement at the charter into which students moved.

Two studies examined the impact of charter schools within a city. Ritter, Jensen, Kisida, and Bowen (2016) examined the impact of charters on racial integration in Little Rock, comparing the racial composition of charter schools to the racial composition of all enrolled public K-12 students in the metro area. They found that 40% of students in TPSs were in hyper segregated schools, compared to 28% of students in charters. Ritter et al. (2016) also computed the absolute difference in racial composition between schools and metro area demographics, and found that charter schools were on average 25 percentage points away from the area composition, while TPSs were 19 percentage points from the area composition. In this study, schools were deemed as less integrated the further their demographics were from the area's racial composition, regardless of whether students of color or White students were overrepresented in the school. Finally, they analyzed student-level moves between TPSs and charters in Little Rock, and found that 73% of student transfers increased integration in TPSs students exited. Parker (2012) compared the percent of students in hyper segregated schools (more than 90% of students of the same race in a school) across charters and TPSs in St. Louis and Kansas City. He found that in St. Louis 61% of TPSs were hyper segregated and 69% of charters were hyper segregated, while in Kansas City 56% of TPSs were hyper segregated, as were 74% of charters.

### *Summary—impacts of charters on racial integration*

The studies reviewed here present a mixed picture of the relationships between charter schools and racial integration, with significant variation between regions. Charters in some areas, such as Chicago, Little Rock, and California, seem to increase integration, while charters in other areas, such as Texas, Philadelphia, North Carolina, St. Louis, and Kansas City, seem to decrease integration. The only dynamic analyses of racial integration in charters (Booker et al., 2005; Ritter et al., 2016) find that student moves into charters have an integrative impact on the system, though neither TPSs nor charters are fully representative of the racial composition of the area. Further, charter schools may have an explicit mission to serve students of color or historically underrepresented groups, which may impact the school's location and recruitment efforts, both of which may affect racial composition. While this consideration does not negate the findings that some charter schools decrease racial integration, it is important to recognize that some stratification in charter schools is due to a deliberate effort to reach underserved students.

## Voucher programs

Vouchers are publicly funded scholarships that allow students to attend private schools. Many participating private schools are religious. Private schools accepting vouchers may or may not face the same governmental regulations as traditional public schools about testing, admissions, or school organization, depending on the design of the voucher program. However, most private schools, voucher-accepting or not, face state regulations (US Department of Education, 2009), and many voucher programs carry additional requirements (Catt, 2014; National Conference of State Legislatures, 2014). Table 4 summarizes the results of the studies examining integration in this context.

One study examined a state-wide voucher program using student-level data. Egalite and Mills (2014) examined a statewide voucher program in Louisiana, and evaluated the dynamic impact of vouchers on racial integration by tracking individual student moves between TPSs and private schools using the Louisiana Scholarship Program (LSP) voucher. They found that 83% of LSP transfers had an integrating effect on the TPSs students left, and 50% had an integrating effect on the private schools students entered. This effect was largely driven by transfers of African American and Hispanic students, who were more likely to make integrative moves than White students.

Seven studies looked at city-wide voucher programs in urban centers. All of the analyses used school level data to evaluate whether private schools with voucher students or TPSs more closely resembled the community around them. In Washington, DC, Greene and Winters (2007) found that 47% of voucher students attended schools where 90% or more of students were of the same race, while 85% of TPS students attended such racially homogenous schools. Further, the racial composition of DC voucher schools more closely resembled the racial composition of the DC metro area than traditional public schools, indicating that voucher-accepting private schools were more integrated than DC TPS. Similarly, in Cleveland, Greene (1999) found that

**Table 4.** Impacts of voucher programs on racial integration.

| Paper | Years of analysis | Location | Research design | Unit of analysis | Comparison group | Main findings |
|---|---|---|---|---|---|---|
| Egalite and Mills (2014) | 2009–2010 through 2012–2013 | Louisiana | Difference in school racial comp, change in difference due to LSP student transfer | Student/school level | Census CBSA | 17% of LSP schools and 34% of public schools are racially homogenous. 83% of LSP transfers have an integrating effect on the sending school; half have an integrating effect on the receiving school. Black and Hispanic moves most likely to be integrative |
| Greene and Winters (2007) | 2004–2005 | Washington, DC | Difference in racial comp; % of students in hyper segregated schools | School | Metro area; voucher private schools vs. TPSs | Voucher schools' racial comp better resembled metro area. 47.3% of voucher schools were 90% racially homogenous or more; 85.4% of TPSs were |
| Greene, Mills, and Buck (2010) | 2006–2007 through 2008–2009 | Milwaukee, WI | Difference in school comp and metro area; % of students in integrated school | School | 5–19-year-old population in Milwaukee metro area | Both MPCP and MPS school substantially different demographically from area; no substantial difference in integration between sectors |
| Greene (1999) | 1999–2000 | Cleveland, OH | Compare CSP schools to TPSs | School | Racial composition of Cleveland | 19% of voucher students are in an integrated school, as are 5.2% of TPS students |
| Fuller and Mitchell (2000) | 1999–2000 | Milwaukee, WI | Difference in school racial comp | School | All students in Milwaukee school system | 50% of students in TPSs, 30% of MPCP students in racially isolated schools. Nonreligious private schools heavily African American, created to serve African-American students |
| Forster (2006a) | 2003 | Cleveland, OH | Segregation Index (statistically adjusted difference in racial comp between school and | School | Cleveland TPSs | Voucher schools were more integrated than public schools by 18 percentage points on the Segregation Index |
| Forster (2006b) | 2003 | Milwaukee, WI | census area) | School | Milwaukee TPSs | MPCP schools more integrated than TPSs by 13 points on Segregation Index |
| Fuller and Greiveldinger (2002) | 2002 | Milwaukee, WI | Compare % of students at racially isolated (90%+ White or 90% students of color) | School | Milwaukee TPSs | 54.4% of students in Milwaukee TPSs are in racially isolated schools; 49.8% of students in MPCP schools are in racially isolated schools |

only 19% of voucher students and 5% of TPS students were in integrated schools, which were defined in the study as demographically similar to the Cleveland area. Forster compared school racial composition to the racial composition of all 5–19 year olds in the Cleveland Census area while statistically controlling for school level and weighting by school size. Forster found that voucher-participating schools in Cleveland were more integrated than traditional public schools in the Cleveland metro area by 18 percentage points.

Four studies examined the impact of the Milwaukee Parental Choice Program (MPCP). Fuller and Mitchell (2000) found that in the 1999–00 school year 50% of TPS students were in racially isolated schools, as were 30% of voucher students attending religious private schools. Fuller and Greiveldinger (2002) used the same definition of racially isolated schools—over 90% White or over 90% students of color—but analyzed data from the 2001–02 school year. They found that 54.4% of students in Milwaukee Public Schools (MPS) attended racially isolated schools while 49.8% of MPCP students attended racially isolated schools. Fuller and Greivldinger also found that 41.8% of MPCP students attending religious private schools were in racially isolated environments, and noted that racial isolation was highest (75.5% of students) at non-religious private schools. Before the MPCP was created, several private schools were established specifically to serve Black or Latino children, as parents felt the MPS schools were not providing an adequate education to such students. The high rate of racial isolation in non-religious private schools was due to this emphasis, rather than the establishment of "white flight" private schools.

Next, Forster (2006b) found that voucher-participating private schools in Milwaukee were more integrated than their MPS counterparts by 13 percentage points on his Segregation Index, a statistically adjusted measure of the difference in racial composition between the school and the 5–19 year old population's racial composition in the Milwaukee Census area. However, Greene, Mills, and Buck (2010) found no substantial differences in the level of integration between MPCP and MPS schools, noting the salience of inter- and intra-district traditional public school choice in the Milwaukee area. When viewed chronologically, the four studies of racial integration in the context of the MPCP suggest that the integrative impact of the program has shifted as the program has matured--at first improving integration, then reaching an equilibrium at which integration levels were similar to those observed in MPS schools.

### *Summary—effects of vouchers on racial integration*

Seven of the eight studies examining the impacts of vouchers on racial integration found that vouchers increased racial integration for participating students. The only study (Egalite & Mills, 2014) to examine the impact of student moves on TPSs also found that students leaving TPSs using a voucher increased the integration of the sending school. These findings may be surprising to some readers given past research (such as Reardon and Yun, 2002) which found high levels of racial segregation in private schools. However, as vouchers are designed to increase access to private schools for disadvantaged populations of students, it is not contradictory to have found that vouchers increased racial integration. Further, past research on the levels of integration of private schools has typically not compared private schools to an external standard, such as the racial composition of the surrounding area, or the racial composition of traditional public schools. Indeed, because of a history of racial segregation in housing, and the reliance of traditional public schools on students' address to assign students to a school, it is perhaps unsurprising that traditional public schools exhibit, to this day, high levels of racial segregation, and that choice programs, including vouchers, that decouple the link between address and school actually increase racial integration.

## Discussion and conclusion

The literature on the impact of choice programs on racial integration is mixed, and varies greatly based on the type and location of choice program. Table 5 summarizes these findings by the type of choice program evaluated[3].

Of the eight studies of district choice, five found that it increased racial integration and three found that it decreased integration. The results for charter schools were even more mixed. Two studies found only positive impacts of charters on racial integration, while three studies found that the impact of charters on racial integration was mediated by the location of the program. One study found that charters had no impact on racial integration, while three found that charters decreased racial integration. While the studies examining voucher programs have generally found positive impacts on racial integration, the question is far from settled. Only one study used the most rigorous research design of examining the dynamic impact of student transfers, and only four separate voucher programs have been evaluated for their impact on racial integration.

While school choice programs have generally been found to increase racial integration, the impact of choice is also mediated by the broader context in which the program is located and program design. More research is needed

**Table 5.** Summary of impacts on integration in all studies, by type of choice program.

| | District choice | Charters | Vouchers |
|---|---|---|---|
| Positive impact | 5 | 3 | 7 |
| Neutral impact | 0 | 1 | 1 |
| Negative impact | 3 | 2 | 0 |
| Impact mixed by geography | 0 | 3 | 0 |

on the local impacts of choice on racial integration, particularly analyses that examine the dynamic impact of student moves on the level of integration in the school's students exit and enter. These analyses allow for a better understanding of how choice programs in specific contexts impact racial integration.

Integration is only partially measured by school demographics. Within-school integration is not examined in this review, but poses a significant question for researchers and policymakers. For example, Cullen, Jacob, and Levitt (2006) find some evidence that students who attend a higher-quality school through an open enrollment lottery process may be placed in lower tracks within those schools. Thus, just because a school appears to be integrated, by whichever definition, within that school there may be higher levels of segregation between classes. Further, these analyses cannot tell us whether students of all backgrounds in an "integrated" school feel affirmed and valued. These questions deserve consideration as researchers continue to study racial integration in schools.

## Disclosure statement

No potential conflict of interest was reported by the authors.

## Notes

1. Interracial exposure reflects the percentage of White students in the average Black student's school. Higher values correspond with higher levels of integration, while lower values correspond to lower levels of integration.
2. Racial imbalance was measured with the index of dissimilarity, which ranges from 0 to 1. The index measures the degree to which a school differs from the racial composition of the district. For example, if a school is 99% Black, and the district is 99% Black, the district would have a score of 0, indicating it was perfectly similar. If the school were 99% Black, and the district were 1% Black, it would have a score of nearly 1, indicating it was practically perfectly dissimilar.
3. Each study is counted once to avoid double-counting of effects. For example, the Koedel et al. (2009) study is counted once as finding that district choice plans increase integration, although the study found positive impacts of both magnet schools, open enrollment, and voluntary busing on racial integration.
4. Included sites were Chicago, San Diego, Philadelphia, Denver, Milwaukee, and the states of Ohio and Texas. The same study included Florida in an analysis of the academic impacts of charter attendance.

## References

Bifulco, R., & Ladd, H. (2007). School choice, racial segregation, and test-score gaps: Evidence from North Carolina's charter school program. *Journal of Policy Analysis and Management*, *26*(1), 31–56. doi:10.1002/(ISSN)1520-6688

Bifulco, R., Ladd, H., & Ross, S. (2009). Public school choice and integration evidence from Durham, North Carolina. *Social Science Research, 38*(1), 71–85. doi:10.1016/j.ssresearch.2008.10.001

Booker, K., Zimmer, R., & Buddin, R. (2005). *The effect of charter schools on school peer composition* (RAND Education Working Paper WR-306-EDU). Santa Monica, CA: RAND Education.

Catt, D. (2014). *Public rules on private schools: Measuring the regulatory impact of state statutes and school choice programs.* Indianapolis, IN: Friedman Foundation for Educational Choice. Retrieved from https://www.edchoice.org/research/public-rules-on-private-schools/

Christenson, B., Eaton, M., Garet, M., Miller, L., Hikawa, H., & DuBois, P. (2003). *Evaluation of the Magnet Schools Assistance Program, 1998 grantees.* Washington, DC: Policy and Program Studies Service, US Department of Education.

Cobb, C., & Glass, G. (2009). School choice in a post-desegregation world. *Peabody Journal of Education, 84*(2), 262–278. doi:10.1080/01619560902810187

Cullen, J., Jacob, B., & Levitt, S. (2000). *The impact of school choice on student outcomes: An analysis of the Chicago Public Schools* (NBER Working Paper 7888). Cambridge, MA: National Bureau of Economic Research.

Cullen, J., Jacob, B., & Levitt, S. (2006). The effect of school choice on participants: Evidence from randomized lotteries. *Econometrica, 74*(5), 1191–1230. doi:10.1111/ecta.2006.74.issue-5

Egalite, A., & Mills, J. (2014). The Louisiana Scholarship Program. *Education Next, 14*(1), 66–69.

Forster, G. (2006a). Segregation levels in Cleveland public schools and the Cleveland voucher program. *School Choice Issues in the State.* Retrieved from http://www.edchoice.org/wp-content/uploads/2015/09/Segregation-Levels-in-Cleveland-Public-Schools-and-the-Cleveland-Voucher-Program.pdf

Forster, G. (2006b). Segregation levels in Milwaukee public schools and the Milwaukee voucher program. *School Choice Issues in the State.* Retrieved from http://www.edchoice.org/wp-content/uploads/2015/09/Segregation-Levels-in-Milwaukee-Public-Schools-and-the-Milwaukee-Voucher-Program.pdf

Fuller, H., & Greiveldinger, D. (2002). *The impact of school choice on racial integration in Milwaukee private schools.* Howard Fuller. Retrieved from howard.fuller@marquette.edu

Fuller, H., & Mitchell, G. (2000). *The Impact of school choice on integration in Milwaukee* (Report MU-CAS-CEI-2000-02). Milwaukee, WI: Marquette University.

Greene, J. (1999). *The racial, economic, and religious context of parental choice in Cleveland.* Washington, DC: Association for Policy Analysis and Management.

Greene, J., Mills, J., & Buck, S. (2010). *The Milwaukee parental choice program's effect on school integration* (SCDP Milwaukee Evaluation Report #20). Retrieved from http://www.uaedreform.org/downloads/2010/04/report-20-the-milwaukee-parental-choice-programs-effect-on-school-integration.pdf.

Greene, J., & Winters, M. (2007). An evaluation of the effect of DC's voucher program on public school achievement and racial integration after one year. *Journal of Catholic Education, 11*(1), 83–101.

Koedel, C., Betts, J. R., Rice, L. A., & Zau, A. C. (2009). The integrating and segregating effects of school choice. *Peabody Journal of Education, 84*(2), 110–129. doi:10.1080/01619560902810096

Miron, G., Urschel, J., Mathis, W., & Tornquist, E. (2010). *Schools with diversity: Education management organizations, charter schools, and the demographic stratification of the American school system.* Boulder, CO: Boulder and Tempe: Education and the Public Interest Center & Education Policy Research Unit.

National Conference of State Legislatures. (2014). *School voucher laws: State-by-state comparison*. Retrieved from http://www.ncsl.org/documents/educ/StateByStateVoucherComparison.pdf

Parker, W. (2012). From the failure of desegregation to the failure of choice. *Journal of Law & Policy, 40*, 117–151.

Rapp, K., & Eckes, S. (2007). Dispelling the myth of "white flight": An examination of minority enrollment in charter schools. *Educational Policy, 21*(4), 615–661. doi:10.1177/0895904806290123

Reardon, S., & Yun, J. (2002). Private school racial enrollments and segregation. In R. D. Kahlenberg (Ed.), *Public school choice vs. Private school vouchers*. New York, NY: Century Foundation Press.

Renzulli, L., & Evans, L. (2005). School choice, charter schools, and white flight. *Social Problems, 52*(3), 398–418. doi:10.1525/sp.2005.52.3.398

Ritter, G., Jensen, N., Kisida, B., & McGee, J. (2010). A closer look at charter schools and segregation. *Education Next, 10*(3), 69–73.

Ritter, G. W., Jensen, N. C., Kisida, B., & Bowen, D. H. (2016). Urban school choice and integration: The effect of charter schools in little rock. *Education and Urban Society, 48*(6), 535–555. doi:10.1177/0013124514546219

Rossell, C., & Armor, D. (1996). The effectiveness of school desegregation plans, 1968-1991. *American Politics Quarterly, 24*(3), 267–302. doi:10.1177/1532673X9602400301

Saporito, S. (2003). Private choices, public consequences: Magnet school choice and segregation by race and poverty. *Social Problems, 50*(2), 181–203. doi:10.1525/sp.2003.50.2.181

Siegel-Hawley, G. (2014). Race, choice, and Richmond public schools: New possibilities and ongoing challenges for diversity in urban districts. *Urban Rev, 46*, 507–534. doi:10.1007/s11256-014-0277-6

Swanson, E., McKenzie, S., & Ritter, G. (2016). Integration in little rock, Part 2: Racial and socioeconomic integration in Llttle rock metro area public schools. *Arkansas Education Report, 13*(3). University of Arkansas: Office for Education Policy. Retrieved from http://www.officeforeducationpolicy.org/downloads/2016/12/integration-in-little-rock-part-2-2.pdf

U.S. Department of Education. (2009). *State regulation of private schools*. Retrieved from https://www2.ed.gov/admins/comm/choice/regprivschl/regprivschl.pdf

Zimmer, R., Gill, B., Booker, K., Lavertu, S., Sass, T., & Witte, J. (2009). Charter schools in eight states: Effects on achievement, attainment, integration, and competition. *RAND Corporation*. Retrieved from https://www.rand.org/content/dam/rand/pubs/monographs/2009/RAND_MG869.pdf

# Evidence on charter school practices related to student enrollment and retention

Kaitlin P. Anderson

**ABSTRACT**

Opponents of charter schools argue these schools "cream-skim" the best students from traditional public schools and push out hard-to-educate students. This paper reviews 22 studies of enrollment issues related to student achievement, special education status, English proficiency, and student discipline in US charter schools. Of the 22 studies, nine use student level data to rigorously test for evidence of strategic enrollment. While the charter sector as a whole tends to serve fewer special education students and English language learners, there is much within-sector variation. Over all, there is very little evidence of systematic "cream-skimming" or "push-out" in US charter schools.

## Introduction

Charter schools, "independently run public schools exempt from many rules and regulations in exchange for increased accountability" (EdChoice, 2016), are a hotly contested form of school choice. Charter schools first appeared in 1992, and now serve over 2.9 million students in the United States (National Alliance for Public Charter Schools, 2015). Opponents of charter schools argue that these schools "cream-skim" the best students from the traditional public schools (TPSs) and push hard-to-educate students out the door. The theoretical motivation for influencing enrollment is that charter schools need student enrollment to survive and may seek out a strong academic reputation by not serving expensive to educate students (Zimmer & Guarino, 2013). One charter school critic has referred to strategic enrollment practices as the "Dirty Dozen" (Welner, 2013). This "Dirty Dozen" includes strategies such as burdensome application forms and interviews, locating or marketing in more advantaged areas, counseling students out, failing to provide services for high-needs students, and disciplining students more harshly. The media has highlighted concerns about these strategies in particular school districts (Brown, 2013; Decker, 2014; Simon, 2013).

On the other side, supporters argue that charters serve more disadvantaged students, citing evidence of growth in the number of charter schools serving ethnically and socioeconomically diverse student populations (Kern, Thukral, & Ziebarth, 2012; Russo, 2013). In the traditional system, school assignment is based on residence, and poor families lack real choices due to their relative inability to move, so market-based strategies may simultaneously promote quality and equity (Hassel, 1999; Schneider, Teske, & Marshall, 2000; Viteritti, 1999).

While some charter schools may actively seek a certain student population, any attempt to paint all charter schools with the same brush will fall short. There are many different types of charters: some have a specific curricular or programmatic focus or a specific target population, some are independent start-ups, some parts of a network or charter management organization, and some are district-conversion schools. Because of this variety, statements about what "charter schools do" are too general to be of use. Further, differences across sectors do not necessarily indicate actions taken by schools. They could, instead, reflect more motivated families utilizing their choice options (Lee & Croninger, 1994; Wells, 1993; Zimmer & Guarino, 2013) or that some families with students in special education might prefer the services in the TPS system. Some selection may be beneficial if it increases the degree of fit between the student and the school, but some other forms of selection may be discriminatory. This article reviews the available evidence on selective enrollment in U.S. charter schools. Given the wide variety of charter schools, this work includes national overviews for a high-level perspective, as well as studies utilizing student-level data in specific contexts. In many cases, studies cannot or do not directly test whether a school is actively creaming or pushing out students; so throughout this article, these terms generally refer to differential enrollment patterns across the sectors, some of which likely is the result of passive selection or "attraction bias".

## *Search and selection process*

I set out to find empirical studies that assess whether there are differences in enrollment patterns for students with disabilities (SWDs), English language learners (ELLs), and students with either high or low prior academic achievement. I used a thorough Internet and library search, snowballing techniques, and expert review. In addition, I included papers that address whether disciplinary rates are different between charter schools and TPSs, and whether this may constitute some sort of push-out. I obtained 48 articles, only 19 of which were empirical studies. The other 29 were theoretical papers, briefs, or news articles not included as a primary source for this review. In addition to these 19 studies, 3 additional papers published in 2017 were included (Winters, 2017; Winters, Carpenter, & Clayton, 2017; Winters, Clayton, & Carpenter, 2017), for a total of 22 empirical studies.

I focus on TPS-charter differences only, ignoring private schools. I exclude articles published prior to 2000, as charter schools served less than 1% of all public school students during the 1999–2000 school year (U.S. Department of Education, National Center for Education Statistics, 2016), and very few large-scale studies would have been conducted before this time. I do not focus on enrollment differences by race or socioeconomic status. While these factors are associated with students' educational options and outcomes, low-income or minority students do not, necessarily, have different learning needs. The student characteristics I focus on of student achievement, ELL status, special education status, and behavioral issues more clearly represent observable characteristics of students that would likely cause them to be more expensive or more difficult to educate, and therefore may be a target for cream-skimming or push-out. Some papers do focus on enrollment issues related to race (Booker, Zimmer, & Buddin, 2005; Zimmer et al., 2009), or income level (Horn & Miron, 2000; Lacireno-Paquet, Holyoke, Moser, & Henig, 2002) and a review of this literature would be a worthwhile, but separate, paper. See Swanson (2017) in this volume for a review of the evidence on the impact of schools of choice on racial integration.

## Review of the literature

The majority (13) of the 22 studies do not test for "cream-skimming" or "push-out" using student-level data. These 13 studies are either qualitative studies or quantitative comparisons at a school level or higher. One of these 13 studies is a review of 7 studies of the Knowledge is Power Program (KIPP) charter network. Of the 22 studies included, 15 (including five of the student-level studies) include enrollment issues related to special education status, 7 (one student-level study) include enrollment issues related to English proficiency, 6 (five student-level studies) include enrollment issues related to academic achievement, and 4 (zero student-level studies) assess discipline-related "push-out." Each of these studies is presented in Table 1. In the sections that follow, I discuss the evidence on each of these four issues.

## Evidence on charter and TPS enrollment and identification of special education students

Charter enrollment of SWDs is a hot topic, with a total of 15 studies addressing this issue. These papers are discussed by data source/type (national comparisons using school-level data, KIPP-specific studies, state-specific studies, and quantitative studies using student-level data).

### *National comparisons across sector using school-level data*

Some studies simply compare student populations across sectors using national data (Malkus, 2016; Miron, Urschel, Mathis, & Tornquist, 2010; U. S. Government Accountability Office, 2012) or nearly national data (Fiore,

**Table 1.** Description of studies.

| | PUBLICATION INFO | | | TYPE OF ANALYSIS | | | | CONTEXT | |
|---|---|---|---|---|---|---|---|---|---|
| | Authors (Year) | Publication Title | Publication Type | Quantitative Assessment? | Qualitative Description? | Entry | Exit | Data Source/Context | Unit of Analysis |
| Special Education Status | Estes (2004) | Choice for All? Charter Schools and Students with Special Needs | PEER REVIEWED: The Journal of Special Education | N | Y | Y | Y | Texas (6 charter schools) | Administrator level interviews |
| | Fiore, Harwell, Blackorby, & Finnigan (2000) | Charter Schools and Students with Disabilities: A National Study. Final Report | Report for the Office of Education Research and Improvement (US Dept. of Ed.) | N | Y | Y | Y | 32 charter schools in 15 states | School-level (and contacted parents, teachers, students, administrators) |
| | Henig (2008) | What do we know about the outcomes of KIPP schools? | Great Lakes Center for Educ. Research and Practice | Y (Review of other studies) | N | Y | Y | KIPP (review of multiple studies) | Review of student-level studies |
| | Horn & Miron (2000) | An evaluation of the Michigan Charter School Initiative: Performance, Accountability, and Impact | The Evaluation Center, Western Michigan University | Y | Y | Y (Qual only) | Y (Qual only) | 51 charter schools, 1997-98 (about half of Michigan charter schools) | School data, surveys, site visits, interviews, document review |
| | Government Accountability Office (2012) | Charter Schools: Additional Federal Attention Needed to Help Protect Access for Students with Disabilities | GAO Report to Congressional Requesters | Y | Y | Y (Qual only) | Y (Qual only) | National (41 states with charter schools in 2008-09 and 2009-10) | School data (and site visits) |
| | Lacireno-Paquet, Holyoke, Moser, & Henig (2002) | Creaming versus Cropping: Charter school enrollment practices in response to market incentives | PEER REVIEWED: Educational Evaluation and Policy Analysis | Y | N | Y | Y | Washington DC; in year with the most charter schools: 30 charter campuses and 147 DCPS schools | School |
| | Lange & Lehr (2000) | Charter schools and students with disabilities: Parent perceptions… | PEER REVIEWED: Remedial and Special Education | N | Y | Y | Y | Minnesota | Surveyed parents |
| | Malkus (2016) | Differences on Balance: National Comparisons of Charter and Traditional Public Schools | American Enterprise Institute | Y | N | N | N | All U.S. public schools; 2011-12 Common Core of Data (CCD) and Civil Rights Data Collection | School |
| | Miron, Urschel, Mathis, & Tornquist (2010) | Schools without diversity: Education management organizations, charter schools, and… | EPIC/EPRU Policy Brief | Y | N | N | N | National (EMO-run schools, 95% of which are charters; from NCES Common Core of Data) | School |
| | Miron, Urschel, & Saxton (2011) | What makes KIPP Work? A study of student characteristics, attrition, and school finance | National Center for the Study of Privatization in Education, Teachers College, Columbia U., and the Study Group on EMOs at Western Michigan U. | Y | N | N | N | KIPP: Common Core of Data (CCD) 2008-09; school-level datasets and KIPP annual report; able to obtain federal data on 60 out of 64 campuses (94%) | District/Charter Level |
| | Nichols-Barrer, Gleason, Gill, & Tuttle (2016) | Student selection, attrition, and replacement in KIPP middle schools | PEER REVIEWED: Educational Evaluation and Policy Analysis | Y | N | Y | Y | 19 KIPP Middle Schools in 9 states and DC | Student |
| | Winters (2013) | Why the gap? Special education and New York City charter schools | Center on Reinventing Public Education (CRPE) Publication | Y | N | Y | Y | New York City Charter Schools and TPSs; Student level data plus lottery data for a sample of 25 charter schools | Student |
| | Winters (2014; 2017) | Understanding the charter school special education gap... (2014); Understanding the gap in special education enrollments... (2017) | Center on Reinventing Public Education (2014) and PEER REVIEWED in Educational Researcher (2017) | Y | N | Y | Y | Denver Charter Schools and TPSs; Student level data including district-wide enrollment system data | Student |
| | Winters, Carpenter, & Clayton (2017) | Does attending a charter school reduce the likelihood of being placed into special education? Evidence from Denver, Colorado | Edcuational Evaluation and Policy Analysis | Y | N | Y | Y | Denver Charter Schools and TPSs; Student level data including district-wide enrollment system data | Student |

(*Continued*)

**Table 1.** (Continued).

| | PUBLICATION INFO | | | TYPE OF ANALYSIS | | | | CONTEXT | |
|---|---|---|---|---|---|---|---|---|---|
| | **Authors (Year)** | **Publication Title** | **Publication Type** | **Quantitative Assessment?** | **Qualitative Description?** | **Entry** | **Exit** | **Data Source/Context** | **Unit of Analysis** |
| English Proficiency | Henig (2008) | What do we know about the outcomes of KIPP schools? | Great Lakes Center for Educ. Research and Practice | Y (Review of other studies) | N | Y | Y | KIPP (review of multiple studies) | Review of student-level studies |
| | Lacireno-Paquet, Holyoke, Moser, & Henig (2002) | Creaming versus Cropping: Charter school enrollment practices in response to market incentives | PEER REVIEWED: Educational Evaluation and Policy Analysis | Y | N | Y | Y | Washington DC; in year with the most charter schools: 30 charter campuses and 147 DCPS schools | School |
| | Malkus (2016) | Differences on Balance: National Comparisons of Charter and Traditional Public Schools | American Enterprise Institute | Y | N | N | N | All U.S. public schools; 2011-12 Common Core of Data (CCD) and 2011-12 Civil Rights Data Collection | School |
| | Miron, Urschel, Mathis, & Tornquist (2010) | Schools without diversity: Education management organizations, charter schools, and… | EPIC/EPRU Policy Brief | Y | N | N | N | National (EMO-run schools, 95% of which are charters; from NCES Common Core of Data) | School |
| | Miron, Urschel, & Saxton (2011) | What makes KIPP Work? A study of student characteristics, attrition, and school finance | National Center for the Study of Privatization in Education, Teachers College, Columbia U., and the Study Group on EMOs at Western Michigan U. | Y | N | N | N | KIPP; Common Core of Data (CCD) 2008-09; school-level datasets and KIPP annual report; able to obtain federal data on 60 out of 64 campuses (94%) | District/Charter Level |
| | Multicultural Education, Training, & Advocacy (2009) | Charter Schools and English Language Learners in Massachusetts… | META Policy Brief | Y | N | N | N | Massachusetts | District/Charter Level |
| | Nichols-Barrer, Gleason, Gill, & Tuttle (2016) | Student selection, attrition, and replacement in KIPP middle schools | PEER REVIEWED: Educational Evaluation and Policy Analysis | Y | N | Y | Y | 19 KIPP Middle Schools in 9 states and DC | Student |
| Student Prior Achievement | Booker, Zimmer, & Buddin (2005) | The Effect of Charter Schools on School Peer Composition | RAND Working Paper | Y | N | Y | N | California and Texas Charter Schools and TPSs | Student |
| | Henig (2008) | What do we know about the outcomes of KIPP schools? | Great Lakes Center for Educ. Research and Practice | Y (Review of other studies) | N | Y | Y | KIPP (review of multiple studies) | Review of student-level studies |
| | Nichols-Barrer, Gleason, Gill, & Tuttle (2016) | Student selection, attrition, and replacement in KIPP middle schools | PEER REVIEWED: Educational Evaluation and Policy Analysis | Y | N | Y | Y | 19 KIPP Middle Schools in 9 states and DC | Student |
| | Winters, Clayton, & Carpenter (2017) | Are low-performing students more likely to exit charter schools?… | PEER REVIEWED: Economics of Education Review | Y | N | N | Y | NYC and Denver | Student |
| | Zimmer, Gill, Booker, Lavertu, Sass, & Witte (2009) | Charter schools in eight states: Effects on achievement, attainment, integration, and competition | RAND Publication | Y | N | Y | N | 2 States (Ohio and Texas) and 5 Urban Districts (Chicago, Denver, Milwaukee, Philadelphia, San Diego) | Student |
| | Zimmer & Guarino (2013) | Is There Empirical Evidence That Charter Schools "Push Out" Low-Performing | PEER REVIEWED: Educational Evaluation and Policy Analysis | Y | N | N | Y | Anonymous, urban, Large school district with 80% FRL students | Student |
| Discipline | Horn & Miron (2000) | An evaluation of the Michigan Charter School Initiative: Performance, Accountability, and Impact | The Evaluation Center, Western Michigan University | Y | Y | N | N | 51 Michigan charter schools during 1997-98 | School data (and surveys, interviews, site visits, document review) |
| | Losen, Keith, Hodson, & Martinez (2016) | Charter schools, civil rights, and school discipline: A comprehensive review | The Center for Civil Rights Remedies at The Civil Rights Project, UCLA | Y | N | N | N | U.S. Department of Education's Office for Civil Rights Dataset from 2011-12 | School |
| | Malkus (2016) | Differences on Balance: National Comparisons of Charter and Traditional Public Schools | American Enterprise Institute | Y | N | N | N | National data: 2011-12 Civil Rights Data Collection | School |
| | Zubrzycki, Cavanagh, & McNeil (2013) | Charter Schools' Discipline Policies Face Scrutiny | Education Week | Y | N | N | N | U.S. Department of Education's Office for Civil Rights Dataset from 2009-10 | School |

Harwell, Blackorby, & Finnigan, 2000). An early national study focuses on schools operated by Educational Management Organizations (EMOs) (Miron et al., 2010). Using the National Center for Education Statistics (NCES)

Common Core of Data (CCD), they find EMO-operated schools, 95% of which are charters, generally serve a lower proportion of SWDs than their host district. However, some EMO schools focus on serving students with special needs. A major limitation is that there is no description of how the "host" district was selected (Miron et al., 2010).

School-level CCD are also used by the Government Accountability Office (GAO, 2012) to study 41 states with charter schools during 2008–2009 and 2009–2010. Country-level comparisons indicate that SWDs are underrepresented in charter schools, but that in eight states (Iowa, Minnesota, Nevada, New Mexico, Ohio, Pennsylvania, Virginia, and Wyoming), charter schools have at least the same proportion of SWDs as TPSs (U.S. Government Accountability Office, 2012). Both Miron et al. (2010) and the GAO (2012) note there are some charter schools that purposively serve SWDs.

The GAO (2012) supplements the CCD with site visits to 13 charter schools and some TPS districts in three states. Unfortunately, the GAO's (2012) qualitative research is anecdotal and fails to fully explain what drives the special education enrollment gap. While some evidence points to "counseling out," charter school officials also indicate that they informed parents about the availability of special education services in a variety of ways: word of mouth, fliers, mailings, or ads in local media, so perhaps some of the gap is due to "attraction bias" if families of SWDs are more attracted to the services in the TPS sector.

Malkus (2016) contributes to the national view by using the CCD to compare charter schools with their five nearest TPS neighbors in terms of distance, jurisdiction, and grade range. He finds that, relative to their nearby TPS peers, charter schools generally serve a lower proportion of special education students. For example, about 50% of charter schools have special education rates of less than 10%, while only 24% of their neighboring TPSs do.

Fiore et al. (2000) visit 32 charter schools in 15 states and interview hundreds of parents of SWDs, teachers, students, and administrators. While their results are not conclusive, they illustrate a variety of experiences. Some parents of SWDs express dissatisfaction with their previous school as a reason for enrolling in a charter school. At more than half the schools, parents say they were encouraged to enroll their child or that their student's disability was not a focus of discussion. However, approximately one-fourth of the schools report discouraging some parents of SWDs from enrolling, often viewing this counseling process as in the student's best interest. Fiore et al.'s (2000) conclusions do not provide one clear answer on the issue of cream-skimming or enrollment. They explain, "charter schools have varying approaches to attracting students" (p. 42), with some specifically targeting SWDs. While there are lower enrollment rates in charters for students with severe disabilities, students with mild disabilities continue to enroll in charters, even if services are not provided.

### *KIPP studies*

Two papers assess enrollment issues for special education students within the KIPP charter network (Henig, 2008; Miron, Urschel, & Saxton, 2011). Henig (2008) reviews seven studies of the participant effects of KIPP, discussing selection issues within the context of explaining KIPP's positive achievement effects. Henig ultimately concludes that the higher performance of KIPP students relative to TPS students is not driven by selective admissions, because KIPP serves many minority and high-needs students. Of the 36 schools covered, only 4 San Francisco Bay Area KIPP schools enrolled fewer SWDs than their surrounding districts (Woodworth, David, Guha, Wang, & Lopez Torkos, 2008).

In a more recent study, Miron et al. (2011) use CCD district level data, limiting their analysis to 37 KIPP campuses in states where charters are treated as individual local education agencies, covering about 58% of KIPP schools at the time. They find that these KIPP schools serve fewer SWDs (5.9% versus 12.1% in the local school district), but acknowledge that this may be due to self-selection of families and not to KIPP selecting particular students. However, combined with concerns about attrition of low-performing students, the authors conclude that "KIPP's practices that result in selective entry and exit result in homogeneous groups of students that mutually benefit from peers who are engaged, have supportive families, and are willing and able to work hard in school" (p. iv).

### *State-based studies*

Four studies covered a specific state or the District of Columbia: one quantitative analysis with school-level data (Lacireno-Paquet et al., 2002), two qualitative studies (Estes, 2004; Lange & Lehr, 2000), and one mixed-methods study (Horn & Miron, 2000).

Lacireno-Paquet et al. (2002) utilize Washington, D.C., data to test the hypothesis that market-oriented or profit-driven charters would engage in "cream-skimming," but other charter schools may serve a disadvantaged population. They find the D.C. charter sector serves similar proportions of special education students as D.C. Public Schools (DCPS), but there are some differences within the charter sector. For example, market-oriented charters serve fewer special education students than DCPS, leading the authors to conclude these schools may "crop off" service to disadvantaged students. While the difference between the proportion of SWDs served in the non-market-oriented charters and DCPS is not statistically significant, the sign of the coefficients indicates non-market-oriented charters serve a larger proportion of these students (Lacireno-Paquet et al., 2002). In summary, while charter schools in D.C., taken as a whole, do not serve an elite population, market-oriented charter schools may be "cropping off" service to SWDs.

Studies in Texas (Estes, 2004) and Minnesota (Lange & Lehr, 2000) provide qualitative findings on charter school enrollment of SWDs. While the Estes (2004) study only includes seven charter school administrators, Lange and Lehr (2000) conduct an extensive study with more than 600 parents of SWDs at the 16 charter schools then operating in Minnesota. The mixed findings across these two studies reflect the types of participants involved.

In Texas, charter school administrators generally do not indicate "counseling out," suggesting, for example, that they tell parents about the services offered and then let the families decide if it is a good fit (Estes, 2004), perhaps generating "attraction bias" rather than "cream-skimming." However, some administrators report concerns about what to do if students with more severe disabilities apply (Estes, 2004).

Lange and Lehr's (2000) study of Minnesota charter school parents finds that about 45% of parents of SWDs chose the school *because of* the services provided. In addition, 72% of parents of SWDs report more satisfaction with the services at the charter school, relative to their previous school, and a majority of parents report greater availability of special education services in the charter school as well (Lange & Lehr, 2000). Despite these positive findings, the authors acknowledge the issue of selective response in this study – all respondents were remaining in the charter sector, and the respondents may have had a particularly positive experience with their school.

Horn and Miron (2000) find more mixed results. They compare charter schools to their host districts using data from 51 charter schools, composing about half of Michigan charters at the time. They find that SWDs make up only 3.7% of enrollment in Michigan charters, but 12.3% of enrollment in the TPS sector, and the SWDs that do attend charters tend to have more mild disabilities (Horn & Miron, 2000).

In addition to reporting school-level enrollment, Horn and Miron (2000) develop several case studies of school districts using surveys, interviews, and document review. Districts report that students returning from charter schools often need special services, and some parents of SWDs report being counseled out of charter schools due to a lack of services. Further, Kalamazoo public school district officials claim that charter schools often hold students until the official count day for funding and then return them to the TPS district without funds, indicating financial incentives may play a role.

### *Quantitative studies using student-level data*

Five studies use student-level data to rigorously assess the extent to which "cream-skimming" or "push-out" based on disability status occurs (Nichols-Barrer, Gleason, Gill, & Tuttle, 2016; Winters, 2013, 2014, 2017; Winters et al., 2017).

Nichols-Barrer et al. (2016) utilize student-level data from 19 KIPP middle schools in nine states and D.C. In general, KIPP students are less likely to be in special education. Students who exited KIPP were not more likely to be special education students, indicating this type of push-out is not occurring. However, students who initially enroll in KIPP in grades higher than the school's entry grade were less likely to be special education students, so in this way, KIPP's population becomes less disadvantaged over time.

Four studies carefully track enrollment and identification of SWDs in the TPS and charter sectors in New York City (NYC) (Winters, 2013) and Denver (Winters, 2014, 2017, 2017; Winters et al., 2017). Winters (2013) uses student-level data for K-3 students in NYC from 2008–2009 through 2011–2012. They track special education students across the sectors over time and also utilize enrollment lottery data from a subsample of 25 NYC elementary charter schools. Schools self-selected into this subsample, so the results of the lottery analysis may not be representative of the entire NYC charter sector.

Using the full set of NYC elementary public school students, Winters (2013) tracks a cohort of students enrolled in kindergarten in 2008–2009 through 2011–2012. In kindergarten, there is a special education gap between charter schools and TPSs of 6.9 percentage points, with charter schools enrolling even fewer students with speech or language disabilities or autism. Winters is unable to identify students with individualized education plans (IEPs) prior to kindergarten, so perhaps some of this gap is due to identification during kindergarten. Utilizing the lottery data, he determines some of the gap is because kindergarten students who apply to charter schools are less likely to have an IEP than those in TPSs. While the gap grows 1.4 percentage points over the next 4 years, this is primarily due to a greater proportion of TPS students newly identified as having a specific learning disability (SLD) after kindergarten entry. While special education students are highly mobile in both sectors, Winters (2013) rules out "push-out" as a major contribution of the special education gap, because students with IEPs do not leave charter schools at significantly higher rates than they leave the TPS sector.

Using a smaller subsample of students who applied to attend an NYC charter school, Winters (2013) compares students who ended up enrolling in charter schools to similar students who applied to charters but did not enroll. Data availability prevented a lottery-based experimental approach; however, within this subsample of applicants, treatment and comparison group students are similar in that they applied to attend a charter. Compared to the full dataset, the initial special education gap within this applicant group at kindergarten entry is much smaller, and the gap increases over time due to greater SLD growth in the TPSs. To explain this further, Winters estimates a linear probability model to predict whether a student was identified as receiving special education in a given year. Conditional on applying to a charter school in kindergarten, enrolling in a charter in kindergarten decreases the likelihood that a student has an IEP by 1.1 percentage points, and for each year of charter schooling, the probability a student has an IEP decreases by 0.87 percentage points.

Winters (2014, 2017) uses student-level data for all Denver K-8 students between 2008–2009 and 2013–2014 as well as data from Denver's district-wide enrollment system since 2012–2013. Importantly, the enrollment data from Denver include the entire public school sector. He finds that while a gap in special education enrollment does exist, it begins because SWDs are less likely to apply to charters in the entry grades of kindergarten and sixth grade, indicating that, rather than active "cream-skimming" or "push-out," there could be "application bias" due to SWDs preferring TPS services or pre-application counseling. Unfortunately, these papers do not distinguish between these two possibilities. The gap then grows partly due to higher rates of identification of SWDs in the TPS sector. Students who enter a Denver charter school in kindergarten are actually less likely to exit during elementary school than SWDs who enter a TPS in kindergarten (Winters, 2014).

Winters et al. (2017) use Denver administrative data 2012–2015 to estimate whether attending a Denver charter school affects the likelihood that students are classified as having a disability in the primary grades. Due to data limitations, they are not able to utilize the lottery's random assignment to test this question. Instead, they use families' preferences for particular schools revealed in the enrollment system data to control for unobservable differences. They claim that attending a charter school reduces the likelihood of receiving an IEP and in particular reduces the likelihood of being classified as having an SLD, as in NYC (Winters, 2013).

### *Summary of special education studies*

Overall, across the nation, the charter sector tends to serve fewer students with special needs than the TPS sector, but there is more nuance within the sector. For example, in eight states charter schools have at least the same proportion of SWDs as TPSs (U.S. Government Accountability Office, 2012), and some charter schools purposively serve SWDs (Miron et al., 2010; U.S. Government Accountability Office, 2012). Further, while market-oriented charter schools may "crop off" service to SWDs, there is less evidence that non-market-oriented schools serve fewer SWDs in D.C. (Lacireno-Paquet et al., 2002).

Looking more at the sources of these gaps, evidence from student-level studies indicates exit rates for SWDs could even be stronger in the TPS districts than in KIPP schools (Nichols-Barrer et al., 2016). In addition, a variety of papers from Denver and NYC suggest that gaps begin because fewer SWDs apply or attend charter schools at entry grades, but the gap grows primarily due to higher identification rates in the TPSs (Winters, 2013, 2014, 2017; Winters et al., 2017).

Thus, while there are overall differences in the enrollment of special education students, and there is qualitative evidence suggesting that this is due at least in part to strategic behaviors on the part of charter schools (Fiore et al., 2000; Horn & Miron, 2000), it is not fair to characterize all charter schools as actively seeking to not serve SWDs.

## Evidence on charter and TPS enrollment of ELLs

Seven studies assess whether students with limited English proficiency are being served by charter schools at the same rates as in TPSs (Henig, 2008; Lacireno-Pacquet et al., 2002; Malkus, 2016; META, 2009; Miron et al., 2010, 2011; Nichols-Barrer et al., 2016).

### *National comparisons across sector using school-level data*

As with SWDs, Miron et al. (2010) and Malkus (2016) find that charter schools tend to serve a lower proportion of ELLs than their "host" districts or similar nearby schools. Miron et al. (2010) find about 4% of students in EMOs were ELLs, compared to 11% in the TPS sector, but that about one-third of EMO schools served a similar share of ELLs as the sending districts. Malkus (2016) finds sector differences that are less stark for ELLs than for SWDs. For example, 77% of charter schools serve less than 10% ELLs compared to 74% of TPSs.

### *KIPP studies*

As with SWDs, ELLs are served at lower rates in some but not all KIPP charter schools, relative to TPS schools. Four out of five KIPP schools in the San Francisco Bay Area enroll fewer ELLs than their surrounding districts (Woodworth et al., 2008, in Henig, 2008). Using CCD data on 38 KIPP campuses, Miron et al. (2011) estimate that these schools serve fewer ELLs (11.5% versus 19.2% in the local school district). Combined with the lower rates of SWDs in KIPP schools, the authors conclude that KIPP does practice selective entry in a way that may be beneficial for the charter schools and the students in them.

### *State-based studies*

Two studies assess this issue using school-level data within Massachusetts (META, 2009) or D.C. (Lacireno-Paquet et al., 2002). According to a study by Multicultural Education, Training, and Advocacy, Inc. (META, 2009),

ELLs are "conspicuously" missing from Massachusetts charter schools (p. 1). In 32 out of 40 charter schools in the Massachusetts districts with ELL student populations, the proportion of charter school enrollment is less than half of the district's ELL percentage (META, 2009). In particular, immigrant ELL students are overwhelmingly enrolled in TPSs. This article does not identify the mechanism creating these gaps, however.

Lacireno-Paquet et al.'s (2002) comparison of market-oriented and non-market-oriented schools in D.C. finds a similar theme for ELL students as for SWDs: The charter sector overall serves similar proportions of ELLs as the TPS sector, but market-oriented charter schools serve fewer ELLs than DCPS, while non-market-oriented charter schools do not. As a result, the authors conclude that market-oriented charter schools may be "cropping off" service to ELLs.

### *Quantitative study using student-level data*

Nichols-Barrer et al. (2016) utilized student-level data from 19 KIPP middle schools and do not find evidence for "cream-skimming" as KIPP tends to admit students that are similarly disadvantaged. In both KIPP schools and the TPSs, early leavers are actually less likely to be ELLs, refuting concerns about actively pushing out these students (Nichols-Barrer et al., 2016).

### *Summary of English proficiency studies*

As with SWDs, ELLs are underserved in charter schools, relative to the TPS sector, but there may be differences within sector based on market orientation (Lacireno-Paquet et al., 2002) and even within particular charter networks (Henig, 2008; Miron et al., 2011). This pattern, combined with very limited student-level analyses, indicates that, compared to SWDs, we know relatively little about what is driving gaps in enrollment patterns for ELLs between charter schools and TPSs.

## Evidence on charter and TPS enrollment based on prior student achievement

No high level, national studies looked specifically at enrollment of high- or low-performing students in charters, in part because, by nature, to address this question, student-level data are required. Thus, the papers reviewed that assess whether "cream-skimming" or "push-out" based on student achievement occurs are either all student-level studies (Booker et al., 2005; Nichols-Barrer et al., 2016; Winters et al., 2017; Zimmer et al., 2009; Zimmer & Guarino, 2013) or a review of KIPP student-level studies (Henig, 2008).

Henig (2008) reviews seven KIPP studies and argues that the higher performance of KIPP students relative to TPS students is not driven by selective admissions. Of the 36 schools included in his review, there is an indication of entry-level selection based on prior student achievement in only one school. In Houston, according to Doran and Drury (as cited in Henig, 2008), students who enter KIPP were making above-average achievement gains even before they enrolled. Henig does note, however, that the students who leave KIPP tend to perform less well than those who stay. Despite these select cases, Henig (2008) does not point to selective entry or exit as contributing to the positive KIPP effects overall.

Booker et al. (2005) utilize data from Texas and a subset of California districts to assess the academic performance of sector switchers. They find that students who move to charter schools are lower performing on average, so there is no evidence of "cream-skimming" based on achievement in these contexts. In Texas, charter school switchers have 0.23 standard deviations lower math scores and 0.16 lower reading scores than their TPS peers. In addition, sector switchers in Texas come from schools with mean scores below the state average, so Texas charter schools tend to draw extremely low-performing students from already low-performing TPS schools (Booker et al., 2005).

Zimmer et al. (2009) also address "cream-skimming" by prior achievement, using student-level data from two states (Ohio and Texas) and five additional urban districts (Chicago, San Diego, Philadelphia, Denver, and Milwaukee). The results vary by context. In Chicago and Philadelphia, charter switchers are higher performing than peers in their previous TPS, potentially signaling "cream-skimming," but they are lower performing in Denver, San Diego, Ohio, and Texas and about the same in Milwaukee. In Ohio and Texas, charter switchers are much lower achieving.

To test for evidence of "push-out," Zimmer and Guarino (2013) utilize 7 years of data from an anonymous, large, urban school district. Zimmer and Guarino (2013) acknowledge students do not just exit from charter schools, but from TPSs as well, so they compare exit rates across sectors. The authors conduct linear probability analysis to predict nonstructural moves. The variables of interest are student performance relative to campus or district performance as well as interactions of low performance with charter attendance and of low performance with TPS attendance. They control for student demographic variables such as race, gender, special needs, and Limited English Proficiency (LEP) status, but not Free and Reduced-price Lunch (FRL) status. In general, they find no empirical evidence to support "push-out." While lower than average students are more likely to make nonstructural moves, the rates are similar across sectors.

Following a similar approach as in Zimmer and Guarino (2013), Winters et al. (2017) use 6 years of NYC and Denver student-level data to assess whether low-performing students are exiting at higher rates in the charter schools in these cities. They focus on exits that are followed by entry to another school within the same district to lessen the chance that these moves are due to moves out of the area, rather than moving due to experiences in the school. While low-performing students in general are more likely to exit both kinds of schools, they conclude there is "no evidence of a differential relationship between prior performance and the likelihood of exiting a school by sector" (p. 1). These results are robust across a variety of definitions of low prior performance.

Finally, Nichols-Barrer et al. (2016) utilize student-level data from 19 KIPP middle schools in 9 states and D.C. and find that KIPP schools tend to replace students who exit with higher achieving students and that fewer students are replaced in later grades. These two factors can make school composition higher achieving over time.

### *Summary of student prior achievement studies*

In sum, charter schools are generally not systematically selecting the highest achieving students or "pushing-out" the lowest achieving. There was no evidence of achievement based push-out in charter schools (Winters et al., 2017; Zimmer & Guarino, 2013), an indication of possible "cream-skimming" by prior achievement in only two geographic locations, Chicago and Philadelphia (Zimmer et al., 2009), and only one indication of selective enrollment in the form of replacing students with higher performing ones (Nichols-Barrer et al., 2016).

## Evidence on student discipline and enrollment in charter and TPSs

Four studies attempt to test whether charter schools use disciplinary consequences to "push-out" students, but fail to provide rigorous evidence to address those claims. Two papers focus solely on discipline issues (Losen, Keith, Hodson, & Martinez, 2016; Zubrzycki, Cavanagh, & McNeil, 2013), while two include discipline issues in addition to the enrollment issues mentioned previously (Horn & Miron, 2000; Malkus, 2016). This issue is somewhat different from those discussed previously, because disciplinary actions could be viewed more as a mechanism for push-out (Brown, 2013; Welner, 2013) than a student characteristic that causes a student to be a target for push-out or cream-skimming.

Horn and Miron (2000) use school-based data from 51 charter schools representing about half of the Michigan charter schools in operation at the time. The other three studies (Losen et al., 2016; Malkus, 2016; Zubrzycki et al., 2013) include national data. Qualitative evidence from district officials in Michigan indicates that behavior and discipline are one of the common reasons students leave the TPS districts for charter schools, but also that frequent suspensions in the charter schools "nearly forced" some students to return to the TPS district (Horn & Miron, 2000). Of course, these are personal reports of district officials and not conclusive evidence of systemic selective enrollment strategies.

Turning to the three national studies, suspension and expulsion rates in the charter schools tend to differ from those in the TPS districts, but due to differences across contexts, as well as limited data availability, making any general statement is nearly impossible (Losen et al., 2016; Malkus, 2016; Zubrzycki et al., 2013). These three national studies all use the Civil Rights Data Collection from the U.S. Department of Education's Office of Civil Rights. A major limitation of these data is that they report "unduplicated counts of suspended students," not accounting for repeat offenses by students (Losen et al., 2016, p. 29). Further, these three studies simply compare rates across sectors, so they are not a true test of disciplinary "push-out."

Losen et al. (2016), for example, use 2011–2012 data from more than 5,250 charter schools and 95,000 public schools and find "deep disparities in discipline practices" at many charter schools (p. 6). However, similar disparities occur within the TPS district as well: In charter schools, about 15.5% of SWDs are suspended at least once, compared to 7% of students without disabilities, but in noncharter public schools the gap is almost as large, at 8 percentage points. Therefore, Losen et al.'s (2016) focus on the "deep disparities" at the charter schools purposefully ignores large disparities in the TPS sector as well.

Similarly, researchers at *Education Week* analyze suspension and expulsion rates and highlight cities where the rates of suspensions at charter schools are about double those of the TPS system (Zubrzycki et al., 2013). A major problem is that there is a lot of variation within a city, so charter schools should be compared to the TPSs the students would have otherwise attended, not the entire city. Further, this work by Zubrzycki et al. (2013) highlights troubling city level disparities across sectors, even though, overall, TPSs have *higher* suspension rates than charter schools (6% versus 4%) and similar expulsion rates (0.20% versus 0.12%).

Malkus (2016) conducts a more reasonable comparison and finds disparities in suspension rates mostly disappear when comparing charters to their *neighboring* public schools, "casting doubt on whether charter discipline is disproportionate" (p. 7). In conclusion, while a few studies have compared charter school and TPS suspension and expulsion rates in response to complaints about "push-out", the findings should be interpreted with these limitations in mind.

## Discussion and conclusions

Overall, the evidence presented here provides evidence of selective enrollment with respect to some characteristics (primary disability status and English proficiency), more so than others, and there is variation within sector as well. Importantly, the nine rigorous analyses using student-level data to track students across sectors (Booker et al., 2005; Nichols-Barrer et al., 2016; Winters, 2013, 2014, 2017; Winters et al., 2017, 2017; Zimmer et al., 2009; Zimmer & Guarino, 2013) find more evidence rejecting, rather than confirming, the hypothesis that charter schools "cream-skim" or "push-out." Among the five original studies using student test scores, there were only two contexts (in a single study) in which "cream-skimming" was indicated (Chicago and Philadelphia, in Zimmer et al., 2009), and only one study finding any evidence of selection in replacement of students who exit (Nichols-Barrer et al., 2016). Rather, evidence indicates charter schools often serve lower performing students or similarly performing students. In the one student-level study looking at LEP status, there was no indication of LEP-based "push-out" (Nichols-Barrer et al., 2016), but more evidence is needed in this area. While there are special education enrollment gaps, it is still unclear whether this is primarily "attraction bias" or could involve some pre-application counseling as well (Winters, 2013, 2014, 2017). Further, although disadvantaged students tend to be mobile, they are mobile in both sectors and in some cases are more likely to exit TPSs than charter schools (Nichols-Barrer et al., 2016; Winters, 2014; Winters et al., 2017; Zimmer & Guarino, 2013).

All of these studies should be interpreted with contextual factors such as location and level of comparison in mind, and policymakers must carefully consider potential unintended consequences. For example, Winters (2013, 2014) cautions policymakers against setting special education enrollment targets for charter schools, because this might incentivize unneeded diagnoses. Obtaining more evidence on this topic is critically important, because many states have or are considering regulations such as caps on the number or size of charter schools (National Alliance for Public Charter Schools, 2017). While this literature review clearly documents that certain types of students (SWDs and ELLs) are underserved in charter schools as a whole, there is also a variety of evidence that indicates some schools are not actively selecting the best students or "pushing-out" the worst, and that in other cases, there is evidence to suggest that the gaps are due, at least in part, to selection by families and not by schools. In addition, there is evidence that decisions to exit charter schools are influenced by school quality (Hanushek, Kain, Rivkin, & Branch, 2007), so this is an important contextual consideration for future research as well. More work is needed to truly understand the practices that charter schools and TPSs as well use to influence and create policies that enable all students to receive the best education possible.

## References

Booker, K., Zimmer, R., & Buddin, R. (2005). *The effect of charter schools on school peer composition*. RAND Working Paper. Retrieved from: http://www.rand.org/pubs/working_papers/WR306.html

Brown, E. (January 5, 2013). D.C. charter schools expel students at far higher rates than traditional public schools. *The Washington Post.* Retrieved from: https://www.washingtonpost.com/local/education/dc-charter-schools-expel-students-at-far-higher-rates-than-traditional-public-schools/2013/01/05/e155e4bc-44a9-11e2-8061-253bccfc7532_story.html?utm_term=.30d677ae0b42

Decker, G. (November 20, 2014). Chancellor Fariña implies some charter schools boosting scores by pushing out students. *Chalkbeat.* Retrieved from: http://www.chalkbeat.org/posts/ny/2014/11/20/farina-implies-some-charter-schools-boosting-scores-by-pushing-out-students/#.VJmrel4DrE

EdChoice. (2016). *Types of school choice.* Retrieved from: https://www.edchoice.org/school-choice/types-of-school-choice/

Estes, M. B. (2004). Choice for all? Charter schools and students with special needs. *The Journal of Special Education, 37*(4), 257–267.

Fiore, T. A., Harwell, L. M., Blackorby, J., & Finnigan, K. S. (2000). *Charter schools and students with disabilities: A national study. Final report.* Washington, DC: Office of Educational Research and Improvement.

Hanushek, E. A., Kain, J. F., Rivkin, S. G., & Branch, G. F. (2007). Charter school quality and parental decision making with school choice. *Journal of Public Economics, 91,* 823–848.

Hassel, B. C. (1999). *The charter school challenge.* Washington, DC: Brookings Institution Press.

Henig, J. R. (2008). *What do we know about the outcomes of KIPP schools?* East Lansing, MI: Great Lakes Center for Education Research & Practice.

Horn, J., & Miron, G. (2000). *An evaluation of the Michigan charter school initiative: Performance, accountability, and impact.* Kalamazoo, MI: The Evaluation Center, Western Michigan University.

Kern, N., Thukral, R., & Ziebarth, T. (May, 2012). *A mission to serve: How public charter schools are designed to meet the diverse demands of our communities.* Washington, DC: National Alliance for Public Charter Schools. Retrieved from http://www.publiccharters.org/wp-content/uploads/2014/01/NAPCS_DiverseModelBrief_5_16_12_20120511T164623.pdf

Lacireno-Paquet, N., Holyoke, T. T., Moser, M., & Henig, J. R. (2002). Creaming versus cropping: Charter school enrollment practices in response to market incentives. *Educational Evaluation and Policy Analysis, 24*(2), 145–158.

Lange, C. M., & Lehr, C. A. (2000). Charter schools and students with disabilities: Parent perceptions of reasons for transfer and satisfaction with services. *Remedial and Special Education, 21*(3), 141–151.

Lee, V., & Croninger, R. G. (1994). Parental choice of schools and social stratification in education: The paradox of Detroit. *Education Evaluation and Policy Analysis, 16,* 434–457.

Losen, D. J., Keith, M. A., Hodson, C. L., & Martinez, T. E. (March, 2016). *Charter schools, civil rights and school discipline: A comprehensive review.* Los Angeles, CA: The Center for Civil Rights Remedies at the Civil Rights Project.

Malkus, N. (2016). *Differences on balance: National comparisons of charter and traditional public schools.* Washington, DC: American Enterprise Institute.

META. (2009). *Charter schools and English language learners in Massachusetts: Policy push without the data.*

Miron, G., Urschel, J. L., Mathis, W. J., & Tornquist, E. (2010). *Schools without diversity: Education management organizations, charter schools, and the demographic stratification of the American school system.* Boulder, CO and Tempe, AZ: Education and the Public Interest Center & Education Policy Research Unit. Retrieved from: http://nepc.colorado.edu/publication/schools-without-diversity

Miron, G., Urschel, J. L., & Saxton, N. (2011). *What makes KIPP work? A study of student characteristics, attrition, and school finance.* New York, NY and Kalamazoo, MI: National Center for the Study of Privatization in Education (Teachers College, Columbia University) and the Study Group on Educational Management (Western Michigan University).

National Alliance for Public Charter Schools. (2015). *Annual report.* Retrieved from http://cdn2.hubspot.net/hubfs/560116/NAPSCAR_Booklet_Digital_V1_WEB.pdf?t=1463430188645

National Alliance for Public Charter Schools. (2017). *Measuring up.* Retrieved from http://www.publiccharters.org/law-database/caps/

Nichols-Barrer, I., Gleason, P., Gill, B., & Tuttle, C. C. (2016). Student selection, attrition, and replacement in KIPP middle schools. *Educational Evaluation and Policy Analysis.* doi:10.3102/0162373714564215

Russo, A. (2013). Diverse charter schools. *Education Next, 13*(1), 28–34.

Schneider, M., Teske, P., & Marshall, M. (2000). *Choosing schools: Consumer choice and the quality of American schools.* Princeton, NJ: Princeton University Press.

Simon, S. (February, 15, 2013). Special report: Class struggle – how charter schools get students they want. *Reuters.* Retrieved from: http://www.reuters.com/article/us-usa-charters-admissions-idUSBRE91E0HF20130215

Swanson, E. (2017). Can we have it all? A review of the impact of school choice on racial integration. *Journal of School Choice, 11*, 4. doi:10.1080/15582159.2017.1395644

U.S. Department of Education, National Center for Education Statistics. (2016). Table 216.30. In U.S. Department of Education, National Center for Education Statistics (Ed.), *Public elementary/secondary school Universe Survey (1999–2000 through 2014–15).* Retrieved from https://nces.ed.gov/programs/digest/d16/tables/dt16_216.30.asp?current=yes

U.S. Government Accountability Office. (June, 2012). *Charter schools: Additional federal attention needed to help protect access for students with disabilities.* Retrieved from: http://www.gao.gov/products/GAO-12-543

Viteritti, J. P. (1999). *Choosing equality: School choice, the constitution, and civil society.* Washington, DC: Brookings Institution Press.

Wells, A. S. (1993). *Time to choose: America at the crossroads of school choice policy.* New York, NY: Hill and Wang.

Welner, K. G. (April, 2013). The dirty dozen: How charter schools influence student enrollment. *Teachers College record.* Retrieved from: http://nepc.colorado.edu/files/welner-charter-enrollment-teachers-college-record.pdf

Winters, M. A. (2017). Understanding the gap in special education enrollments between charter and traditional public schools: Evidence from Denver, Colorado. *Educational Researcher, 44*(4), 228–236.

Winters, M. A. (June, 2014). *Understanding the charter school special education gap: Evidence from Denver, Colorado.* Seattle, WA: Center on Reinventing Public Education.

Winters, M. A. (September, 2013). *Why the gap? Special education and New York City charter schools.* Seattle, WA: Center on Reinventing Public Education.

Winters, M. A., Carpenter, D. M., II, & Clayton, G. (2017). Does attending a charter school reduce the likelihood of being placed into special education? Evidence from Denver, Colorado. *Educational Evaluation Policy Analysis.* Prepublished February 20, 2017. doi:10.3102/0162373717690830

Winters, M. A., Clayton, G., & Carpenter II, D. M. (2017). Are low-performing students more likely to exit charter schools? Evidence from New York City and Denver, Colorado. *Economics of Education Review, 56*, 110–117.

Woodworth, K., David, J. L., Guha, R., Wang, H., & Lopez Torkos, A. (2008). *San Francisco Bay area KIPP schools: A study of early implementation and achievement, final report*. Menlo Park, CA: SRI International.

Zimmer, R., Gill, B., Booker, K., Lavertu, S., Sass, T. R., & Witte, J. (2009). *Charter schools in eight states: Effects on achievement, attainment, integration, and competition*. Santa Monica, CA: Rand Corporation. Retrieved from http://www.rand.org/pubs/monographs/MG869.html

Zimmer, R. W., & Guarino, C. M. (2013). Is there empirical evidence that charter schools "push out" low-performing students? *Education Evaluation Policy and Analysis*, *35*(4), 461–480.

Zubrzycki, J., Cavanagh, S., & McNeil, M. (February, 19 2013). *Charter schools' discipline policies face scrutiny*. Bethesda, MD: Education Week. Retrieved from http://162.230.210.194/RandD/Education%20Week/Charter%20Schools'%20Discipline%20Policies%20Face%20Scrutiny.pdf

# Do self-interested schooling selections improve society? A review of the evidence

Corey A. DeAngelis

**ABSTRACT**

I review the literature that quantifies the effects of private school choice programs on three important civic outcomes for students in the United States: tolerance, civic engagement, and social order. Out of the 11 studies on private school choice that examine these civic outcomes, the impacts are null to positive for tolerance, null to positive for civic engagement, and positive for social order. None of the studies indicates that private school choice negatively affects these vital civic outcomes.

## Introduction

Opponents of private school choice claim that a uniform system of public schooling is necessary to teach children various civic values (Apple & Beane, 1995; Durkheim, 1956; Gutmann, 1999; Wolfe, 2009). Without public schools instilling these essential civic values, they argue, democratic societies will not be able to function properly (Boyles, 2004; Molnar, 2013; Saltman, 2000). Early advocates of the common school movement in the United States argue that only uniform public schools could teach children common civic and social virtues that would erase or blur sectarian, philosophical, or regional differences (Mann, 1855; Rush, 1786). E.D. Hirsch (2010) also claims that an education system needs to instill a uniform knowledge base in order to create a shared public culture and a functional democracy.

Civic values such as tolerance, respect, social order, and democratic participation are all important for social cohesion, but it is unclear whether public schooling is necessary for this to occur. In fact, private schools may have an advantage with inculcating these values to children in the United States. Private schools have an incentive to cater to the needs of individual families, and parents value the citizenship skills of their children (Friedman & Friedman, 1990; Neal, 2002). Additionally, private school choice allows for an improved match between the interests of children and educators, which increases the likelihood that children will be engaged at school. If children are more engaged in school, they will be more likely to learn the civic values being taught, and less likely to feel rebellious against social order.

Perhaps most importantly, since public schools explicitly aim to instill a uniform set of values and ideas, a system of private schooling may increase the likelihood that students will be introduced to alternative viewpoints and engage in discussion. Essential debates and dialogue may be less likely to take place in the public sphere, so private schools may be better equipped to diminish intolerance between people holding competing views. If sufficient evidence indicates that private schools are more effective at teaching these social values, decision makers should promote policies designed to increase the magnitude of private school choice programs in the United States.

A vast majority of the evaluations of private school choice programs focus on student achievement as measured by standardized test scores. Around the world, experimental evidence indicates that additional options generated through private school choice programs produce slightly higher student achievement in the form of test scores (Shakeel, Anderson, & Wolf, 2016). Only three recent experimental evaluations of private school choice show negative impacts on student achievement; two studies examine the Louisiana Scholarship Program (LSP) (Abdulkadiroglu, Pathak, & Walters, 2015; Mills & Wolf, 2017a), and one looks at the Opportunity Scholarship Program (OSP) in D.C. (Dynarski, Rui, Webber, Gutmann, & Bachman, 2017). Notably, the voucher experiment in Louisiana finds that children in private schools catch up to their control group counterparts in achievement by the end of the third year of the program (Mills & Wolf, 2017b).

While the impacts of private school choice have been generally small and positive for student test scores, all of the research on school choice and student attainment has found large positive impacts, indicating that private schools may be most beneficial through improving noncognitive skills of students such as motivation and determination (Cowen, Fleming, Witte, Wolf, & Kisida, 2013; Neal, 1997; Warren, 2008; Wolf et al., 2013). In particular, Cowen et al. (2013) found that the Milwaukee Parental Choice Program (MPCP) improved graduation rates by 7 percentage points and Wolf et al. (2013) found that the D.C. OSP improved graduation rates by over 20 percentage points.

While these results are clearly positive for academic student outcomes, less than 1% of the students in the United States are enrolled in private school choice programs.[1] We should be cautious about generalizing these outcomes to the rest of the student population when interpreting effects. Theoretically, since most private school choice programs in the United States are targeted to the least-advantaged children in society, the effects of choice could be smaller, or even negative, for more-advantaged groups of students. Alternatively, impacts on students and society could be much more positive if supply-side developments of market-entry and shutdown conditions are allowed to take place in the long run through expanded educational choice. Furthermore, if private schools can shape noncognitive skills and graduation rates, they may also be able to shape character and citizenship skills that are valuable to society as a whole. However, the theoretical arguments surrounding private schooling and citizenship skills are complex and compelling on both sides, so it is necessary to study the existing empirical evidence.

In this review of the literature, I examine the effects of private school choice programs on tolerance, civic engagement, and social order for students in the United States. For tolerance, I use studies that examine any type of tolerance of others as an outcome measure. For civic engagement, I use research that examines voting behavior, charitable giving, and volunteering. For social order, I use studies that examine criminal activity.

## Theory

Although there are several theories for how school choice could accomplish goals that are beneficial to society overall, I outline three of the strongest in Figure 1.

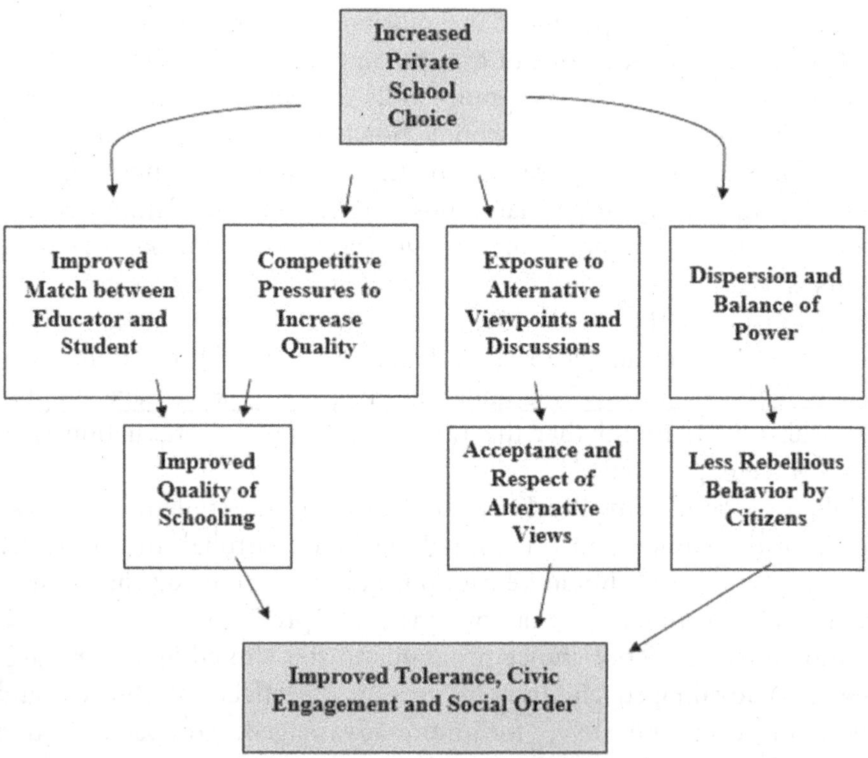


**Figure 1.** How Private School Choice Influences Civic Values

The first, and perhaps the clearest, argument relates to basic economic principles. The current system of schooling allows public schools to have a monopoly on public funding, which ultimately grants them monopoly power. As in any industry, the large presence of monopoly power generally leads to lower quality service at a higher price (Smith, 1776). Since public schools have a monopoly on public funding, they do not face a substantial threat of competition from private schools. Consequently, they may not have a sufficient incentive to improve quality or decrease expenses (Chubb & Moe, 2011; Hoxby, 2003). Alternatively, they may even have an incentive to increase expenditures each year rather than become more efficient (Niskanen, 1971). Alongside the competitive pressures to increase quality is the potential benefit of specialization. School choice programs can improve the match between educator and student and increase the quality of the educational experience overall. This allocative efficiency is particularly important in the education sector since all children are unique; they have diverse interests, learning abilities, and learning styles. The increase in quality in schooling could improve test scores as well as citizenship skills of children. Enhanced citizenship skills could increase the likelihood that the student will be tolerant of others, engage in civic activity, and follow implicit and explicit laws of society.

Secondly, since a system of private schooling decreases the monopoly that public institutions have on information and biases in schools, private school choice could increase the likelihood that a student will become exposed to alternative viewpoints within their school and in society. This increased exposure to alternative viewpoints could lead individual students to become more respectful, accepting, and knowledgeable about the arguments of other groups (Short, 2002). Additional experience considering diverse views would result in improved citizenship skills for students in private school choice programs and even may indirectly affect those in public schools. In addition, students and educators in private schools may be more open about discussing topics that would appear controversial in the public sphere. Since selection into and out of private schools is voluntary, and based on interests, students may feel more encouraged to discuss alternative viewpoints. On the other hand, students in a public setting may be more likely to fear insulting or offending other groups of students, so controversial discussions may not happen at all (Berkman & Plutzer, 2010). When argumentative exchanges do not occur, students are less likely to recognize the views of those groups, and therefore less likely to be tolerant of those with which they disagree when disagreements inevitably arise in the future.

Lastly, school choice can lead to a dispersion and balance of power within the realm of education. A private school choice program reduces the monopoly that public schools and their leaders currently hold on power by shifting authority to the families. The resulting balance of power could lead to citizens feeling more in control of their own lives (Stewart & Wolf, 2014). The feeling of control and autonomy could reduce the likelihood that citizens will engage in rebellious behavior such as breaking implicit or explicit laws in society. While this specific theory has not been empirically tested, there is significant evidence that autonomy leads to increased satisfaction and decreased stress (Finn, 2001). Greater levels of happiness and lower levels of stress lead to less irrational behaviors such as criminal activity and disrespect of others (Artello & Williams, 2014).

However, there are also strong theoretical arguments which lead to a less-optimistic conclusion: that private school choice could negatively impact society overall. Theoretically, if school quality includes the ability of schools to alter civic behavior, and private schools are of lower quality, then private school choice could harm civic outcomes.

Critics of private schooling argue that since individuals are self-interested, they will not demand the type of schooling that improves social outcomes. Moreover, individuals exercising private school choice may self-select into environments that reinforce their pre-existing interests and biases against other groups of people (Cheng & DeLany, 1999; Ladd, 2002; Mathews, 2006).

Perhaps most prominent is the historical argument that public schools are necessary for a stable democratic society since they force children from diverse backgrounds to spend time with one another. If children from a wide array of backgrounds, religions, and races are in the same classroom, they may become more accepting of each other since they would have the opportunity to discuss opposing views (Mann, 1855). In addition, government-run schools may have a strong interest in inculcating character skills that result in significant benefits accruing to third parties.

Since there are possibly equally strong theoretical arguments on either side of this issue, a review of the empirical evidence is necessary.

## Review content

In my review of the evidence, I found 11 evaluations of school choice programs in the United States that focused on civic outcomes. Six of these evaluations examined tolerance as an outcome measure. Two of the evaluations were of the D.C. Washington Scholarship Fund (WSF), one was of the MPCP, one was of the LSP, and two were of the nationwide Children's Scholarship Fund (CSF).[2]

## Tolerance

Political tolerance is the willingness to extend legal and constitutional protections to groups with whom one disagrees (Wolf, 2005). It is a vital civic value in a democratic republic to prevent disagreements among citizens from resulting in

**Table 1.** The effect of school choice on tolerance.

| Study | Program | Design | Finding |
|---|---|---|---|
| Campbell (2002) | CSF | RFT | + |
| Howell and Peterson (2006) | D.C. WSF | RFT | Null |
| Mills, Cheng, Hitt, Wolf, and Greene (2016) | LSP | RFT | Null |
| Peterson and Campbell (2001) | CSF | RFT | Null |
| Wolf et al. (2001) | D.C. WSF | RFT | + |
| Fleming et al. (2014) | MPCP | Matching QED | + |

*Null* indicates that the study did not detect any statistically significant effect on tolerance of others. A box highlighted in gray indicates that the study found statistically significant positive effects on tolerance of others. RFT is randomized field trial, QED is quasi-experimental design, CSF is Children's Scholarship Fund, WSF is Washington Scholarship Fund, LSP is Louisiana Scholarship Program, and MPCP is Milwaukee Parental Choice Program.

the persecution of people for their views. As presented in Table 1, the evaluations of the WSF, LSP, and CSF were all experimental randomized field trials; however, three out of five did not detect any effect on tolerance of others. Two experimental evaluations, one of the D.C. WSF, and one of the CSF, found positive impacts of private school vouchers on tolerance of others (Campbell, 2002; Wolf, Peterson, & West, 2001). Based on responses to three survey questions about tolerance of others, Wolf et al. (2001) found that the simple offer of private schooling increased tolerance levels between 6.7 and 8.2 percentage points. They found that the effect of actually going to a private school in D. C. increased tolerance levels by over twice as much, between 16.4 and 20.2 percentage points. David Campbell (2002) found that switching from a public to a private school increased students' political tolerance index score by 0.8 points, which represented over a one standard deviation increase in political tolerance.

The only nonexperimental study of the effect of private schooling on tolerance of others found positive results in Milwaukee (Fleming, Mitchell, & McNally, 2014). The authors reported that student voucher status was associated with a 0.15-point increase in the 4-point political tolerance scale and a higher likelihood of students stating that their schools promote political tolerance. While this was not an experiment, researchers used a sophisticated algorithm that matched students on geographic location, baseline test scores, and other demographic characteristics. Methodological literature has shown that this type of matching technique is one of the best at replicating experimental results (Bifulco, 2012).

## Civic engagement

Five studies were found on the impacts of private school choice on civic engagement as measured by political participation, voting activity, charitable giving, and volunteer activity. As presented in Table 2, three studies examining the relationship between private school choice and civic engagement found positive results and one did not find an impact. There were two

**Table 2.** The effect of school choice on civic engagement.

| Study | Program | Type | Design | Finding |
|---|---|---|---|---|
| Bettinger and Slonim (2006) | CSF Ohio | Charitable giving | RCT | + |
| Carlson et al. (2017) | SCSF | Voting | RFT | Null |
| DeAngelis and Wolf (2016b) | MPCP | Voting | Matching QED | Null |
| Fleming (2014) | MPCP | Political participation | Matching QED | + |
| Fleming et al. (2014) | MPCP | Political participation, volunteering | Matching QED | + |

*Null* indicates that the study did not detect any statistically significant effect on tolerance of others. A box highlighted in gray indicates that the study found statistically significant positive effects on tolerance of others. RCT is randomized controlled trial, RFT is randomized field trial, QED is quasi-experimental design, CSF is Children's Scholarship Fund, SCSF is School Choice Scholarships Foundation Program, and MPCP is Milwaukee Parental Choice Program.

**Table 3.** The effect of school choice on social order.

| Study | Program | Type | Design | Finding |
|---|---|---|---|---|
| DeAngelis and Wolf (2016a) | MPCP | Adult crime | Matching QED | + |

A box highlighted in gray indicates that the study found statistically significant positive effects on social order. QED is quasi-experimental design and MPCP is Milwaukee Parental Choice Program.

experimental evaluations: one of the New York School Choice Scholarships Foundation Program and the CSF of Toledo, Ohio (Bettinger & Slonim, 2006; Carlson, Chingos, & Campbell, 2017). The other three program evaluations examined the MPCP and used quasi-experimental matching methods to determine program effects on political participation and volunteering (DeAngelis & Wolf, 2016b; Fleming, 2014; Fleming et al., 2014).

The lab experiment performed by Bettinger and Slonim (2006) found that winning an educational scholarship through the CSF in Toledo, Ohio, positively affected student's charitable activity. Conversely, they did not find significant evidence that vouchers affected parent's altruism. Specifically, they found that, in a lab setting, voucher winners offered to give about 23% more money to charity than lottery losers. However, the amount of money involved in the experiment was quite small; on average, voucher winners gave $4.08, while losers donated only $3.33.

The randomized field trial by Carlson et al. (2017) found that the offer of a private school voucher in New York City did not have any impact on voter registration or voter turnout. Moreover, this study did not find any impacts of the school choice voucher on any of the elections or subgroups examined.

Fleming (2014) used the matched-student data from the state-mandated evaluation of the MPCP and focused on the resulting political engagement of parents. He found that voucher parents were more than twice as likely to say that they had contacted a government official and had a 7-percentage point higher likelihood of saying that their child's school experience taught them about government. Also, voucher parents had a 4-percentage point higher likelihood of saying that the government influenced their child's school, indicating that the program increased the visibility of educational policy.

Furthermore, voucher parents had a 9-percentage point higher likelihood of saying that their child's school experience increased their own political activity.

Fleming et al. (2014) used the same MPCP dataset and matching procedure, but focused on the political impacts for students. Overall, they found that voucher students displayed moderately higher levels of civic skills, political participation, and volunteer activity. Their preferred model found that voucher students had an 11-percentage point higher likelihood of stating they would certainly vote in the future and were more likely to partake in civic skill-building activities in school. Finally, they found that voucher students had an 11-percentage point higher likelihood of volunteering within the previous year and also were more likely to believe in the importance of volunteer activity. However, when students were asked if they thought they would volunteer as adults, no statistically significant effect was detected.

The two previous studies found that parents and students were more likely to say they would vote in future elections; however, the researchers were not able to observe actual voting behavior. DeAngelis and Wolf (2016b) used the same student-level dataset from the state-mandated evaluation of the MPCP and found different results regarding student civic behaviors. They examined the matched students in 2012 and 2016, or when they were around 19–26 years old, and found no difference in voter participation. While it is unclear if the MPCP increased voter activity, it is possible that access to the program developed the citizenship skill of understanding society's expectations even if the young adults did not fulfill those expectations at significantly higher rates.

## Social order

The least explored area of research within this review is how private school choice relates to social order, perhaps because social order is so difficult to quantify and measure. The amount of law-breaking done by students and the amount of trust within a society can both be proxies for social order. As shown in Table 3, the only study examining the relationship between private school choice and crime finds that increases in school choice reduce the likelihood of students becoming criminals (DeAngelis & Wolf, 2016a).

DeAngelis and Wolf (2016a) use the same MPCP dataset and matching procedure as Fleming (2014) and find that participating in the voucher program for at least 4 years reduces the likelihood of being accused of any crime between 21% and 50%. Also, 4-year persistence in the program is associated with students being less than half as likely to commit a misdemeanor or a felony by the time that they are around 22–25 years old.

**Table 4.** Overall vote-counting results.

| Outcome | Positive | Null | Negative |
|---|---|---|---|
| Tolerance | 3 | 3 | 0 |
| Civic engagement | 3 | 2 | 0 |
| Social order | 1 | 0 | 0 |

## Overall results

As presented in Table 4, a majority of the studies find statistically significant positive results, indicating that private school choice leads to improved civic outcomes for families and society overall. None of the reviewed studies found statistically significant results indicating that private school choice harmed tolerance of others, charitable giving, political participation, volunteering, civic skills, or social order.

In particular, half of the six studies examining tolerance found that private school choice increased tolerance, while the remaining half found no significant difference. Three of the five studies examining the effects of private school choice on civic engagement found clearly positive impacts on society through increased political participation, volunteer activity, charitable giving, and civic skills. The only study examining impacts on criminal activity found that access to school choice reduced adult crime, leading to improved social order.

## Need for further research

While the literature on the impacts of private school choice on student achievement does not suffer from a shortage of studies, the same cannot be said of the research on social impacts. It is difficult to make an informed policy decision when solely relying on information about student test scores, especially since there are many claims that private schooling can harm society as a whole while benefitting individuals. Surely, if private schooling only benefitted individual students by slightly increasing standardized test scores at the expense of intolerance, democratic disengagement, and social disorder, we would not want to contribute to such an arrangement through public financing.

However, if we find sufficient evidence to suggest that private schooling benefits individuals and society overall, we may feel more comfortable with policy proposals leading toward those ends. Currently, we have plenty of evidence indicating that school choice slightly benefits academic outcomes as measured by standardized test scores, but we lack substantial evidence on each of the civic outcomes covered in this review. While this review finds that existing evidence indicates improved civic outcomes of private school choice, we must be cautious of the implications, specifically because the evidence is scarce. Additional causal research on all of these topics is especially welcome and highly policy-relevant. Learning more about the impacts of private schooling on society will allow us to understand what type of educational system is necessary for a democratic society to flourish.

## Conclusion and policy implications

This review of the literature finds that private school choice programs are generally beneficial to overall social goals such as tolerance, civic engagement, and order. In particular, out of the 11 studies on private school choice that examine these civic outcomes, the impacts are null to positive for tolerance, null to positive for civic engagement, and positive for social order. None of the studies indicates that private school choice has negative effects on civic outcomes. However, this does not mean that private school choice does not, or cannot, negatively influence civic outcomes. Furthermore, the studies included in this review largely focus on the private school choice programs in Milwaukee and D.C., which are not representative of the country as a whole.

The literature on this topic is scarce, and existing evidence only pertains to specific groups of students, so decision makers should be cautious about using these results for policy decisions. In addition, the effects found in all of these studies are for students that elect to use private school choice programs. Students left behind in public schools could do worse on civic outcomes through negative peer effects; however, public institutions may also increase their focus on character skills in order to remain competitive. Nonetheless, the current research indicates that private school choice programs such as vouchers, tuition tax credits, and education savings accounts can improve tolerance of others, civic engagement, and social order for children in the United States.

Researchers should take advantage of this hole in the literature by asking more questions related to the civic outcomes of school choice and education in general. However, this literature gap may be due to severe data limitations rather than a lack of research questions. Decision makers should focus on policies that improve the amount of information available to researchers on nonacademic outcomes of students in the United States. In particular, individual student information such as name and date of birth is necessary for researchers to find impacts of school choice programs on civic outcomes such as political participation and criminal activity. Efforts to make such information more available to scholars would be welcome.

## Notes

1. https://www.edchoice.org/school-choice/.
2. The D.C. WSF and the CSF were privately funded K-12 scholarship programs. The CSF still operates nationally. The WSF was replaced by the publicly funded D.C. Opportunity Scholarship Program incrementally from 2004 to 2010.

## References

Abdulkadiroglu, A., Pathak, P. A., & Walters, C. R. (2015). *Free to choose: Can school choice reduce student achievement?*. NBER Working Paper No. 21839. Retrieved from http://www.nber.org/papers/w21839

Apple, M. W., & Beane, J. A. (1995). *Democratic schools*. Association for Supervision and Curriculum Development, 1250 North Pitt Street, Alexandria, VA 22314.

Artello & Williams. (2014). Stress and crime. In W. C. Cockerham, R. Dingwall, & S. R. Quah (Eds.), *The Wiley Blackwell encyclopedia of health, illness, behavior, and society*. Hoboken, NJ.

Berkman, M., & Plutzer, E. (2010). *Evolution, creationism, and the battle to control America's classrooms*. Cambridge, UK: Cambridge University Press.

Bettinger, E., & Slonim, R. (2006). Using experimental economics to measure the effects of a natural educational experiment on altruism. *Journal of Public Economics, 90*(8), 1625–1648.

Bifulco, R. (2012). Can nonexperimental estimates replicate estimates based on random assignment in evaluations of school choice? A within-study comparison. *Journal of Policy Analysis and Management, 31*(3), 729–751.

Boyles, D. R. (Ed.). (2004). *Schools or markets? Commercialism, privatization, and school-business partnerships*. Mahwah, NJ: Lawrence Erlbaum Associates.

Campbell, D. E. (2002). The civic side of school reform: How do school vouchers affect civic education? *Center for the Study of Democratic Politics Working Paper*.

Carlson, D., Chingos, M. M., & Campbell, D. E. (2017). The effect of private school vouchers on political participation: Experimental evidence from New York City. *Journal of Research on Educational Effectiveness, 10*(3), 545–569.

Cheng, H., & DeLany, B. (1999). Quality education and social stratification: The paradox of private schooling in China. *Current Issues in Comparative Education, 1*, 2.

Chubb, J. E., & Moe, T. M. (2011). *Politics, markets, and America's schools*. Washington, DC: Brookings Institution Press.

Cowen, J. M., Fleming, D. J., Witte, J. F., Wolf, P. J., & Kisida, B. (2013). School vouchers and student attainment: Evidence from a state-mandated study of Milwaukee's parental choice program. *Policy Studies Journal, 41*(1), 147–168.

DeAngelis, C., & Wolf, P. J. (2016a). The school choice voucher: A get out of jail card? EDRE Working Paper 2016-03. Retrieved from SSRN: https://ssrn.com/abstract=2743541.

DeAngelis, C., & Wolf, P. J. (2016b). *Can democracy survive private school choice? The effect of the Milwaukee parental choice program on voting behavior* (Unpublished Manuscript).

Durkheim, E. (1956). *Education and sociology*. New York, NY: Simon and Schuster.

Dynarski, M., Rui, N., Webber, A., Gutmann, B., & Bachman, M. (2017). Evaluation of the DC opportunity scholarship program: Impacts after one year. NCEE 2017-4022. U.S. Department of Education.

Finn, C. (2001). Autonomy: An important component for nurses' job satisfaction. *International Journal of Nursing Studies, 38*(3), 349–357.

Fleming, D. J. (2014). Learning from schools: School choice, political learning, and policy feedback. *Policy Studies Journal, 42*(1), 55–78.

Fleming, D. J., Mitchell, W., & McNally, M. (2014). Can markets make citizens? School vouchers, political tolerance, and civic engagement. *Journal of School Choice, 8*(2), 213–236.

Friedman, M., & Friedman, R. (1990). *Free to choose: A personal statement*. Orlando, FL: Houghton Mifflin Harcourt.

Gutmann, A. (1999). *Democratic education*. Princeton, NJ: Princeton University Press.

Hirsch, E. D., Jr. (2010). *The schools we need: And why we don't have them*. New York, NY: Anchor Books.

Howell, W. G., & Peterson, P. E. (2006). *The education gap: Vouchers and urban schools.* Washington, DC: Brookings Institution Press.

Hoxby, C. M. (2003). School choice and school productivity. Could school choice be a tide that lifts all boats? In C. M. Hoxby (Ed.),*The economics of school choice* (pp. 287–342). Chicago, IL: University of Chicago Press.

Ladd, H. F. (2002). School vouchers: A critical view. *The Journal of Economic Perspectives, 16* (4), 3–24.

Mann, H. (1855). *Lectures on education.* Boston, MA: WB Fowle and N. Capen.

Mathews, F. D. (2006). *Reclaiming public education by reclaiming our democracy.* Dayton, OH: Kettering Foundation Press.

Mills, J. N., Cheng, A., Hitt, C., Wolf, P. J., & Greene, J. P. (2016). *Measures of student non-cognitive skills and political tolerance after two years of the Louisiana scholarship program (Louisiana scholarship program evaluation report #2. School Choice Demonstration Project, University of Arkansas, Fayetteville, AR. Education Research Alliance),* New Orleans, LA: Tulane University.

Mills, J. N., & Wolf, P. J. (2017a). Vouchers in the bayou: The effects of the Louisiana scholarship program on student achievement after 2 years. *Educational Evaluation and Policy Analysis, 39*(3), 464–484.

Mills, J. N., & Wolf, P. J. (2017b). The effects of the Louisiana scholarship program on student achievement after three years. School Choice Demonstration Project, University of Arkansas, Fayetteville, AR. Education Research Alliance for New Orleans, Tulane University, New Orleans, LA.

Molnar, A. (2013). *School commercialism: From democratic ideal to market commodity.* New York, NY: Routledge.

Neal, D. (1997). The effects of catholic secondary schooling on educational achievement. *Journal of Labor Economics*, 15(1, Part 1), 98–123.

Neal, D. (2002). How vouchers could change the market for education. *The Journal of Economic Perspectives, 16*(4), 25–44.

Niskanen, W. A. (1971). *Bureaucracy and representative government.* New Brunswick, NJ: Transaction Publishers.

Peterson, P. E., & Campbell, D. E. (2001). An evaluation of the children's scholarship fund (KSG Working Paper No. RWP02-020).

Rush, B. (1786). Thoughts upon the mode of education proper in a republic. In F. Rudolph (1966) (Ed.), *Essays on education in the early republic.* Cambridge, MA: Harvard University Press.

Saltman, K. J. (2000). *Collateral damage: Corporatizing public schools–A threat to democracy.* Lanham, MD: Rowman & Littlefield.

Shakeel, M., Anderson, K. P., & Wolf, P. J. (2016). *The participant effects of private school vouchers across the globe: A meta-analytic and systematic review* (EDRE Working Paper No. 2016-07). Retrieved from SSRN: https://ssrn.com/abstract=2777633.

Short, G. (2002). Faith–based schools: A threat to social cohesion? *Journal of Philosophy of Education, 36*(4), 559–572.

Smith, A. (1776). *The wealth of nations, Book 1.* London, UK: Methuen & Co.

Stewart, T., & Wolf, P. J. (2014). *The school choice journey: School vouchers and the empowerment of urban families.* New York, NY: Palgrave Macmillan.

Warren, J. R. (2008). *Graduation rates for choice and public school students in Milwaukee.* School Choice Wisconsin. Retrieved from http://www.bradleyfdn.org/On-Lion-Letter/ID/286/Graduation-rates-for-Milwaukee-school-choice-students-higher-than-for-public-school-students

Wolf, P. J. (2005). School choice and civic values. In J. R. Betts, & T. Loveless (Eds.), *Getting choice right: Ensuring equity and efficiency in education policy* (pp. 210–244). Washington, DC: Brookings.

Wolf, P. J., Kisida, B., Gutmann, B., Puma, M., Eissa, N., & Rizzo, L. (2013). School vouchers and student outcomes: Experimental evidence from Washington, DC. *Journal of Policy Analysis and Management, 32*(2), 246–270.

Wolf, P. J., Peterson, P. E., & West, M. R. (2001). *Results of a school voucher experiment: The case of Washington, DC after two years* (KSG Working Paper No. RWP02-022).

Wolfe, A. (Ed.). (2009). *School choice: The moral debate.* Princeton, NJ: Princeton University Press.

# What's the secret ingredient? Searching for policies and practices that make charter schools successful

Philip M. Gleason

**ABSTRACT**

The charter-school sector in the United States has grown steadily since the first charter school opened in 1992 and nearly 7,000 charter schools currently serve nearly 3 million students. Research suggests that the average charter school performs about the same as nearby traditional public schools, but there is great variation in the effects of charter schools. Some are successful in boosting student achievement and others are not, raising the question of what distinguishes good charter schools from bad. This article summarizes the research on factors associated with successful charter schools. The research suggests that urban charter schools have more positive impacts on student achievement than other charter schools. The policies most consistently found to be associated with positive charter-school impacts include long school days or years, comprehensive behavioral policies with rewards and sanctions, and a mission that prioritizes boosting student achievement. In addition, moderately strong evidence suggests that high-dosage tutoring, frequent feedback and coaching for teachers, and policies promoting the use of data to guide teachers' instructional practices are positively associated with charter schools' achievement impacts.

## Introduction

Charter schools are a central component of current efforts to reform the public education system in the United States. These schools are publicly financed but free of many of the regulations that govern traditional public schools, such as those involving staffing, curriculum, and budget decisions. The first charter schools opened in Minnesota in 1992, and the charter-school sector has grown steadily since that time. There are now nearly 7,000 charter schools serving roughly 3 million students in forty-two states and the District of Columbia with Kentucky recently added as the forty-third charter state.

One of the original hopes for charter schools was that they would serve as a sort of educational laboratory, that without the oversight and regulations of traditional public school districts they would be free to innovate and test out new ideas. Some charter schools would fail, but the hope was that others would succeed and the new ideas and approaches that they successfully tested out could be used in other schools. In a May 2014 proclamation of National Charter Schools Week, President Barack Obama highlighted this point, saying that charter schools "that are successful can provide effective approaches for the broader public education system."

In recent years, many good research studies have examined the effects of charter schools on student learning and achievement. Some have taken advantage of the fact that popular charter schools typically conduct admissions lotteries to admit students, allowing a comparison of subsequent outcomes among participants who were and were not admitted by lottery. This experimental approach provides strong evidence on charter-school effects but can only be applied to schools that hold lotteries. Other studies have used rigorous non-experimental methods to produce evidence of the effects of broader groups of charter schools.

Among studies that have examined the effects of both urban and nonurban charter schools, the research suggests that the average charter school performs about as well, but no better, than nearby traditional public schools in terms of boosting student achievement. Among non-experimental studies examining broad sets of charter schools, for example, CREDO (2013a) found that average student achievement among charter-school students in 27 states was no more than 0.01 standard deviations different from that of similar traditional public school students. Zimmer, Gill, Booker, Lavertu, and Witte (2012), examining charter schools in seven states, found that in most cases there were no statistically significant charter-school effects. Studies using lottery-based methods to study broad sets of charter schools have had similar findings. An Institute of Education Sciences study that examined 36 charter schools in 15 states found no significant achievement effects on average (Clark, Gleason, Tuttle, & Silverberg, 2015; Gleason, Clark, Tuttle, & Dwoyer, 2010). Using both lottery-based and non-experimental methods, Furgeson et al. (2012) studied charter schools in 22 charter management organizations (CMOs) around the country and found no significant impacts on average.

However, these studies also suggest that there is great variation in the effects of charter schools. Some charters are successful in boosting student achievement and others are not. CREDO (2013a) found that 25–29% of charter schools had positive effects on students' math and reading achievement, while 19–31% had negative effects and the remainder had no significant effects. Gleason et al. (2010) found that impacts on reading achievement ranged from −0.43 to +0.33 standard deviations, with even greater variation in math impacts. Furgeson et al. (2012) found that among the 22 CMOs they studied, 11 had significant positive effects and 7 had significant negative effects in math. Angrist and his colleagues (Angrist, Pathak, & Walters, 2013) found impacts of over 0.30 standard deviations per year of attendance at oversubscribed urban charter schools in Massachusetts, while Carlson and Lavertu (2016) estimated that the lowest performing charter schools in Ohio have impacts of about −0.20 to −0.30 standard deviations.[1]

This heterogeneity in charter-school effects raises questions. What characteristics distinguish good charter schools from bad ones? Under what conditions are charter schools most likely to be successful? Can we identify the policies and practices that make a charter school successful? Can these policies and practices of successful charter schools be replicated in other schools—charter or traditional public schools—equally successfully?

This article addresses these questions by summarizing the research on factors associated with successful charter schools. The first section presents a framework for understanding how different factors might influence the success of a charter school. The second section introduces the studies that have explored this issue systematically and summarizes their methodology. The next section reviews the findings of these studies, and the final section discusses their implications.

## Framework for analyzing what makes a charter school successful

### *Defining school success*

A successful charter school should lead to positive short- and long-term student outcomes. In the short run, students should master the important material covered by a school. In the long run, they should do well throughout their educational careers and become productive and happy adults. However, prior research studies have typically focused on the short-run outcome of student achievement as measured by performance on standardized assessments in reading and math. A smaller number of studies have examined charter schools' impacts on non-achievement outcomes including students' attitudes and behaviors, educational attainment, and earnings (see Epple, Romano, & Zimmer, 2015 for a review). However, these studies have not typically focused on the question of which charter schools are most successful in terms of positively affecting these non-achievement outcomes.

Charter-school success has also typically been measured in relative terms, based on comparisons of charter schools with other schools that their students might otherwise have attended. In other words, the research has defined a successful charter school as one in which student test scores are better than they would have been in this alternative, or counterfactual, set of schools. The set of schools used as a comparison or control group depends on the study's design and methodology. Lottery-based studies follow lottery losers to whatever schools they attended in the years following the lottery. Many non-experimental studies select a comparison group of students from traditional public schools in the same district as the charter school, with the students having similar characteristics and baseline achievement levels as the charter-school students.

This definition of what makes a charter school successful has implications for research on factors that lead to charter-school success. Based on this definition, what makes a charter school successful depends on which factors lead to better student performance on achievement tests rather than on which factors lead to other possible dimensions of success. Furthermore, the success of a charter school depends in part on what is happening at nearby traditional public schools.

### *The three Cs*

Weiss, Bloom, and Brock (2014) characterize factors that may affect sources of variation in program impacts—that is, what explains why some programs have more positive impacts than others—as the three Cs: treatment contrast, clients, and context. *Treatment contrast* is the difference in services received by treatment group members who participate in the program being evaluated and control group members who do not. This difference rather than simply the quantity and quality of program services mediates the program's impacts, as program participants who experience greater service contrast demonstrate larger program impacts (see, e.g., Howell, W., & Peterson, P.E., with Wolf, P. J., & Campbell, D.E., 2006, on school vouchers). The *clients* are those served by the program who make up the treatment group. Client characteristics may moderate program impacts, as some types of clients may benefit from the program more than others. The *context* in which the program operates is another possible moderator—for example, some programs may work better during economic booms than during recessions (or vice versa).

The framework developed by Weiss et al. (2014) helps us understand factors related to charter-school success. The treatment contrast represents differences in the experiences of students attending charter schools versus those of students attending the comparison schools. These student experiences are captured using school characteristics, policies, and practices, such as

- Amount of instruction received (e.g., length of the school day)
- Curriculum and instructional approach
- Approach to regulating student behavior
- Quality of teachers and school leaders
- Characteristics of student peers in the school

Ideally, studies examining heterogeneity in charter-school impacts would measure the treatment contrast using differences in these characteristics between the charter schools being evaluated and the comparison schools.

In practice, most studies only have detailed information on the charter schools' characteristics, policies, and practices, and not on those of the nearby traditional public schools.[2] Rather than measuring the treatment contrast, these studies measure charter-school characteristics alone. They cannot examine whether one reason for variation in charter-school impacts is that some charters are surrounded by traditional public schools that differ more in quality or services from them than are other charters. However, they can explain variation in impacts associated with characteristics of the charter schools themselves.

A charter school's clients are the students who attend the school. Different kinds of students may respond differently to charter schools, so these schools may be most successful for a particular kind of student. For example, students who are low achieving at the time they enter charter schools may benefit most from a charter school. If so, one would expect to see larger impacts for charter schools serving larger proportions of low-achieving students.

Finally, measures of the context in which charter schools operate include characteristics of their neighborhoods, perhaps because the neighborhood influences schools' ability to attract good teachers or students' ability to complete homework during non-school hours. More generally, charter schools in urban settings may have different impacts than those in nonurban settings because of the characteristics of traditional public school districts in these respective areas.[3]

## Methods for identifying factors related to charter-school success

To understand how particular policies or practices influence a charter school's success, one would ideally randomly assign these policies and practices to a group of charter schools and then measure their influence on the schools' impacts. This type of experimental approach to evaluating the impacts of specific school characteristics has been conducted in traditional public schools, with a set of schools randomly assigned to implement a particular set of practices and other schools randomly assigned to a control group not implementing these practices. This approach has been used to evaluate the effects of school-wide implementation of data-driven instruction (Carlson, Borman, & Robinson, 2011; Slavin, Cheung, Holmes, Madden, and Chamberlain 2013; Konstantopoulos, Miller, & Van Der Ploeg, 2013), a school-wide positive behavior supports approach to managing student behavior (Bradshaw, Mitchell, & Leaf, 2010; Horner et al., 2009), professional development for teachers (Garet et al., 2011), and instructional or curricular interventions in reading (Drummond et al., 2011) and math (Agodini, Harris, Seftor, Remillard, & Thomas, 2013). Fryer (2014) randomly assigned a set of traditional public schools to implement a set of practices, including extensive teacher feedback, data-driven instruction, high-dosage tutoring, and expanded instructional time.

Randomly assigning practices to schools is particularly challenging in the charter-school sector, however. An essential feature of charter schools is their autonomy, which allows leaders to implement the educational approach they believe will be most successful for their students. Randomly assigning a particular practice to these schools would work against this autonomy. In addition, charter schools typically implement a bundle of policies and practices, which define their identities. For example, No Excuses charter schools emphasize a particular approach to maintaining student discipline, high expectations for academic achievement, a focus on traditional reading and math skills, increased instructional time, and selective teacher hiring (Carter, 2000; Thernstrom & Thernstrom, 2003). Research suggests that the collection of policies and practices used in No Excuses schools has been successful in boosting student achievement (Cheng, Hitt, Kisida, & Mills, 2017), but imposing a single policy or practice into this mix may have little effect or be counterproductive.

Studies that have examined what factors are responsible for the success of certain charter schools have used a non-experimental or observational approach. This approach involves observing how charter schools' characteristics, policies, and practices are correlated with measures of the schools' success, which are typically the estimated impacts of the school on student achievement using lottery-based or strong non-experimental designs. To measure charter schools' characteristics, policies, and practices in some detail, the studies typically use surveys of school leaders or staff.

Once the studies have estimated impacts and measured the policies and practices of a sample of charter schools, they estimate the correlation between factors thought to influence charter-school success and the schools' impacts on student achievement. In some cases, this correlational analysis is bivariate, where the basic question being addressed is whether charter schools with a particular feature have, on average, more positive (or negative) impacts than charter schools without that feature. In other cases, the analysis is multivariate, with statistical controls added to the analysis for other relevant features of the school (Wolf & Lasserre-Cortez, 2017).

This methodology for assessing which factors explain charter-school success has several limitations, most importantly that correlation is not the same as causation. In observational studies, policies and practices correlated with positive charter-school impacts may be correlated with other, unobserved characteristics, policies, and practices that are actually driving a school's observed success. Without random assignment, one cannot be certain that the factors included in the analysis are causally related to charter-school impacts.

Another limitation of these observational studies is that they typically rely on small samples of about 30 charter schools. Thus, the statistical power of these analyses is low, in that a relationship between a particular factor and charter-school impacts would have to be quite strong to be statistically significant. This "Low-N" problem is made worse by the fact that the number of factors that could potentially influence a charter school's success is large. Although the typical study has a sample of about 30 to 40 charter schools to analyze, the number of different characteristics, policies, or practices that could conceivably influence the schools' impacts on student achievement probably exceeds 30 to 40.[4]

Finally, many factors that might be the most important contributors to a charter school's ability to boost student achievement are difficult to measure and are not included in these analyses. The effectiveness of a school's principal and teachers likely matters a lot. Studies have used proxies for teacher or principal effectiveness using measures such as certification status, experience, and educational attainment, but these objective measures are weak proxies for true teacher and principal quality (Aaronson, Barrow, & Sander, 2007; Rivkin, Hanushek, & Kain, 2005).

## Factors associated with charter-school success

### *Description of studies*

The findings presented here are from studies that set out explicitly to examine a wide range of factors that might explain charter-school success. Other studies have presented evidence on how one or two individual factors are related to charter-school impacts, but they did not aim to systematically explain factors related to charter-school success. Those studies are not reviewed here.

A brief description of each study that has systematically explored factors that may explain charter-school success is presented below. Although many of them used experimental methods to determine the overall impact of charters compared to a control group of students, none of them randomly assigned specific school characteristics to the charter students so their findings regarding charter features and achievement are merely correlational. Table 1 shows additional details about these studies.

- Hoxby, Murarka, and Kang (2009): Lottery-based study that estimated impacts of 32 New York City charter schools. Used data on characteristics of the charter schools, and conducted bivariate and multivariate analysis of the relationships between these charter-school characteristics and their impacts on student achievement.

**Table 1.** Summary of studies systematically examining factors related to charter-school impacts.

| Study | Location | Years | Number of charter schools | Number of factors examined | Design for estimating impacts | Data source for measuring school characteristics and other factors related to charter-school impacts | Design for estimating relationship between factors and charter-school impacts |
|---|---|---|---|---|---|---|---|
| Hoxby et al. (2009) | New York City | 2000–2001 through 2007–2008 | 33 | 28 | Lottery-based | Charter school administrators, NYC Dept. of Education (measured for charter schools only) | School-level bivariate and multivariate analysis[a] |
| Berends et al., 2010 | National | 2002–2003 through 2005–2006 | 76 | 12 | Non-experimental | Teacher and principal surveys (charter schools and traditional public schools) | Student-level regression model[b] |
| Gleason et al. (2010) | 15 states | 2004–2005 through 2007–2008 | 36 | 18 | Lottery-based | Principal survey (charter schools and traditional public schools) | School-level bivariate and multivariate analysis[a] |
| Furgeson et al. (2012) | 8 states | 2002–2003 through 2009–2010 | 22 CMOs, 68 schools | 6 (43)[c] | Non-experimental/ lottery-based[d] | Principal survey (charter schools and traditional public schools) and teacher survey (charter schools only) | School-level bivariate and multivariate analysis[a] |
| Angrist et al. (2013) | Massa-chusetts | 2001–2002 through 2010–2011 | 33 | 11 (42)[e] | Non-experimental/ lottery-based[d] | School administrator survey (charter schools only) | School-level bivariate and multivariate analysis[a] |
| Dobbie and Fryer (2013) | New York City | 2003–2004 through 2010–2011 | 39 | 9 (40)[f] | Non-experimental/ lottery-based[d] | Principal, teacher, and student surveys and video observations (charter schools only) | School-level bivariate and multivariate analysis[a] |

(*Continued*)

**Table 1.** (Continued).

| Study | Location | Years | Number of charter schools | Number of factors examined | Design for estimating impacts | Data source for measuring school characteristics and other factors related to charter-school impacts | Design for estimating relationship between factors and charter-school impacts |
|---|---|---|---|---|---|---|---|
| Tuttle et al. (2013) | 13 states | 2003–2004 through 2010–2011 | 36 | 17 | Non-experimental/ lottery-based[d] | Principal survey (charter schools only) | School-level bivariate and multivariate analysis[a] |
| Knechtel et al. (2015) | 9 states | 2013–2014 | 34 | 13 | Non-experimental/ lottery-based[d] | Principal survey (charter schools only) | School-level bivariate and multivariate analysis[a] |
| Chabrier et al. (2016) | Multiple districts and states[g] | 2001–2002 through 2010–2011 | 87 | 11 | Lottery-based | Principal survey (charter schools only) | School-level bivariate and multivariate analysis[a] |

[a]The bivariate analysis involved regressing a measure of charter-school impacts on a single characteristic of charter schools or examining this relationship between school characteristics and impacts in some similar way. The multivariate analysis involved regressing impacts on several school characteristics simultaneously.

[b]Berends et al. (2010) estimated a regression model in which student achievement was regressed on the student's prior achievement level, demographic characteristics, and characteristics of the student's school (regardless of whether or not the school was a charter school). One of the school characteristics included in the regression was charter-school status. Thus, this study used variation in school characteristics across schools in the charter and traditional public school sectors to capture the relationship between school characteristics and student achievement.

[c]Furgeson et al. (2012) conducted the primary, confirmatory analysis using six factors, but conducted exploratory analysis with a total of 43 factors.

[d]Non-experimental estimates were the primary estimates used in estimating the relationship between charter-school characteristics and impacts, though as part of the larger study impacts were estimated using lottery-based methods as well.

[e]Angrist et al. (2013) conducted the primary, confirmatory analysis using 11 factors but conducted exploratory analysis with a total of 42 factors.

[f]Dobbie and Fryer (2013) conducted the primary, confirmatory analysis using 9 factors but conducted exploratory analysis with a total of 40 factors.

[g]Chabrier et al. (2016) conduct their analysis using an aggregated data set based on data from three prior studies (Angrist et al., 2013; Dobbie & Fryer, 2013; Gleason et al., 2010), with lottery-based impact estimates from those studies only.

CMO = charter management organization.

- Berends, Goldring, Stein, and Cravens (2010): Non-experimental study that examined a national sample of 76 charter schools. School characteristics data obtained from teacher and principal surveys administered at both the charter schools and a matched set of traditional public schools. Unlike the other studies reviewed here, this study did not estimate separate impacts for each charter school in the analysis and examine correlations between school characteristics and impacts. Rather, it used a multivariate regression model to examine the relationship between individual school characteristics and student achievement for both types of schools simultaneously.
- Gleason et al. (2010): Lottery-based study that estimated impacts of 36 charter schools in 15 states. Used survey and administrative data on school characteristics in both these charter schools and the traditional public schools that lottery losers attended. Conducted bivariate and multivariate analysis of the relationships between school characteristics—contrasting charter and traditional public schools when possible—and impacts on student achievement.
- Furgeson et al. (2012): Lottery-based and non-experimental study that estimated impacts of 22 CMOs with 68 schools in 8 states. Collected survey data on school characteristics in the CMO schools and in one traditional public school for each CMO school. Conducted bivariate and multivariate analysis of relationships between CMO school characteristics—contrasting CMO and traditional public schools when possible—and impacts on student achievement.
- Angrist et al. (2013): Lottery-based and non-experimental study that estimated impacts of 33 Massachusetts charter schools. Used survey data on charter-school characteristics. Conducted bivariate and multivariate analysis of relationships between charter-school characteristics and impacts on student achievement.
- Dobbie and Fryer (2013): Lottery-based and non-experimental study that estimated impacts of 39 New York City charter schools. Used survey and observational data on charter-school characteristics. Conducted bivariate and multivariate analysis of relationships between charter-school characteristics and impacts on student achievement.
- Tuttle et al. (2013): Lottery-based and non-experimental study that estimated impacts of 36 KIPP (Knowledge Is Power Program) charter schools. Used survey data on KIPP school characteristics. Conducted bivariate and multivariate analysis of relationships between characteristics of KIPP schools and impacts on student achievement.
- Knechtel et al. (2015): Lottery-based and non-experimental study that estimated impacts among a sample of 34 KIPP charter schools. Used survey data on KIPP school characteristics—with a focus primarily on the schools' leadership practices. Conducted bivariate and multivariate

analysis of relationships between characteristics of KIPP schools and impacts on student achievement.

- Chabrier, Cohodes, and Oreopoulos (2016): Study used an aggregated data set compiled from prior studies, including many of those described above, to examine factors correlated with charter-school impacts based on 113 charter schools. Conducted bivariate and multivariate analysis of relationships between charter-school characteristics and impacts on student achievement.

Conclusions about the findings of these research studies were based on the following rules of thumb. Findings were based on strong evidence if at least four studies found a consistent statistically significant relationship between a particular characteristic and charter-school impacts with no strong counter evidence.[5] Findings were based on moderate evidence if at least two studies found a consistent significant relationship and there was minimal evidence to the contrary. A conclusion of no relationship between a characteristic and charter-school impacts was made if at least two studies had examined the relationship and found no significant relationship with no more than minimal evidence to the contrary.

### *Key findings—school characteristics, policies, and practices consistently associated with positive charter-school impacts*

Several charter-school policies or practices were positively related to impacts on student achievement consistently across a number of different studies.

- ***The most successful charter schools are those located in urban areas.***

Just three of these studies directly examined the association between a charter school's urban location and its achievement impacts, but each study found a strong positive relationship. Angrist et al. (2013) found that among Massachusetts middle schools, a year at an urban charter school compared with nearby traditional public schools led to a statistically significant increase of 0.15 standard deviations in English/language arts achievement by students, whereas the impact of nonurban charter schools was negative and significant (–0.14). The difference between urban and nonurban charter schools impacts in math was even larger. Among a sample of charter schools in multiple states, Gleason et al. (2010) found that after 2 years the impact of being admitted to an urban charter school on student math achievement was positive and significant (0.16) while the impact of nonurban charter schools was negative and significant (–0.14). Chabrier et al. (2016) also found a significant positive relationship between urban status and impacts on math and English/language arts achievement.

Some studies have not examined urban–nonurban differences because they focus entirely on urban charter schools. However, the overall pattern of results across studies supports the finding of more positive impacts in urban charter schools. Studies focusing entirely on urban charter schools have generally found positive impacts, including charter-school studies in Boston (Abdulkadiroglu, Angrist, Dynarski, Kane, and Pathak 2011), Chicago (Hoxby & Rockoff, 2005), and Los Angeles (CREDO, 2014), and New York City (CREDO, 2013b; Dobbie & Fryer, 2013; Hoxby et al., 2009). By contrast, broader studies that include urban and nonurban charter schools have found impacts that are close to zero and not statistically significant (Bifulco & Ladd, 2006; CREDO, 2013a; Furgeson et al., 2012; Gleason et al., 2010; Sass, 2006; Zimmer et al., 2012).

An important caveat about this evidence of a relationship between a charter school's urban status and impacts on achievement is that these studies do not examine random samples of urban or nonurban schools. Most importantly, the lottery-based studies examine only oversubscribed schools that hold admissions lotteries. If the nature of selection of schools into these studies differs in urban and nonurban areas, that differential selection could lead to an artificial difference in impacts between urban and nonurban charter schools.

- ***The most successful charter schools consistently enforce a comprehensive behavior policy with rewards for positive behavior and sanctions for negative behavior.***

Although different studies used different measures of schools' behavior policies, several found that charter schools that had high expectations for student behavior and strictly enforced their rules governing behavior had more positive impacts on student achievement:

- Furgeson et al. (2012) found that "comprehensive behavior policies" were positively associated with student impacts. This behavior measure was based on whether the school used "consistent behavior standards and disciplinary policies," zero-tolerance policies for potentially dangerous behaviors, rewards and sanctions, and parent or student responsibility agreements.
- Hoxby et al. (2009) found more positive impacts among schools with disciplinary policies "based on the idea that expecting small courtesies and punishing small infractions. . .is important." They contrast this with policies that focused mainly on preventing large infractions.
- Dobbie and Fryer (2013) found more positive impacts among schools with higher values on a 10-item index aimed at capturing the extent to which schools had a "strict disciplinary policy."

- Angrist et al. (2013) found that the extent to which the school emphasized "discipline and comportment" was positively correlated with impacts. They argued that this policy is an important part of schools' No Excuses identity, which they also found to be strongly correlated with achievement impacts. Chabrier et al. (2016) had a similar finding.

Finally, several studies found positive impacts among charter-school networks known for an emphasis on high expectations for student behavior. Teh, McCullough, and Gill (2010) found positive impacts among schools in the Achievement First and Uncommon Schools CMOs. KIPP schools have also been found to have strong positive impacts on student achievement (Angrist, Dynarski, Kane, Pathak, & Walters, 2012; Gleason, Tuttle, Gill, Nichols-Barrer, & Teh, 2014; Tuttle et al., 2015). All KIPP schools use an approach that includes high expectations for student behavior, but Tuttle et al. (2013) found that even among KIPP schools, those with the most positive impacts had higher ratings for behavior standards and discipline policies with rewards and sanctions enforced consistently across the school.

Most schools with the type of comprehensive behavior policy described here have a well-known reputation in their communities. As a result, these schools presumably attract and retain students and families who are aware of these policies and willing to comply with them. The nature of their student populations likely makes enforcement of these policies easier than it would be for non-choice schools. The correlation between a charter school's behavior policy and impacts does not prove that the policy itself caused the school to be effective. Other factors such as the nature of the student population or other policies used by the schools could be driving their impacts.

- ***Charter schools with longer school days, school years, or both tend to have more positive impacts on student achievement.***

Nearly all studies reviewed here found a positive association between a charter school's instructional time (length of the school day or year) and impacts on student achievement (Angrist et al., 2013; Chabrier et al., 2016; Dobbie & Fryer, 2013; Furgeson et al., 2012; Gleason et al., 2010; Hoxby et al., 2009). However, several found that although this relationship was statistically significant in bivariate models, it was not significant in multivariate models (Angrist et al., 2013; Chabrier et al., 2016; Furgeson et al., 2012; Gleason et al., 2010). Thus, it may not be the additional time in school that leads to more positive impacts, but rather some other policies or practices associated with time in school.

KIPP schools displayed an interesting relationship between time in school and impacts (Tuttle et al., 2013). The average KIPP school day is 9 h, much longer than the average public school day. The positive impacts of KIPP

(Gleason et al., 2014) support the notion that long school days contribute to positive impacts. The KIPP school day varies from about 8–10 h, and Tuttle et al. (2013) found that those with the longest days had less positive impacts than those with shorter days.[6] Upon further exploration, however, they found that what happened during the school day mattered. Schools that spent more time on core instructional activities had more positive achievement impacts, whereas those that spent more time on activities other than core instruction had less positive impacts. In other words, they found that a long school day still was associated with more positive impacts so long as the time was spent on core instruction. Hoxby et al. (2009) and Angrist et al. (2013) also found a significant positive relationship between instructional time on core subjects and charter-school impacts.

Research on extended time in traditional public schools also suggests that extra time may have beneficial effects only if it is devoted to instruction in core subjects. A non-experimental evaluation of the expanded learning time (ELT) initiative in Massachusetts, which added at least 300 h to the school year but did not restrict the additional time to instructional activities, found that the additional time did not significantly affect student achievement (Checkoway et al., 2012). By contrast, Cortes, Goodman, and Nomi (2015) found that a double dose of algebra instruction had positive impacts on student achievement and educational attainment.

- ***Charter schools that prioritize the objective of boosting students' academic achievement above other possible educational objectives have more positive impacts on student test scores.***

Several studies used measures designed to capture schools' focus on improving their students' academic achievement. All schools presumably want their students to perform at high levels, but these studies attempted to measure which schools placed more emphasis on this goal than on other goals. Berends et al. (2010) measured "focus on achievement" using teachers' ratings on items such as the extent to which they expected students to complete assignments and the extent to which they set high expectations for students' academic work. Hoxby et al. (2009) measured the extent to which the school's mission statement emphasized academic performance. Furgeson et al. (2012) used school principals' reports on whether the school places high importance on students "exceeding state academic standards." Dobbie and Fryer (2013) used principals' reports on whether the school places a "relentless focus on academic goals and having students meet them," noting that other potential priorities not selected by these schools involved "the social and emotional needs of the whole child" and "building a student's self-esteem through positive reinforcement." Angrist et al. (2013) used a measure of the extent to which a school's philosophy emphasized measurable results in terms of achievement gains. In all of these studies, the authors found a positive correlation between charter schools' focus on academic achievement and impacts on students' math or English/language arts scores.

The alignment between this characteristic of charter schools and the measure of charter-school success—positive achievement impacts—may explain this finding. Charter schools that prioritize student achievement over other goals tend to have more positive achievement impacts. A key question not addressed by these studies, however, is how these schools affect other possible outcomes, such as non-cognitive outcomes or long-term educational attainment. One hypothesis is that achievement and other outcomes are substitutes and, because these schools prioritize achievement, they may neglect and have negative impacts on other aspects of students' development. Alternatively, achievement and other outcomes may be complements, and schools that prioritize achievement may also have positive impacts on other outcomes.

### *Key findings—school policies and practices with moderate evidence of positive associations with charter-school impacts*

Based on somewhat more limited evidence, the research has identified several additional factors potentially related to charter-school impacts.

- ***Some evidence suggests that charter schools providing frequent feedback and coaching to teachers have more positive impacts on student achievement.***

Dobbie and Fryer (2013) and Furgeson et al. (2012) developed indexes of how much coaching and feedback charter-school teachers receive on their instructional practices. Angrist et al. (2013) measured the extent to which schools use videotaped lessons as a means of providing feedback. Each found that the most successful charter schools provided teachers with the most coaching and feedback, based on both the bivariate and multivariate analysis, as did Chabrier et al. (2016). Among KIPP schools, on the other hand, Tuttle et al. (2013) found no significant relationship between KIPP impacts and a measure of teacher professional development and mentoring. Among traditional public schools, Glazerman et al. (2010) studied a teacher induction intervention that provided teachers with various forms of coaching and support. They found positive impacts of this intervention but only after teachers had been exposed to it for 3 years.

- ***Charter schools that promote the use of student data to guide teachers' instructional practices may be more successful in boosting student achievement.***

A popular approach to helping teachers improve their instructional practices involves using data from interim student assessments to provide real-time information to teachers on students' mastery of particular concepts (Hamilton et al., 2009). Often called formative assessment, several studies offered some support for the promise of this data-driven instruction approach in charter schools. Hoxby et al. (2009) found that charter schools using more internal diagnostic assessments per year had more positive impacts. Angrist et al. (2013) found that using informal tests to gauge understanding was positively correlated with impacts. Dobbie and Fryer (2013) found that an index of data-driven instruction was positively associated with impacts, although not significantly. Chabrier et al. (2016) also found data-driven instruction to be significantly related to impacts. Finally, Furgeson et al. (2012) found no significant association between a school's efforts to provide student data to teachers, but a measure of how much teachers actually used data to help with their instruction was positively associated with impacts. By contrast, Knechtel et al. (2015) found a negative and significant relationship between KIPP schools' use of data-driven instruction and impacts.

Evidence from traditional public schools has not shown a strong positive relationship between data-driven instruction and student achievement. Carlson et al. (2011), Slavin et al. (2013), Konstantopoulos et al. (2013), and West, Morton, and Herlihy (2016) all found either no significant effects of data-driven instruction on student achievement or small positive effects. These studies examined interventions that focused largely on producing student data and getting it to teachers rather than on helping the teachers figure out how to use the data to improve their instruction.

- ***Limited evidence suggests that high-dosage tutoring helps charter schools improve student achievement.***

Dobbie and Fryer (2013) measured the extent to which charter schools offered students high-dosage tutoring or frequent instruction in small groups of six or fewer students four or more times a week. They found a positive association between tutoring and charter-school impacts, particularly in English/language arts. Angrist et al. (2013) also found a positive relationship between a measure of tutoring for all students and charter-school impacts in math. Other studies did not directly examine the relationship between the availability of tutoring in charter schools and the schools' impacts. Research in traditional public schools is mixed, but a recent study of the provision of supplemental educational services such as tutoring and other academic services under the No Child Left Behind (NCLB) Act shows no evidence of positive impacts on student test scores (Deke, Gill, Dragoset, & Bogen, 2014).

### *Key findings—school policies and practices not associated with charter-school impacts*

Studies have also identified policies and practices that do not appear to be related to impacts. These findings do not necessarily mean that these policies and practices are not relevant or important, given the limitations of the studies' research designs. Just as we cannot necessarily conclude that factors correlated with charter-school impacts are responsible for these schools' success, we cannot rule out the possibility that factors not significantly correlated with charter schools' impacts do contribute to their success. However, the evidence to date shows no significant relationships between the following factors and charter-school impacts:

- ***Class size.*** Several studies found no relationship between class size or student-teacher ratio and charter-school impacts (Dobbie & Fryer, 2013; Hoxby et al., 2009; Furgeson et al., 2012; Tuttle et al., 2013). Gleason et al. (2010) found a significant relationship but in a counterintuitive direction, with impacts more positive in charter schools with a larger student-teacher ratio. Knechtel et al. (2015) found significantly more positive impacts in schools with smaller classes, though this relationship was not significant in the multivariate analysis. In the largest experimental study on the effects of class size in traditional public schools, Finn and Achilles (1990) found positive effects of small kindergarten to 3rd grade classes (13–17 students) relative to larger classes.
- ***Teacher qualifications.*** Dobbie and Fryer (2013) and Chabrier et al. (2016) found no significant association with charter-school impacts of two measures of teacher qualifications, certification and having a master's degree.[7] Gleason et al. (2010) and Tuttle et al. (2013) found no association between a charter school's proportion of experienced teachers and the school's impacts. These findings are largely consistent with research in traditional public schools, which has found no consistent link between student learning and teacher qualifications, with the exception of a teacher's experience in teaching (Aaronson et al., 2007; Rivkin et al., 2005).
- ***Charter management organization affiliation.*** Overall, studies have not found a strong relationship between a charter school's CMO status—that is, whether the school is part of a CMO or operates independently—and the school's impacts (Gleason et al., 2010; Hoxby et al., 2009).[8] Studies that directly estimated impacts across multiple CMOs found that average impacts were not large. For example, Furgeson et al. (2012) and CREDO (2013c) found no statistically significant impact of attending a CMO school, while CREDO (2017) found a statistically significant but small effect size of 0.03. Some individual CMOs, such as Uncommon Schools

and KIPP, have been found to have strong positive impacts on student achievement (Gleason et al., 2014; Teh et al., 2010).

- ***Policies promoting parent involvement.*** Some charter schools make a special effort to involve parents in their students' education. Dobbie and Fryer (2013) developed an index of parent engagement capturing feedback provided to parents on students' behavior, academic performance, and other issues. Hoxby et al. (2009) and Angrist et al. (2013) measured whether schools use parent contracts. Tuttle et al. (2013) developed an index of parent involvement. In each case, the researchers found no significant relationship between these measures of parent involvement and charter-school impacts.
- ***Charter-school age.*** Charter schools may become more effective as they mature. However, Hoxby et al. (2009) and Gleason et al. (2010) found no significant relationship between the age of a charter school and its impacts on student achievement. One caveat is that both studies were lottery-based and focused on oversubscribed charter schools, so very young charter schools may have been underrepresented. In addition, this relationship may be nonlinear, with schools struggling during an initial start-up period but improving thereafter.[9]
- ***Enrollment.*** Furgeson et al. (2012) found that enrollment was not significantly related to charter-school impacts. Similarly, Berends et al. (2010) found no significant relationship between enrollment and student achievement. Gleason et al. (2010) found a significant negative relationship between total enrollment and charter-school impacts. However, the relationship between enrollment per grade and impacts was not statistically significant, suggesting that the enrollment effect may have been related to the number of grades served.

### Mixed evidence for some measures

The evidence is mixed on the relationship between some charter-school policies or practices and impacts on student achievement. Angrist et al. (2013) found that charter schools that required students to wear uniforms had significantly more positive impacts than other schools, but Hoxby et al. (2009) found no significant relationship. Conversely, Hoxby et al. (2009) found a positive relationship between a school's use of pay for performance or merit pay and their impacts, while Angrist et al. (2013) found no significant relationship.

There is also no consensus on instructional practices that have been examined across multiple studies. Gleason et al. (2010) found more positive impacts among schools making use of ability grouping of students, while Furgeson et al. (2012) found no significant relationship. Knechtel et al. (2015)

found that KIPP schools using more individualized instruction had more positive impacts than other schools, but Angrist et al. (2013) failed to find this relationship.

Finally, the evidence is mixed on whether charter-school funding or expenditures are related to their impacts. Angrist et al. (2013) and Dobbie and Fryer (2013) failed to find a statistically significant relationship between charter schools' per pupil expenditures and impacts. By contrast, Gleason et al. (2010) and Chabrier et al. (2016) found a significant bivariate relationship between per pupil revenues and impacts in math, though the relationship was no longer significant in the multivariate model. A big caveat with this research is that it is difficult to accurately measure charter-school funding, given complexities of revenues and costs associated with school facilities as well as serving special needs students (Maloney & Wolf, 2017). Moreover, none of these studies accounted for the funding at nearby traditional public schools, which could presumably also influence estimated impacts.

One issue not addressed by the primary studies reviewed here involves whether schools with an online or virtual approach to education differentially affect student achievement. However, CREDO (2015) estimated impacts specifically for online charter schools and found that they had large negative impacts on student achievement. In terms of success as defined here, evidence suggests that brick and mortar charter schools are more successful than online schools, as currently organized.

## Discussion: what do we know and how can we learn more?

We naturally desire to understand what explains the success of certain charter schools. By understanding factors linked to their success, these policies and practices might be used successfully in other charter schools or traditional public schools. Charter-school networks that employ these policies and practices might be expanded, or traditional public schools and new charter schools might be encouraged to use the same approaches.

**What do we know?** The research provides evidence that some policies and practices are correlated with more positive charter-school impacts on student achievement. The most successful charter schools tend to be urban schools, consistently enforce a comprehensive behavior system, have long school days and/or years, and/or put their highest priority on helping students meet high expectations for academic achievement. More limited evidence suggests that successful charter schools give teachers frequent feedback and coaching, encourage and facilitate the use of student data to help teachers improve their practices, and/or provide high-dosage tutoring to students.[10] Other charter-school policies and practices have been found to be uncorrelated with impacts, including the school's age, CMO affiliation, funding, average class size, teacher qualifications, and how much they encourage parent involvement.

The research is useful but has substantial limitations—small samples, focus on just the single student outcome of achievement, and limited ability to control for confounding factors. The policies and practices found in successful charter schools may simply be correlated with other factors that are actually responsible for the schools' success. For example, charter-school impacts may be driven by a principal's ability to identify and hire effective teachers, and such principals may also happen to work in schools with long school days. Because we cannot observe a principal's ability to hire good teachers, we only see a positive correlation between the school day's length and charter-school impacts. If a new charter school with a long school day opened, that school may not be successful because it may not have a principal who can identify and hire good teachers.

Even if the correlations found in these studies are causal, believing that these policies and practices would work equally well in traditional public schools requires an even greater leap. Charter schools are schools of choice, and may have attributes that are unappealing to certain types of students. Unmotivated students would be unlikely to choose to attend a school with 9-h school days, for example. Traditional public schools, by contrast, typically must serve all students living in a particular geographic area. It is difficult to know whether the policies and practices that are effective in boosting student achievement in a school of choice would be equally effective in a traditional public school serving all students who live in a given neighborhood.

Scaling up successful charter-school networks brings other challenges. For networks to remain successful as they grow, they must be able to maintain the policies and practices that made them successful. Maintaining these policies and practices may make it challenging for these schools to attract enough of the right kind of students to fill the seats in the new schools they wish to open. Similarly, they must be able to continue to attract the kind of teachers and school leaders who made them successful in the first place. As these networks grow, they will likely have to open schools in different contexts and face competition from different kinds of traditional public schools. If the early success of charter schools in the network was driven in part by the fact that the schools were being compared to low-performing traditional public schools (i.e., a weak counterfactual), network schools opening in different areas may have less success. Finally, as CMOs grow, they face increasing administrative burden, and their internal bureaucracy presumably must grow to meet this burden. This growing internal bureaucracy could lead to unanticipated problems.

**How can we learn more?** Given the limitations of the research on the factors associated with charter-school success, findings from these studies should be thought of as generating hypotheses about what policies and practices led to the schools' success and might be successful elsewhere. The best strategy for learning more about the effectiveness of these promising policies and practices involves testing them out elsewhere and carefully measuring their effects. In particular, a set of policies and practices found to be correlated with charter-school impacts could be purposefully implemented in new schools. This purposeful implementation would allow researchers to set up research designs that can provide more rigorous evidence about their effects on student achievement.

In practice, such studies could be implemented in two ways. First, a package of policies and practices associated with successful charter schools could be randomly assigned to a group of schools that agreed to participate in a research study. By randomly assigning these policies and practices to selected schools and tracking student outcomes in these schools and a set of control schools, studies could generate causal impact estimates. Second, researchers could study trends in impacts of successful charter-school networks already implementing many of these policies and practices as the networks expand. Key questions would be whether impacts of the newly opened schools are smaller than those of network schools operating when the network was smaller, and whether impacts at all network schools declined as the network grew.

Fryer (2014) provides an excellent example of the first approach to learning more about charter-school policies and practices. The author identified a bundle of five policies and practices found by Dobbie and Fryer (2013) to be consistently present in successful New York City charter schools and implemented these practices in a set of traditional public schools in Houston, Texas. These practices included increased instructional time, strategies to increase human capital of teachers and administrators, high-dosage tutoring, frequent use of data to inform instruction, and a culture of high expectations. In one set of schools, random assignment was used to determine which schools would implement the practices. In a second set of schools, non-experimental methods were used to determine the effect of the practices on student outcomes. The implementation of the bundle of charter-school policies and practices in Houston led to an annual increase in student achievement of 0.206 standard deviations in math and 0.043 standard deviations in reading. The intervention also led to a modest increase in attendance at the secondary school level, although the impact at the elementary school level was not statistically significant.

We know less about the extent to which successful charter-school networks maintain positive impacts as they grow and reach a scale at which they could struggle to replicate their practices effectively. Most charter-school networks are relatively small, especially in terms of their presence in a single city or district. KIPP is currently the largest network, with about 200 schools as of the 2016–2017 school year, and only a few individual districts have a large number of KIPP schools—with 26 schools operating in the largest district. Tuttle et al. (2015) examined trends in impacts at 37 KIPP middle schools using data from 2001–2002 to 2013–2014, and found that impacts were highest at the earliest part of that period, declined but remained positive and significant through the middle years, and then stabilized at that level through the end of that time period.

Overall, learning more about the policies and practices likely to lead to success among charter schools, and potentially among traditional public schools, requires continuing research in three areas. First, researchers should continue conducting studies using rigorous methods to estimate charter-school impacts and how these impacts are correlated with school policies and practices. Second, researchers should work with policymakers to purposefully implement packages of the most promising factors in other schools and investigate their effects. Third, as successful charter-school networks expand, researchers should examine whether schools in the network remain as effective as the size of the network increases.

## Notes

1. One might question whether there is similar variation in the impacts of individual traditional public schools. Zimmer et al. (2012) examined this issue and found significantly greater variation in school-level impacts in the charter-school sector than in the traditional public school sector in most of the states they examined.
2. There are exceptions. Gleason et al. (2010) and Furgeson et al. (2012) measured a treatment contrast for selected school characteristics using charter school and traditional public school differences based on data from a principal survey. Berends et al. (2010) used a different methodology and did not directly measure a treatment contrast but did account for the characteristics of both charter schools and traditional public schools based on both principal and teacher surveys. Chabrier et al. (2016) examine variation in charter-school impacts after accounting for average test scores in students' "fallback" traditional public schools.
3. Conceptually, the characteristics of the relevant set of traditional public schools should be reflected in measures of the treatment contrast. As described above, however, it is difficult to accurately measure these characteristics and, as a result, a contextual variable such as an indicator for being located in an urban area may serve as a proxy for traditional public-school characteristics.
4. The studies reviewed here have explicitly tried to limit the number of factors they've examined given the limited degrees of freedom in analysis based on a sample of 30–40, but still have examined correlations with charter-school impacts of between 11 and 43 different factors.
5. Evidence was also considered strong if three studies found a significant relationship and there was compelling supporting evidence.
6. By contrast, Knechtel et al. (2015) found no statistically significant relationship between time in school and the impacts of KIPP schools.
7. Chabrier et al. (2016) found no significant association between teachers having a master's degree and impacts in the bivariate analysis, but did find a significant positive association in the multivariate analysis.

8. One study did find some evidence of a relationship between CMO status and charter-school impacts. Dobbie and Fryer (2013) found that New York City charter schools affiliated with a CMO had significantly more positive impacts at the elementary school level, though differences at the middle-school level were not significant. In addition, CREDO (2017) found that impacts among CMO schools were slightly larger than those of independently operated charter schools (e.g., with effect sizes of 0.03 versus 0.01 in math) but did not test the significance of this difference.
9. Zimmer et al. (2011) examined patterns of impacts among first-year versus third-year charter schools in eight states. In three of the states, impacts were substantially more positive in the third year than in the first year, while in the other states there were not substantial differences in the schools' impacts between their first and third years. The authors did not test the statistical significance of any of these differences. Buddin and Zimmer (2005) found significant differences in the impacts of new versus more established charter schools, but the direction of these differences was not consistent. For some types of charter schools, more established schools performed better than new schools but the reverse was true for other types of charter schools.
10. Some evidence suggests that successful charter schools tend to use most or all of these policies and practices in clusters, rather than just one or two of them (Angrist et al., 2013; Dobbie & Fryer, 2013; Furgeson et al., 2012). However, the research focuses on the correlations between individual factors and impacts, either in a bivariate or multivariate model, and does not examine whether there are interactions between factors in their correlation with charter-school impacts.

## References

Aaronson, D., Barrow, L., & Sander, W. (2007). Teachers and student achievement in the Chicago public high schools. *Journal of Labor Economics, 25*(1), 95–135. doi:10.1086/508733

Abdulkadiroglu, A., Angrist, J. D., Dynarski, S. M., Kane, T. J., & Pathak, P. A. (2011). Accountability and flexibility in public schools: Evidence from Boston's charters and pilots. *Quarterly Journal of Economics, 126*(2), 699–748. doi:10.1093/qje/qjr017

Agodini, R., Harris, B., Seftor, N., Remillard, J., & Thomas, M. (2013). *After two years, three elementary math curricula outperform a fourth.* Washington, DC: Institute of Education Sciences, U.S. Department of Education.

Angrist, J. D., Dynarski, S. M., Kane, T. J., Pathak, P. A., & Walters, C. R. (2012). Who benefits from KIPP? *Journal of Policy Analysis and Management, 31*(4), 837–860. doi:10.1002/pam.2012.31.issue-4

Angrist, J. D., Pathak, P. A., & Walters, C. R. (2013). Explaining charter school effectiveness. *American Economic Journal: Applied Economics, 5*(4), 1–27.

Berends, M., Goldring, E., Stein, M., & Cravens, X. (2010). Instructional conditions in charter schools and students' mathematics achievement gains. *American Journal of Education, 116* (3), 303–335. doi:10.1086/651411

Bifulco, R., & Ladd, H. F. (2006). The impact of charter schools on student achievement: Evidence from North Carolina. *Education Finance and Policy, 1*(1), 50–90. doi:10.1162/edfp.2006.1.1.50

Bradshaw, C. P., Mitchell, M. M., & Leaf, P. J. (2010). Examining the effects of school-wide positive behavioral interventions and supports on student outcomes: Results from a randomized controlled effectiveness trial in elementary schools. *Journal of Positive Behavior Interventions, 12*(3), 133–148. doi:10.1177/1098300709334798

Buddin, R., & Zimmer, R. (2005). Student achievement in charter schools: A complex picture. *Journal of Policy Analysis and Management, 24*, 2. doi:10.1002/pam.20093

Carlson, D., Borman, G. D., & Robinson, M. (2011). A multistate district-level cluster randomized trial of the impact of data-driven reform on reading and mathematics achievement. *Educational Evaluation and Policy Analysis, 33*(3), 378–398. doi:10.3102/0162373711412765

Carlson, D., & Lavertu, S. (2016). Charter school closure and student achievement: Evidence from Ohio. *Journal of Urban Economics, 95*(1), 31–48. doi:10.1016/j.jue.2016.07.001

Carter, S. C. (2000). *No Excuses: Lessons from 21 high-performing, high-poverty schools.* Washington, DC: Heritage Foundation.

Chabrier, J., Cohodes, S., & Oreopoulos, P. (2016). What can we learn from charter school lotteries? *Journal of Economic Perspectives, 30*(3), 57–84. doi:10.1257/jep.30.3.57

Checkoway, A., Gamse, B., Velez, M., Caven, M., De La Cruz, R., Donoghue, N., . . . Woodford, M. (2012). *Evaluation of the Massachusetts Extended Learning Time (ELT) initiative.* Cambridge, MA: Massachusetts Department of Elementary and Secondary Education.

Cheng, A., Hitt, C., Kisida, B., & Mills, J. (2017). 'No excuses' charter schools: A meta-analysis of the experimental evidence on student achievement. *Journal of School Choice, 11*(2), 209–238. doi:10.1080/15582159.2017.1286210

Clark, M. A., Gleason, P. M., Tuttle, C. C., & Silverberg, M. K. (2015). Do charter schools improve student achievement? *Educational Evaluation and Policy Analysis, 37*(4), 419–436. doi:10.3102/0162373714558292

Cortes, K. E., Goodman, J. S., & Nomi, T. (2015). Intensive math instruction and educational attainment: Long-run impacts of double-dose algebra. *Journal of Human Resources, 50*(1), 108–158. doi:10.1353/jhr.2015.0004

CREDO. (2013a). *National charter school study: 2013.* Stanford, CA: Stanford University Center for Research on Educational Outcomes.

CREDO. (2013b). *Charter school performance in New York City.* Stanford, CA: Stanford University Center for Research on Educational Outcomes.

CREDO. (2013c). *Charter school growth and replication.* Stanford, CA: Stanford University Center for Research on Educational Outcomes.

CREDO. (2014). *Charter school performance in Los Angeles.* Stanford, CA: Stanford University Center for Research on Educational Outcomes.

CREDO. (2015). *Online charter school study.* Stanford, CA: Stanford University Center for Research on Educational Outcomes.

CREDO. (2017). *Charter management organizations.* Stanford, CA: Stanford University Center for Research on Educational Outcomes.

Deke, J., Gill, B., Dragoset, L., & Bogen, K. (2014). Effectiveness of supplemental educational services. *Journal of Research on Educational Effectiveness, 7*(2), 137–165. doi:10.1080/19345747.2013.809178

Dobbie, W., & Fryer, R. G., Jr. (2013). Getting beneath the veil of effective schools: Evidence from New York City. *American Economic Journal: Applied Economics, 5*(4), 28–60.

Drummond, K., Chinen, M., Duncan, T. G., Miller, H. R., Fryer, L., Zmach, C., & Culp, K. (2011). *Impact of the thinking reader software program on grade 6 reading vocabulary, comprehension, strategies, and motivation (NCEE 2010-4035).* Washington, DC: Institute of Education Sciences, U.S. Department of Education.

Epple, D., Romano, R., & Zimmer, R. (2015). *Charter Schools: A survey of research on their characteristics and effectiveness.* Cambridge, MA: National Bureau of Economic Research (NBER Working Paper No. 21256).

Finn, J. D., & Achilles, C. M. (1990). Answers and questions about class size: A statewide experiment. *American Educational Research Journal, 27*(3), 557–577. doi:10.3102/00028312027003557

Fryer, R. G. (2014). Injecting charter school best practices into traditional public schools: Evidence from field experiments. *Quarterly Journal of Economics, 129*(3), 1355–1407. doi:10.1093/qje/qju011

Furgeson, J., Gill, B., Haimson, J., Killewald, A., McCullough, M., Nichols-Barrer, I., ... Lake, R. (2012). *Charter-School Management Organizations: Diverse strategies and diverse student impacts.* Cambridge, MA: Mathematica Policy Research.

Garet, M. S., Wayne, A. J., Stancavage, F., Taylor, J., Eaton, M., Walters, K., ... Doolittle, F. (2011). *Middle school mathematics professional development impact study (NCEE 2011-4024).* Washington, DC: Institute of Education Sciences, U.S. Department of Education.

Glazerman, S., Isenberg, E., Dolfin, S., Bleeker, M., Johnson, A., Grider, M., & Jacobus, M. (2010, June). *Impacts of comprehensive teacher induction: Final results from a randomized controlled study.* Washington, DC: Institute of Education Sciences, U.S. Department of Education.

Gleason, P., Clark, M., Tuttle, C. C., & Dwoyer, E. (2010). *The evaluation of charter school impacts: Final report (NCEE 2010-4029).* Washington, DC: Institute of Education Sciences, U.S. Department of Education.

Gleason, P. M., Tuttle, C. C., Gill, B., Nichols-Barrer, I., & Teh, B. (2014). Do KIPP schools boost student achievement? *Education Finance and Policy, 9*(1), 36–58. doi:10.1162/EDFP_a_00119

Hamilton, L., Halverson, R., Jackson, S. S., Mandinach, E., Supovitz, J. A., & Wayman, J. C. (2009). *Using student achievement data to support instructional decision making. Institute of Education Sciences Practice Guide (NCEE 2009-4067).* Washington, DC: Institute of Education Sciences, U.S. Department of Education.

Horner, R. H., Sugai, G., Smolkowski, K., Eber, L., Nakasato, J., Todd, A. W., & Esperanza, J. (2009). A randomized, wait-list controlled effectiveness trial assessing school-wide positive behavior support in elementary schools. *Journal of Positive Behavior Interventions, 11*(3), 133–144. doi:10.1177/1098300709332067

Howell, W., & Peterson, P.E., Wolf, P.J., & Campbell, D.E. (2006). *The education gap: Vouchers and urban schools. In (Revised edition).* Washington, DC: Brookings.

Hoxby, C. M., Murarka, S., & Kang, J. (2009). *How New York City's Charter Schools affect student achievement.* Cambridge, MA: New York City Charter Schools Evaluation Project.

Hoxby, C. M., & Rockoff, J. E. (2005). Findings from the city of big shoulders. *Education Next, 5*(4), 52–58.

Knechtel, V., Anderson, M. A., Burnett, A., Coen, T., Sullivan, M., Tuttle, C. C., & Gleason, P. (2015). *Understanding the effect of KIPP as it scales: Volume II, leadership practices at KIPP.* Washington, DC: Mathematica Policy Research.

Konstantopoulos, S., Miller, S. R., & Van Der Ploeg, A. (2013). The impact of Indiana's system of interim assessments on mathematics and reading achievement. *Educational Evaluation and Policy Analysis, 35*(4), 481–499. doi:10.3102/0162373713498930

Maloney, L. D., & Wolf, P. J. (2017). *Charter school funding: Inequity in New York City.* Fayetteville, AR: School Choice Demonstration Project. Retrieved from http://www.uaedreform.org/wp-content/uploads/charter-school-funding-inequity-in-new-york-city.pdf

Rivkin, S. G., Hanushek, E. A., & Kain, J. F. (2005). Teachers, schools, and academic achievement. *Econometrica, 73*(2), 417–458. doi:10.1111/ecta.2005.73.issue-2

Sass, T. R. (2006). Charter schools and student achievement in Florida. *Education Finance and Policy, 1*(1), 91–122. doi:10.1162/edfp.2006.1.1.91

Slavin, R. E., Cheung, A., Holmes, G. C., Madden, N. A., & Chamberlain, A. (2013). Effects of a data-driven district reform model on state assessment outcomes. *American Educational Research Journal, 50*(2), 371–396. doi:10.3102/0002831212466909

Teh, B., McCullough, M., & Gill, B. P. (2010). *Student achievement in New York City middle schools affiliated with achievement first and uncommon schools.* Cambridge, MA: Mathematica Policy Research.

Thernstrom, A., & Thernstrom, S. (2003). *No excuses: Closing the racial gap in learning.* New York, NY: Simon and Schuster.

Tuttle, C. C., Gill, B., Gleason, P., Knechtel, V., Nichols-Barrer, I., & Resch, A. (2013). *KIPP Middle Schools: Impacts on achievement and other outcomes.* Washington, DC: Mathematica Policy Research.

Tuttle, C. C., Gleason, P., Knechtel, V., Nichols-Barrer, I., Booker, K., Chojnacki, G., … Goble, L. (2015). *Understanding the effect of KIPP as it scales: Volume I, impacts on achievement and other outcomes.* Washington, DC: Mathematica Policy Research.

Weiss, M. J., Bloom, H. S., & Brock, T. (2014). A conceptual framework for studying the sources of variation in program impacts. *Journal of Policy Analysis and Management, 33*(3), 778–808. doi:10.1002/pam.21760

West, M. R., Morton, B. A., & Herlihy, C. M. (2016). *Achievement network's investing in innovation expansion: Impacts on educator practice and student achievement.* Cambridge, MA: Harvard University, Center for Education Policy Research.

Wolf, P. J., & Lasserre-Cortez, S. (2017). *Features of New Orleans charter schools associated with student achievement growth based on an exploratory analysis.* Washington, DC: U.S. Department of Education, Institute of Education Sciences, National Center for Education Evaluation and Regional Assistance, Regional Educational Laboratory Southwest. Retrieved from http://ies.ed.gov/ncee/edlabs

Zimmer, R., Gill, B., Booker, K., Lavertu, S., Sass, T., & Witte, J. (2011). *Charter schools in eight states: Effects on achievement, attainment, integration, and competition.* Santa Monica, CA: RAND Research Corporation.

Zimmer, R., Gill, B., Booker, K., Lavertu, S., & Witte, J. (2012). Examining charter school achievement effects across seven states. *Economics of Education Review, 31*(2), 213–224. doi:10.1016/j.econedurev.2011.05.005

# A review of the research on parent satisfaction in private school choice programs

Evan Rhinesmith

**ABSTRACT**
I review the research literature on parent satisfaction with private school choice programs providing vouchers, scholarships, or education savings accounts. The reviewed studies make use of parent surveys to measure satisfaction, often comparing the responses of parents of scholarship lottery winners to those of parents of students who lost scholarship lotteries or comparing parent satisfaction in their current private school of choice to satisfaction with their previous public school. Results of all these studies show parents who can choose private schools are more satisfied with their child's school. These studies also find higher levels of satisfaction when comparing choice parents to public school parents. More research is needed to explain why parents choose specific schools and whether parents choose schools that satisfy specific qualities they have deemed important when choosing a new school.

## Introduction

After President Donald Trump tabbed American Federation for Children Chairwoman Betsy DeVos (Brown, 2016) as the pick for US Secretary of Education, school choice moved to the forefront of education policy debates (Donald J. Trump for President, Inc, 2016). School choice programs offer parents the chance to enroll their children in public or private schools using public money. Supporters of school choice argue that it provides parents the opportunity to choose the school setting that best fits their child's needs without having to move to a different public school district.

Under our current education system, most children are assigned to schools based on their home address. Giving parents choices in education removes the barrier imposed through the common neighborhood assignment process. School choice exists in multiple forms (Wolf & Egalite, 2016). The most common is choice through mortgage, which families can exercise by buying a home or renting an apartment in a different public school district. Other growing forms of choice include public charter schools and private school choice programs offering vouchers, scholarships, and tax credits to cover at least a portion of tuition for a private school. For this review, I focus on the various forms of private school choice and research regarding parent satisfaction after participating in these programs.

During the 2016–2017 school year, 31 states and the District of Columbia offered 61 different private school choice programs (EdChoice, 2017). These programs exist in multiple forms, including school vouchers, education savings accounts (ESAs), scholarship tax credit programs, and programs targeted specifically to children with special needs. The potential high watermark for school choice came when Nevada's State Legislature passed the nation's first near-universal private school choice program, which has not enrolled any students because a state court found it to be legal in all aspects of its design except its funding mechanism (Brown, 2015; Chereb, 2015).

While school choice advocates experienced many victories in 2015, there were multiple lawsuits and court decisions concerning school choice programs. One of the biggest cases concerned the Douglas County, Colorado choice program, where a plurality in the Colorado Supreme Court found the program to be unconstitutional (Gorski, 2015), effectively continuing the hold on the program that has been in place since 2011 after more than 90% of the first group of applicants chose to attend religious schools. Colorado Supreme Court Justice Allison Eid dissented, writing,

> [A] more serious error on the part of the plurality is its steadfast refusal to consider whether section 7 is unenforceable due to possible anti-Catholic bias. The plurality applies what it believes to be (erroneously in my view) the 'plain language' of the section. But the plurality cannot sweep the possibility of anti-Catholic bigotry under the plain language rug. (*Taxpayers for Public Education v. Douglas County School District, 2015*).

Defendants of the Douglas County program have appealed to the US Supreme Court.

During 2016 and 2017, there have been heated debates over proposed school choice initiatives in multiple states and state legislators have pushed for more choice in education. With states like Arkansas and Tennessee passing a special education voucher and ESA program, respectively. Similarly, studies on statewide school voucher programs in Indiana and Louisiana have made the debates on private school choice more heated, as they have reported initial negative test-score effects that take several years to fade (Berends & Waddington, 2016; Mills & Wolf, 2017).

To date, most of the research on various school choice programs has focused on student achievement on standardized tests, student attainment such as graduation and college enrollment, and systemic effects of school choice programs on public schools, finding that students using private school choice often outperform their peers or, at the very least, do no worse. A recent meta-analysis from Greg Forster (2016) examined the academic outcomes of students using private school choice programs as reported in empirical analyses using random assignment methodologies. Forster found that of the 18 studies using the "gold standard" method, 14 found positive outcomes for students in school choice programs, 2 found no significant impact, and 2 found negative effects at least in the short-term. Both studies with negative school choice achievement findings are of the Louisiana Scholarship Program (Abdulkadiroglu, Pathak, & Walters, 2015; Mills & Wolf, 2016), where concerns about government regulations led two-thirds of the private schools in the state to decline the invitation to participate (Kisida, Wolf, & Rhinesmith, 2015). A more formal statistical meta-analysis of the achievement effects of private school choice programs worldwide largely confirms Forster's findings from the USA. Choice tends to boost student achievement, especially several years after first switching from public to private school, particularly in reading, and most strongly in developing countries (Shakeel, Anderson, & Wolf, 2016).

Despite the controversy surrounding the issue, legislators, researchers, and interest groups continue to push for more choice in education. Perhaps school choice initiatives continue to pop up in the face of such fierce opposition is the impact these programs have on parent satisfaction. After all, parents, unlike children, can vote (Peterson, 1993). Parental satisfaction is not a new topic in educational research, as the US Department of Education often conducts surveys of parents with school-aged children (Snyder, De Brey, & Dillow, 2016). Recent survey studies from Barrows, Peterson, and West (2017) found that charter school parents are "considerably more satisfied with their schools" compared to parents who enroll their children in a traditional public school (TPS). Similarly, parents in the survey sample who enrolled their children in a private school reported higher levels of satisfaction compared to charter school parents (Barrows et al., 2017). Phillip Vassallo's "More Than Grades: How Choice Boosts Parental Involvement and Benefits Children" (2000, p. 12) finds overall, that "parents are overwhelmingly satisfied with their new schools than they were with their previous schools on a range of measures..." Vassallo's results form the foundation of the current review. We build substantially upon that foundation by including the results of more private school choice programs and more recent studies while excluding the results of charter schools. The question driving this review is: What does research on private school choice programs reveal about levels of parental satisfaction in school when parents are given the opportunity to choose?

A common criticism of these programs and parental satisfaction ratings is Hawthorne or placebo effects (see Duflo, Glennerster, & Kremer, 2008), where treatment group parents are more satisfied and happier simply because they know that they are receiving an experimental treatment. This awareness may cause them to think that their child's school is better, at least initially, just because it is different. Also, since parents choose their child's school in voucher, scholarship, and ESA programs, higher levels of school satisfaction may be the result of cognitive dissonance, as parents filter out negative information about the school to confirm in their own mind that they made a good choice. However, studies of parental satisfaction that go beyond the first year of a private school choice program can alleviate these effects and temper these criticisms, as placebo effects and cognitive dissonance are likely to weaken substantially over time.

Studies of parental satisfaction in private school choice programs have used a combination of random assignment and observational methods to produce estimates of parental satisfaction due to increased amounts of choice in schools. This study reviews both the experimental and non-experimental studies of parental satisfaction when participating in private school choice programs. Table 1 shows the full list of studies included in this review, along with a summary of the findings. In total, there are 19 studies that examine parental satisfaction in private school choice programs in the United States.

The following section describes the methodology for finding and selecting studies included in the review. The section after that describes the studies of private school choice programs that have attempted to measure parental satisfaction using experimental, quasi-experimental, and observational methods and reviews the findings. The subsequent section discusses the research implications, and the final section concludes.

## Methodology

This literature review is organized by study methodology. The first subsection of results is limited to studies that use experimental methods to compare parent satisfaction with their child's school. These studies compare the results of families that won a school choice lottery to those of a control group of families who wanted to exercise school choice but lost the lottery. In some cases the researchers use statistical techniques to account for lottery winners who decline to use their vouchers and control group students who attend private schools outside of the program.

These studies make use of surveys to measure levels of parental satisfaction. Many of the private school choice program analyses compare voucher/scholarship winners to voucher/scholarship losers, leaving them vulnerable to the "sour grapes" criticism and not providing a valid picture of satisfaction in the TPSs. As Howell and his colleagues (2002, p. 178) describe, "Simply having applied for a voucher, participants in the voucher programs registered a certain measure of discontent with their local public schools. . .Observed impacts on measures of satisfaction may have been due to an especially low opinion of public schools by parents who

**Table 1.** Summary of impacts of private school choice programs on parent satisfaction.

| Location | Program name | Author (year) | Methods | Satisfaction impacts |
|---|---|---|---|---|
| Arizona | Arizona Empowerment Scholarship Accounts | Butcher and Bedrick (2013) | Parent surveys | No parents responded as neutral or a level of dissatisfaction with their new school compared with their previous school, 71% reported being "very satisfied" |
| Charlotte, NC | Children's Scholarship Fund | Greene (2001) | RCT | Private school parents more likely to give their school an A compared to public school parents; choice parents more likely to report being "very satisfied" |
| Cleveland, OH | Cleveland Scholarship and Tutoring Program | Metcalf (1999) | Parent surveys | Scholarship-winning parents more satisfied on all aspects of school than scholarship losers and non-applicants |
| Cleveland, OH | Cleveland Scholarship and Tutoring Program | Peterson et al. (1999) | Multivariate regression | Private school parents 16 percentage points more satisfied than public school parents |
| Dayton, OH | Parents Advancing Choice in Education | Howell and Peterson (2002) | RCT | 1.14 of a standard deviation improvement in year 1 |
| Edgewood ISD, San Antonio, TX | Horizon Scholarship Program | Peterson et al. (1999) | Parent surveys | Effect size of 0.58 of a standard deviation on program participants reporting being "very satisfied" |
| Florida | McKay Scholarship Program for Students with Disabilities | Greene and Forster (2003) | Parent surveys | Current and former participants were more satisfied with their chosen school; former participants equally satisfied with school facilities and equipment |
| Georgia | Georgia GOAL Scholarship Program | Kelly and Scafidi (2013) | Parent surveys | 84% of GOAL parents were very satisfied with new private school compared to previous school |
| Indiana | Indiana Choice Scholarship Program & Indiana School Scholarship Tax Credit | Catt and Rhinesmith (2016) | Parent surveys | 13 percentage point advantage for choice program participants being "very satisfied" with their choice school over non-program private school parents. |
| Indiana | Indiana Choice Scholarship Program & Indiana School Scholarship Tax Credit | DiPerna (2014) | Parent surveys | 57.2% of parents were dissatisfied with their previous school; 89.7% were "very satisfied" with their chosen private school |
| Indianapolis, IN | Educational Choice Charitable Trust | Weinschrott and Kilgore (1998) | Parent surveys | 90% of parents in private schools reported being satisfied compared to previous public school |
| Milwaukee, WI | Milwaukee Parental Choice Program | Witte (2001) | Parent surveys | Choice parents gave grades 0.3 points higher than public school parents and were more satisfied than public school parents |
| Milwaukee, WI | Milwaukee Parental Choice Program | Witte et al. (2008) | Parent surveys | 12 percentage point advantage for MPCP parents giving their school an A or B over public school parents |

(*Continued*)

**Table 1.** (Continued).

| Location | Program name | Author (year) | Methods | Satisfaction impacts |
|---|---|---|---|---|
| Mississippi | Mississippi's Special Needs ESA | Kittredge (2016) | Parent surveys | 98% of participating parents reported being at least somewhat satisfied |
| New York, NY | School Choice Scholarships Fund | Howell and Peterson (2002) | RCT | 1.01 of a standard deviation improvement in year 1 |
| USA | Children's Scholarship Fund | Howell and Peterson (2002) | RCT | 0.95 of a standard deviation impact on parent satisfaction |
| USA | Children's Scholarship Fund | Peterson and Campbell (2001) | RCT | Choice parents more likely to give their school an A and say "very satisfied" |
| Washington, DC | Washington Scholarship Fund | Howell and Peterson (2002) | RCT | 0.66 of a standard deviation improvement in year 1 |
| Washington, DC | DC Opportunity Scholarship Program | Kisida and Wolf (2015) | RCT | Increased average school grade by 0.34–0.53 of a standard deviation |

used a voucher." To that end, a second subsection examines the outcomes of quasi-experimental and observational studies of parent satisfaction. Those survey studies compare satisfaction of parents intentionally enrolling their children in private schools through choice programs to satisfaction levels of parents intentionally enrolling their children in TPS or to their levels of satisfaction when their child was in public schools.

The studies included in this review were collected via a combination of internet searches using Google and Google Scholar; database searches of Academic Search Premier, EBSCOHost, ERIC (Education Resources Information Center), and JSTOR; and the examination of networked citations in studies included in the review. The search strings consisted of combinations of numerous synonyms for and varieties of "parental satisfaction," "private school choice programs," and "school choice satisfaction".

Identified studies were included in this review if they used generally acceptable experimental, quasi-experimental, or observational methods to study private school choice programs. Studies were included if they surveyed parents who enrolled their children in private schools using public dollars through a program like a voucher, tax credit scholarship, or ESA. While this review attempts to be comprehensive, it is always possible that some studies measuring and comparing parental satisfaction levels were missed.

While the methodologies of the studies varied, the conclusions at which these studies arrive are still important. The next section reviews the existing research on parental satisfaction in private school choice programs and reports the findings.

## Review of content

This section reviews studies of parental satisfaction in private school choice programs. It begins with experimental studies that compare school satisfaction levels of families randomly assigned to schools of choice to those of families who sought choice but lost the scholarship lottery. While the ideal study makes use of random assignment, this is not always possible. Sometimes the best comparison is available is between the parents of students who choose to enroll in a private school and those who choose to remain in a public school. By matching students on key characteristics or controlling for those factors, such studies can be viewed as quasi-experimental. Finally, sometimes parental satisfaction measurements are only obtainable through observational surveys asking parents to compare their current schools of choice to their previous TPS. This section begins by reviewing studies using experimental designs to assign families to treatment and control who are then surveyed to measure satisfaction. This is followed by the results from quasi-experimental and observational studies.

### *Experimental studies*

To date, random assignment studies and quasi-experimental studies have found that parents participating in private school choice programs are often more satisfied with their schools of choice than their counterparts whose children enroll in TPS. While there are myriad reasons to choose, voucher programs appear to increase satisfaction on multiple outcomes. As Wolf (2008, p. 435) says, "Voucher programs appear especially to increase parent satisfaction regarding curriculum, safety, parent-teacher relations, academics, and the religious environment of schools." Not only do voucher programs have positive impacts on parental satisfaction, but these results are often large, "averaging three-tenths of a standard deviation" (Wolf, 2008, p. 435).

The Children's Scholarship Fund (CSF) awarded 40,000 scholarships by lottery to low-income families nationwide. The lottery allowed for a randomized control trial to evaluate the impacts of the program. In 2001, Paul Peterson and David Campbell surveyed 2,300 applicants to the program, finding that parents able to enroll their child in a private school were more likely to give their school of choice an 'A' and more likely to say that they were "very satisfied" with aspects of their school compared to their public school counterparts. When Peterson and Campbell (2001, p. 17) asked parents to grade their school, "72 percent of private school parents gave their child's school an A, compared to 16 percent of public school parents." Private school parents said they were more satisfied specifically with school academics, safety, discipline, and teaching values.

In a study of a private school voucher program in Charlotte, Jay Greene (2001) analyzed the impact of receiving a private school voucher by lottery for children grades 2 through 8. Along with the achievement measures, Greene surveyed parents to examine their opinions regarding their child's school. After one year of participation in the program, the parents of just over 450 students (40% of those invited to participate) completed satisfaction surveys. Nearly twice as many parents enrolling their students in private schools assigned their school an A as their public school counterparts. As Greene (2001, p. 57) writes, "Choice parents were also far more likely to report being 'very satisfied' with virtually all aspects of their children's school..."

William Howell and colleagues (2002) examine the impacts of vouchers in urban schools in *The Education Gap*. They include a chapter on satisfaction in urban schools by examining randomized control trials in New York City, Dayton, the national CSF, and Washington, DC as well as observational data from Cleveland and the Edgewood school district in San Antonio. They write (p. 170), "Overall, the findings are unambiguous. The effects on parents' initial satisfaction with their child's switch from a public to a private school.. .were large, clear, sustained and positive." To account for any potential placebo effect, they include responses from years one, two, and three, finding only small drops in satisfaction over time. Also, the study accounts for "sour grapes" by tracking satisfaction with parents who did not win a voucher, finding that satisfaction levels were higher in the private sector. The authors also aggregate the responses from all the programs to scale the responses to represent an effect size. All the urban private school programs (DC, New York, and Dayton) create an average impact of 0.92 of a standard deviation increase in parental satisfaction during the first year of parent participation, which is very large. This effect size shrinks slightly over time, falling to 0.89 of a standard deviation increase in parental satisfaction in the second year and 0.85 in the third year (Howell et al., 2002, p. 175). Though the overall effect size shrinks slightly over time, the sustained impact of attending a private school on parent satisfaction is still quite large. The program in Dayton had the largest first year effect of 1.14 standard deviations, which fell to 0.59 in year 2. The impact of the CSF program on parent satisfaction was similar to the three individual urban programs, with an effect size of 0.95 of a standard deviation. In all cases, parents using a private school voucher were more satisfied than their public school counterparts.

The Opportunity Scholarship Program in Washington, DC randomly assigned students to receive a voucher for private schools by lottery (Wolf et al., 2010). In a follow-up to the Congressionally-mandated evaluation of the program, Kisida and Wolf (2015) analyzed the impact of the program on parent satisfaction with their child's school. They found that access to private schooling through the voucher program increased the average grade that parents assigned to their child's school by .34 to .53 standard deviations, moving it from a solid C+ to above a B (Kisida & Wolf, 2015, p. 273). The pattern of satisfaction effects across time revealed no evidence of a placebo effect, as the highest satisfaction ratings of the treatment group were in Year 4 of the study, and only modest evidence of sour grapes, with control group ratings only slightly lower immediately after losing the lottery than several years later. The moderately-large positive impacts of the OSP on parent satisfaction were closely replicated when researchers used a 12-item satisfaction scale as the outcome measure instead of parent grade of school (Kisida & Wolf, 2015, p. 275). Results were consistent across subgroups based on student gender, baseline achievement, previous exposure to failing public schools, and grade level. When researchers examined satisfaction impacts on individual aspects of schools, they found that treatment parents were significantly more satisfied than control parents with academic quality, teacher and parent communication, safety, school facilities, and class sizes (Kisida & Wolf, 2015, p. 275). Parent satisfaction with services for students with special needs was statistically similar for the treatment and control group parents.

The next section reviews results from studies relying on quasi-experimental and observational methods. Most of these studies rely on self-reported information resulting from surveys administered to parents enrolling in an assortment of choice and TPS programs.

### Quasi-experimental and observational studies

By relying on survey reports, parent satisfaction levels appear to be very high in private school choice programs. Teske and Schneider (2001, p. 615) write, "Researchers agree almost completely on at least one outcome: Parents who choose report being more satisfied with the school than those who do not choose." However, there is disagreement about the cause of these higher levels of satisfaction.

In many cases of experimental studies, parents who win a voucher through a lottery are compared to parents who were not awarded a voucher through the same lottery. While this helps to remove the issue of selection bias when comparing achievement and attainment, it leads to what Peterson, Myers, and Howell (1999) refer to as "sour grapes" criticisms. The argument claims that parents who did not win a scholarship through a lottery would not be representative of the typical public school parents because they were likely to be unusually dissatisfied with the public schools. Therefore, showing that treatment group families were more satisfied than these "sour grapes" did not prove much of anything.

To address this and the placebo effect criticisms more directly, Greene, Howell, and Peterson (1999a) use a multivariate regression to analyze what exactly led to the different levels of parent satisfaction in the Cleveland Scholarship Program. This study uses a survey of 2,020 Cleveland Scholarship and Tutoring Program applicants, 1,014 scholarship recipients and 1,006 applicants who chose not to enroll in the program. The results of their satisfaction surveys show that the "most prominent finding is that the parents with students attending established private schools were as much as 16 percentage points more satisfied than parents whose children voluntarily decided to remain in public schools" (Greene, Howell, & Peterson, 1999b, p. 372). These results were large and statistically significant, finding that private school parents were, on average, more satisfied than public school parents. Also, this study sample accounts for "sour grapes" criticisms as the results do not just reflect the "dissatisfaction felt by a small subset of public school parents who could not get their children into the program" (Greene et al., 1999a, p. 373).

The Educational Choice Charitable Trust (ECCT) provided private school tuition vouchers on a first-come, first served basis to low-income students enrolled in Indianapolis Public Schools. Weinschrott and Kilgore (1998) used results from a multiyear evaluation conducted by the Hudson Institute. For parental satisfaction, the researchers used parent surveys that were administered in the fall of each year of the program. The sample consists of parents whose children enrolled in public schools prior to enrolling in the ECCT program and were enrolled in their ECCT school for at least 2 years. These surveys look back to the previous year and compare responses for satisfaction. Analyzing satisfaction levels in the Indianapolis program shows, "In all dimensions more than 90% of respondents were satisfied or very satisfied with the private school environment. Satisfaction in the second year of private school dropped in some categories, but in most cases 80% of the respondents were at least satisfied with the private school setting." (Weinschrott & Kilgore, 1998, p. 324) In all cases, the differences were significant, showing that parents were more satisfied in the private school settings compared to public schools.

In a separate study of the Cleveland Scholarship and Tutoring Program from 1996–99, Kim Metcalf compared satisfaction levels of 468 scholarship recipients to 487 families enrolling in public schools and 526 applicants for the scholarship program who did not receive a scholarship in the third year of the program. Metcalf's (1999, pp. 19–20) results showed that "parents of scholarship students tend to be much more satisfied with their child's school than other parents." In a possible example of sour grapes, parents who applied for and did not receive a scholarship are less satisfied overall than the other two groups of parents. However, the inclusion of the parents of public school students who did not apply show that parents able to partake in choice were still more satisfied when given the chance to choose.

The Horizon Scholarship Program was the first voucher program to offer a private school voucher to all low-income families living in the Edgewood Independent School District of San Antonio, Texas. The unique circumstances of this program allowed Peterson et al. (1999) to compare voucher parents to a multitude of public school parents in the Edgewood district. The results of the satisfaction surveys were similar to those of the Cleveland studies. Parents enrolling their children in private schools with a voucher were more satisfied than parents enrolling their children in Edgewood Public School. They write, "The percentage of Horizon parents who reported they were 'very satisfied' with specific dimensions of their child's school was considerably higher than the percentage of public school parents." (Peterson et al., 1999, p. 28)

John F. Witte's study of the Milwaukee Parental Choice Program included an analysis of its effects on parent satisfaction. As a means of measuring satisfaction, Witte administered surveys to parents in the voucher program and parents whose children were enrolled in Milwaukee Public Schools (MPS). In total, 611 choice parents and 1,541 MPS parents responded to the surveys. In the initial surveys, choice parents were asked to rate their previous public school, showing that choice parents were "approximately two points less satisfied with their prior schools, than were nonchoosing MPS parents" (Witte, 2001, pp. 67–68). These results were reversed when choice parents were asked about their private schools, as parents were, on average, "very satisfied" to "somewhat satisfied". According to Witte (p. 118), "Interestingly, the two measures on which parents were least satisfied in the public schools—educational environment and discipline—were the areas of greatest satisfaction in private schools." Also, choice parents' grades for their private schools increased from year to year, improving from an average grade of 3.0 in 1991 to 3.1 in 1995, compared to 2.8 for the MPS parents in the control group (Witte, 2001). Parents participating in the Milwaukee Parental Choice Program were, on average, more satisfied with the private school of choice compared to their previous public school.

A follow-up study focuses on the Milwaukee program from 2006 to 2012. The evaluation includes a sample of 2,727 voucher-participating students matched with the same number of observationally similar MPS students, with surveys administered to their parents. The study reports: "About 87 percent of MPCP parents gave their child's school an A or B. About 75 percent of MPS respondents gave their children's school a similar high grade." (Witte, Wolf, Cowen, Fleming, & Lucas-McLean, 2008, p. 27). Researchers further reported that MPCP parents were almost 16 percentage points more likely to say they plan to keep their child in their current school compared to MPS parents (Witte et al., 2008, pp. 27–28).

In a survey of 300 parents in Denver and Washington, DC, Teske, Fitzpatrick, and O'Brien (2009) surveyed 300 parents in each city. The main focus of this study was to understand the barriers that transportation poses to school choice. They found that over half of the survey sample had children who did not attend their neighborhood public school or the school closest to their home. Parents who chose a school other than their local public school had higher levels of satisfaction. However, if parents were unable to enroll their child in the school they chose due to transportation, they were more likely to report dissatisfaction with their current school (Teske et al., 2009, p. 19).

The Georgia GOAL Scholarship Program administered surveys to parents of K-12 scholarship recipients in 2013. Nine hundred sixty-two of the participants responded to the GOAL survey, 754 of whom completed the entire survey (Kelly & Scafidi, 2013). Of the parents who responded, 84% were very satisfied with their new private school compared to their previous school, along with nearly 15% saying they were satisfied with their new private school (Kelly & Scafidi, 2013). The parents who participated in this program were more likely to assume a large financial burden, as the GOAL scholarship does not cover the full tuition charged at Georgia private schools.

The state of Florida enacted the McKay Scholarship Program for Students with Disabilities in 1999, with the purpose of providing school vouchers to special education students in Florida public schools. In 2003, Greene and Forster conducted an evaluation of the McKay Scholarship Program's impacts on participants on a variety of outcomes including parental satisfaction. Using a telephone survey, Greene and Forster (2003) used contact information provided by the Florida Department of Education for McKay Program participants in the 2001–2002 and 2002–2003 school years to survey families that left the program between the two years and those families who participated during the 2002–2003 school year. This resulted in a list of 9,202 participants in 2002–2003 and 1,050 former participants, creating a survey sample of 600 current and 215 former participants. The results showed that current McKay participants were more satisfied with their McKay school than their public school, with the exception being former participants stating they are roughly equally satisfied with facilities and equipment in their public school and McKay school, while current participants are more satisfied with their McKay school (Greene & Forster, 2003, p. 6). Along with the reported satisfaction levels of current program participants, Greene and Forster (2003) show that former participants "overwhelmingly endorse the program's continued availability" (Greene & Forster, 2003, p. 12).

A revolutionary idea in school choice is Arizona's ESA program. Proposed by the Goldwater Institute in 2005 and enacted in 2011, ESAs offer the greatest level of autonomy to parents to direct their child's education by depositing 90% of the per pupil funding to parents of eligible students in private accounts. Parents are then able to use the ESA to pay tuition in a different K-12 school meeting Arizona's ESA law requirements or tutoring programs for their children. They also can save funds and use them for their child's post-secondary education (Arizona Empowerment Scholarship Accounts, 2012). In the first examination of parent satisfaction in Arizona's ESA program Butcher and Bedrick (2013) surveyed 179 parents who participated in an online ESA message board in the spring of 2013. This sample represents more than half of the 300 families using ESAs in the 2012–13 school year (Butcher & Bedrick, 2013). Of the parents who used their ESA funds to enroll their child in a new school, 71% reported being "very satisfied", 19% said they were "satisfied", and the remaining 10% reported being "somewhat satisfied" (Butcher & Bedrick, 2013).

In 2015, Mississippi became the third state to provide families educational options through an ESA. Much like the early years of Arizona's ESA, Mississippi's program is available only to students with special needs or who have received an IEP in the five years prior to enrolling in the program. There were 425 accounts available during the 2016–2017 school year awarded via lottery. Many families awarded an account used the money to pay for tuition at an eligible private school (Kittredge, 2016). During the 2015–2016 school year, Empower Mississippi surveyed just over 10% of the participating families to measure their levels of satisfaction. These results are remarkably similar to those of the Butcher and Bedrick study in Arizona, as an overwhelming majority (98%) of parents reported being at least somewhat satisfied, 71% of whom said they were very satisfied (Kittredge, 2016). The survey also asked parents how satisfied they were with their previous school, finding that two-thirds of parents were at least somewhat unsatisfied with their previous school.

Indiana has one of the broadest school voucher programs in the country, with nearly 4,000 families using vouchers to enroll in private schools in the program's first year of 2011–2012. Enrollment more than doubled in year two and participation surged to nearly 20,000 participants by the third school year of 2013–14 (DiPerna, 2014). Indiana policymakers were interested in knowing why parents were enrolling in choice scholarship schools. Over 4,000 Indiana private school choice parents participated in the survey, with nearly 60% of parents reporting dissatisfaction with their previous school and nearly 90% of parents saying they were "very satisfied" with their choice school (DiPerna, 2014).

The Indiana choice program continued to grow, with over 32,000 participants in the voucher program. In a follow-up to the 2014 survey alongside a larger survey sample of choice and non-choice private school parents, Catt and Rhinesmith (2016) examined parent satisfaction and why parents chose to leave their neighborhood public schools. With over 2,000 responses to the survey, the authors found that over half of choice-program respondents were at least "somewhat satisfied" with their previous neighborhood public school (Catt & Rhinesmith, 2016, p. 19). While parents were seemingly happy with the schools they were actively trying to leave, Indiana choice program parents were overwhelmingly satisfied with their current private schools. They found that 92% of parents were at least "somewhat satisfied" and 81% of choice parents said they were "very satisfied" (Catt & Rhinesmith, 2016, p. 12). A similar percentage of non-choice program private school parents said they were at least "somewhat satisfied" with their current school, but only 68% said they were "very satisfied".

Parents were asked what specifically made them want to leave their previous schools and why they were choosing their new schools. Over one-third of choice parents said they left their previous school because of a "lack of religious environment/instruction", and similar percentages of parents said they were unhappy with the academic quality and a "lack of (values) instruction" in their neighborhood public school. As this shows, even though choice program participants were satisfied with their previous school, parents were happier when they could enroll their child in a private school that offered better academics and a religious environment in which their children could learn.

The literature on parent satisfaction in choice programs points to higher levels of satisfaction when parents can choose a school outside of their government assigned school. These results hold in more rigorous studies comparing treatment and control groups in random assignment studies and in quasi-experimental and observational survey studies where parents self-sort into school sectors. The strength of the experimental studies is their ability to prevent self-selection bias in the comparisons across groups. The strength of the observational studies is in their ability to respond to "sour grapes" and placebo effect criticisms. Unfortunately, these reports of high levels of satisfaction do not explain why parents are more satisfied or if parents were able to get what they chose for from their school. The following section discusses the implications for research on parent satisfaction in school choice programs.

## Research implications

While the research on private school choice programs shows that, overall, parents are satisfied with the schools they have chosen, there is little to explain why parents are so satisfied. Researchers would do well to ask parents about their level of satisfaction with the programs themselves, as this could offer some explanation as to why parents are so satisfied with their chosen school. These studies have used parent surveys asking parents to rate or grade their private school of choice, often comparing their current school to their previous public school. Other studies compared the satisfaction levels of parents enrolling their children in private schools of choice to satisfaction levels of parents of children in public schools.

As Fuller, Elmore, and Orfield (1996, p. 19) argue, "Researchers are still not digging into the critical issue of why private or non-neighborhood schools at times boost parental satisfaction." Teske and Schneider (2001, p. 616) point out that parents' high levels of satisfaction may be an "ex post" rationalization of the choices made after the effort parents must exert to choose a charter school or enroll in a private school voucher program. The responses of high levels of satisfaction may result from a justification of their investment. Similarly, Wolf (2008, p. 435) writes, "Since parents themselves selected their child's new school, they might feel vested in the outcome of the choice and filter their perceptions in such ways that the voucher schools look better to them even if, objectively, they are no better than the child's previous public school."

Future research that could alleviate these concerns needs to focus on both how parents choose and whether parents get what they chose for from their school of choice. Wolf (2008, p. 435) writes, "Although it is indisputable that parents are more satisfied with their child's school if they have been given a voucher, we do not yet know why they are so much more satisfied." Some studies have speculated as to why these parents are more satisfied, but none has been able to definitively answer the question of why choosing parents are more satisfied. Providing an answer to these questions would support the argument that parents are able to make good choices in schools and that school choice programs are able to provide services that parents desire in their schools.

## Conclusion

This article has reviewed literature on parent satisfaction in school choice programs. It includes studies that randomly-assigned students to receive a private school choice opportunity or not. Such experimental studies are impervious to self-selection bias but are vulnerable to "sour grapes" or placebo effects. It also includes quasi-experimental and observational studies that survey parents who have self-sorted their children into private or public schools. Such studies are vulnerable to self-selection bias but are less prone to sour grapes or placebo effects. If methodology is behind the results, we would expect the experimental and observational studies to differ dramatically in their results. They do not.

Whether students enrolled in their choice program through lottery or self-sorted into their private school of choice, the results have shown that providing choice in education leads to higher levels of parent satisfaction. This is an important finding for school choice programs, especially for arguments in support of removing government involvement in school assignment.

While these results are encouraging and useful, they show some of the shortcomings of parental satisfaction research. It is difficult to defend against self-selection bias and to trust parent self-reporting in satisfaction surveys. Often, surveys are asking parents to compare their current school to their previous school, a comparison that is perfectly confounded with time. Also, multiple survey studies lack a valid counterfactual, as they are unable to accurately compare satisfaction levels of choice parents to those of public school parents. While some research looks to explain why parents elect to participate in school choice programs and why they choose certain schools, little research has sought to explain whether parents get what they choose for. This is an important aspect of satisfaction research in school choice and would support claims of parents being able to make good choices in schools.

Future research aside, the current literature shows that choosing parents are satisfied with their schools. This overwhelming wave of support from parents in school choice programs could explain legislators' willingness to continually push for more choice, despite the near certainty of a legal challenge. The political power of customer satisfaction appears undeniable when considering the results of parent school choice satisfaction research.

## References

Abdulkadiroglu, A., Pathak, P. A., & Walters, C. R. (2015). *School vouchers and student achievement: First-year evidence from the Louisiana scholarship program*. NBER Working Paper 21839. Cambridge, MA: National Bureau of Economic Research. Retrieved from http://www.nber.org/papers/w21839

*Arizona Empowerment Scholarship Accounts*. A.R.S. 15.2401-04. (2012).

Barrows, S., Peterson, P. E., & West, M. R. (2017). What do parents think of their children's schools? *EducationNext*, *17*(2). Retrieved from http://educationnext.org/what-do-parents-think-of-childrens-schools-ednext-private-district-charter/

Berends, M., & Waddington, R. J. (2016). School choice in Indianapolis: Effects of charter, magnet, private, and traditional public schools. *Education Finance and Policy*, 1–53.

Brown, E. (2015). "ACLU sues to stop Nevada's new school voucher program". 27 August 2015, *Washington Post*. Retrieved from https://www.washingtonpost.com/local/education/aclu-says-its-suing-to-stop-nevadas-new-school-voucher-program/2015/08/27/db57dcd2-4cd0-11e5-902f-39e9219e574b_story.html

Brown, E. (2016). Trump picks billionaire Betsy DeVos, school voucher advocate, as education secretary. 23 November 2016, *Washington Post*. Retrieved from https://www.washing

tonpost.com/local/education/trump-picks-billionaire-betsy-devos-school-voucher-advocate-as-education-secretary/2016/11/23/c3d66b94-af96-11e6-840f-e3ebab6bcdd3_story.html?utm_term=.eeabb1f04dcb

Butcher, J., & Bedrick, J. (2013). *Schooling satisfaction: Arizona Parents' opinions on using education saving accounts.* Retrieved from http://www.edchoice.org/wp-content/uploads/2013/10/SCHOOLING-SATISFACTION-Arizona-Parents-Opinions-on-Using-Education-Savings-Accounts-NEW.pdf

Catt, A. D., & Rhinesmith, E. (2016). *Why parents choose: A survey of private school and school choice parents in Indiana.* Indianapolis, IN: Friedman Foundation for Educational Choice. Retrieved from https://www.edchoice.org/research/why-parents-choose/

Chereb, S. (2015). "Gov. Sandoval signs Nevada school choice bill." 13 April 2015, *Las Vegas Review Journal.* Retrieved from http://www.reviewjournal.com/leg-edu/gov-sandoval-signs-nevada-school-choice-bill.

DiPerna, P. (2014). *Why Indiana Voucher parents choose private schools.* Retrieved from http://www.edchoice.org/Research/Reports/Why-Indiana-Voucher-Parents-Choose-Private-Schools.aspx

Donald J. Trump for President, Inc. (2016). *Education.* Retrieved from https://www.donaldjtrump.com/policies/education

Duflo, E., Glennerster, R., & Kremer, M. (2008). Using randomization in development economics research: A Toolkit. In Schultz & Strauss (Eds.), *Handbook of development economics,* Vol. 4. North Holland, Netherlands.

EdChoice. (2017). *The ABCs of school choice: The comprehensive guide to every school choice program in America.* Retrieved from https://www.edchoice.org/wp-content/uploads/2017/02/The-ABCs-of-School-Choice-1.pdf

Forster, G. (2016). *A win-win solution: The empirical evidence on school choice.* 4th ed. Indianapolis, IN: Friedman Foundation for Educational Choice. Retrieved from http://www.edchoice.org/wp-content/uploads/2016/05/A-Win-Win-Solution-The-Empirical-Evidence-on-School-Choice.pdf

Fuller, B., Elmore, R., & Orfield, G. (1996). Policy-making in the Dark: Illuminating the school choice debate. In B. Fuller, R. Elmore, & G. Orfield (Eds.), *Who chooses? Who loses? Culture, institutions, and the unequal effects of school choice.* New York, NY: Teachers College Press.

Gorski, E. (2015, June 29). "Colorado supreme court rejects Douglas county voucher program". *Denver Post.* Retrieved from http://www.denverpost.com/news/ci_28401042/colorado-supreme-court-rejects-douglas-county-voucher-program

Greene, J. P. (2001). Vouchers in Charlotte: Vouchers and the test-score gap. *Education Next, 1*(2), 55–60.

Greene, J. P., & Forster, G. (2003). *Vouchers for special education students: An evaluation of Florida's McKay scholarship program.* Manhattan Institute for Policy Research.

Greene, J. P., Howell, W. G., & Peterson, P. E. (1999a). *An evaluation of the Cleveland voucher program after two years.* Program on Education Policy and Governance, Harvard University.

Greene, J. P., Howell, W. G., & Peterson, P. E. (1999b). Lessons from the Cleveland Scholarship Program. In P. Peterson, & B. Hassel (eds.), *Learning from school choice.* Washington, DC: Brookings Institute.

Howell, W. G., Peterson, P. E., With Wolf, P. J., & Campbell, D. E. (2002). *The education gap: Vouchers and urban schools.* Washington, DC: Brookings Institution Press.

Kelly, J. P., & Scafidi, B. (2013). *More than scores: An analysis of why and how parents choose private schools.* Retrieved from www.edchoice.org/CMSModules/EdChoice/FileLibrary/1031/More-Than-Scores.pdf.

Kisida, B., & Wolf, P. J. (2015). Customer satisfaction and educational outcomes: Experimental impacts of the market-based delivery of public education. *International Public Management Journal, 18*(2), 265–285.

Kisida, B., Wolf, P. J., & Rhinesmith, E. (2015). *Views from private schools: Attitudes about school choice programs in three states.* American Enterprise Institute for Public Policy Research.

Kittredge, B. (2016). *The special needs ESA: What families enrolled in the program are saying after year one.* Retrieved from http://empowerms.org/wp-content/uploads/2016/12/ESA-Report-final.pdf.

Metcalf, K. K. (1999). *Evaluation of the Cleveland scholarship and tutoring grant program, 1996–1999.* Bloomington, IN: Indiana Center for Evaluation.

Mills, J. N., & Wolf, P. J. (2016). *The effects of the Louisiana scholarship program on student achievement after two years.* Retrieved from http://educationresearchalliancenola.org/files/publications/Report-1-LSP-Y2-Achievement.pdf doi: 10.2139/ssrn.2738805

Mills, J. N., & Wolf, P. J. (2017). *The effects of the Louisiana Scholarship Program on student achievement after three years.* Fayetteville, AR: School Choice Demonstration Project, University of Arkansas. Retrieved from http://www.uaedreform.org/the-effects-of-the-louisiana-scholarship-program-on-student-achievement-after-three-years/

Peterson, P. E. (1993). An immodest proposal. *Daedulus, 121*(4), 18–23.

Peterson, P. E. (1998). School choice: A report card. In P. Peterson, & B. Hassel (Eds.), *Learning from school choice.* Washington, DC: Brookings Institute.

Peterson, P. E., & Campbell, D. E. (2001). *An evaluation of the children's scholarship fund* (Research Paper PEPG01-03, May 2001). Harvard: Program on Education Policy and Governance.

Peterson, P. E., Myers, D., & Howell, W. G. (1999). *An evaluation of the horizon scholarship program in the Edgewood independent school district, San Antonio, Texas: The First Year.* Mathematica Policy Research; Cambridge, MA: Program on Education Policy and Governance.

Shakeel, M. D., Anderson, K. P., & Wolf, P. J. (2016). The participant effects of private school vouchers across the globe: A meta-analytic and systematic review. *EDRE Working Paper 2016-07.* Retrieved from http://www.uaedreform.org/downloads/2016/05/the-participant-effects-of-private-school-vouchers-across-the-globe-a-meta-analytic-and-systematic-review-2.pdf

Snyder, T. D., De Brey, D., & Dillow, S. A. (2016). *Digest of Education Statistics 2014, NCES 2016-006* (p. 134). Washington, DC: U.S. Department of Education, National Center of Statistics. table 206.50. Retrieved from http://nces.ed.gov/pubs2016/2016006.pdf

*Taxpayers for Public Education v. Douglas County School District.* 351 P.3d 461 (Col. S.C. 2015).

Teske, P., Fitzpatrick, J., & O'Brien, T. (2009). *Drivers of choice: Parents, transportation, and school choice.* Bothell, WA: Center on Reinventing Public Education.

Teske, P., & Schneider, M. (2001). What research can tell policymakers about school choice. *Journal of Policy Analysis and Management, 20*(4), 609–631. doi:10.1002/(ISSN)1520-6688

Vassallo, P. (2000). *More than grades: How choice boosts parental involvement and benefits children.* Washington, DC: Policy Analysis, Cato Institute, No. 383.

Weinschrott, D. J., & Kilgore, S. B. (1998). Evidence from the Indianapolis Voucher Program. In P. Peterson, & B. Hassel (Eds.), *Learning from School Choice.* Washington, DC: Brookings Institute.

Witte, J. F. (2001). *The market approach to education: An analysis of America's first voucher program.* Princeton, NJ: Princeton University Press.

Witte, J. F., Wolf, P. J., Cowen, J. M., Fleming, D. J., & Lucas-McLean, J. (2008). *MPCP longitudinal educational growth study baseline report.* Fayetteville, AR: School Choice

Demonstration Project. Retrieved from http://www.uaedreform.org/downloads/2008/02/report-5-mpcp-longitudinal-educational-growth-study-baseline-report.pdf

Wolf, P. J. (2008). School voucher programs: What the research says about parental school choice. *Brigham Young University Law Review, 2008*(2), 415–446.

Wolf, P. J., & Egalite, A. J. (2016). *Pursuing innovation: How can educational choice transform K-12 Education in the U.S.* Indianapolis, IN: Friedman Foundation for Educational Choice. Retrieved from http://www.edchoice.org/wp-content/uploads/2016/04/2016-4-Pursuing-Innovation-WEB-2.pdf

Wolf, P. J., Gutmann, B., Puma, M., Kisida, B., Rizzo, L., Eissa, N., & Carr, M. (2010). *Evaluation of the DC Opportunity Scholarship Program: Final Report*, U.S. Department of Education, Institute of Education Sciences, National Center for Education Evaluation and Regional Assistance, Washington, DC: U.S. Government Printing Office, NCEE 2010-4018.

# A systematic review of the empirical research on selected aspects of homeschooling as a school choice

Brian D. Ray

**ABSTRACT**

This article gives the demographic characteristics of the U.S. homeschooling population and the reasons that parents choose to homeschool, summarizes the findings of studies on the homeschool learner outcomes of academic achievement, social development, and success in adulthood, and proposes future research on parent-led home-based education. The majority of peer-reviewed studies on academic achievement reveal a positive effect for the homeschooled students compared to institutional schooled students, while a few studies show mixed or negative results. Regarding social and emotional development, a large majority of studies show clearly positive outcomes for the homeschooled compared to those in conventional schools. A majority of the studies on the relative success of the home-educated who later became adults show positive outcomes for the homeschooled compared to those who had been in conventional schools. I recommend that the existing literature be enhanced by well-controlled non-experimental designs to examine adults who were homeschooled in terms of an array of knowledge, attitudes and behaviors regarding lifelong learning, rates of public welfare dependency, and degree of personal agency or self-efficacy.

## Introduction

Parent-led home-based education is an educational choice that has existed for millennia around the globe. Most people today call it homeschooling. Focusing on the United States and its early history, the practice of parents being the main educators of their children went from being the norm in the colonial period to being the clear minority practice by 1900 (Ray, 2017a). In many developed western nations, homeschooling was nearly extinct by the mid-twentieth century.

The homeschool movement startled the U.S. public and the education establishment by mushrooming from only 13,000 K-12 students in the early 1970s to now roughly 2.4 million students (Lines, 1991; Ray, 2016; Redford, Battle, & Bielick, 2017). The reasons for this mammoth growth will be discussed in this article.

First, however, some perspective is needed regarding homeschooling as a school choice. Homeschool students represented only about 0.03% of U.S. school-age children in the mid-1970s (Lines, 1991). One of the most careful estimates of the size of the homeschool population placed it at 3.4% of school-age children in 2012 (Redford et al., 2017). This 113-fold growth occurred over roughly four decades. A nearly equal number of children are being homeschooled as are enrolled in Catholic schools (National Catholic Educational Association, 2014). By some estimates, there are only slightly more students in public charter schools than are being home educated (National Alliance for Public Charter Schools, 2017). Egalite and Wolf (2016) succinctly put the growth of homeschooling into perspective with the following comment:

> Notably, all three of these choice mechanisms [homeschooling, public charter schools, and school voucher or tax-credit scholarship programs] have experienced remarkable growth in the past decade, a cause for alarm among school choice opponents and celebration among supporters. (p. 442)

With such growth in the homeschool option over the past thirty years, there has also come an accompanying burgeoning of research on the topic. It is therefore challenging to keep reviews of research on the topic current and meaningful. The base of scholarly research on homeschooling has grown from a handful articles and studies in the mid-1980s to now a plethora of theses, dissertations, chapters in books, books, and a quickly growing number of basic qualitative and quantitative studies. This rapid growth in research is offering more empirical evidence to help inform what have sometimes been highly theoretical or polemical articles on the merits or demerits of the homeschooling educational choice, and what research does or not tell us about the effects of homeschooling on students and society (Apple, 2006; Fineman, 2009; Murphy, 2012; Ray, 2013).

Many of the past surveys of research on homeschooling have not offered clear or tight guidelines for the inclusion of articles or studies for review. With that in mind, I have noticed a remarkable expansion of studies on homeschooling in peer-reviewed journals over the past five years and this fact has guided the approach for this review. Therefore, I am offering something new to the class of overviews of homeschool research. This article will be a systematic review that relies solely on peer-reviewed empirical studies for gaining an understanding of the effects of homeschooling on learner outcomes such as academic achievement, social development, and how well home-educated students are doing in life once they reach adulthood. Although there has been ongoing scholarly debate about the relative value of studies that appear in peer-reviewed research journals, peer review still holds high value in the academic world (Goldbeck-Wood, 1999; Jefferson, 2006; Jennings, 2006; Roberts, 1999; Sampson, 2014; Sieber, 2006). Besides being a new approach to the inclusion of research on homeschooling for review, using this criterion serves as a reducing filter for an article that has only limited space available. Finally, such a selection criterion serves to keep conclusions about the effects of a currently minority approach to schooling conservatively bound and reduces the likelihood that any author will make biased claims in any direction about the value of home-based education (Roberts, 1999).

The purpose of this article is to offer (a) a brief glimpse of the demographic characteristics of the homeschooling population and the reasons that parents choose to homeschool; (b) a summary of specially selected studies on the homeschool learner outcomes of academic achievement, social development, and success in adulthood; and (c) some concluding remarks for future research on homeschooling.

## Methods

To seed this review and address its purpose, I searched and scoured the entirety of the English-language set of homeschool research and scholarship. Key sources for the searches were the government-sponsored Education Resources Information Center (ERIC), Google Scholar and other online databases, and an annotated bibliography that focuses on homeschooling that has been continuously updated by Ray (2017b) since about 1983. Throughout the literature exploration process, I searched for terms such as homeschooling, home schooling, home education, unschooling, academic achievement, social development, reasons, and motivations. The reference lists from key texts that included reviews of homeschool research (e.g., Murphy, 2012; Rothermel, 2015), most of which the author was already aware of, were used to generate additional possibilities, and the reference lists from those texts were used in a snowballing process. At some point, the fact that no new relevant references appeared gave me a strong signal that no additional pertinent pieces were going to be found.

Only peer-reviewed sources were noted and included for the aspect of this review that deals with the selected learner outcomes of academic achievement, social development, and degree of success in adulthood. The purpose is to compare homeschool students to those who were educated in conventional or institutional schools such as traditional public, charter, or private schools.

This is the first review of homeschool research that I know of to use this approach. This tactic enhances discipline and consistency in the review. It reduces the opportunity for the reviewer to be arbitrary, capricious, or biased in what is selected for inclusion. It theoretically enhances the methodological soundness of the studies included in the overview, and thus makes the conclusions based on the data more dependable. The key effort regarding the learner outcomes studies is to provide succinct summaries of the studies as data with minimal micro-evaluation of each individual study. The one exception to the peer-reviewed criterion for inclusion was that state-provided academic achievement data were included where they were available.

Observers of empirical research on the student outcomes of homeschooling have voiced various concerns and cautions. First, a continuous note for three decades has been that consumers of the studies should be careful about assigning causation to a form of schooling when it comes to significant differences in dependent variables such as achievement test scores, measures of social development, and college GPA (e.g., Murphy, 2012; Ray, 1986, 1988, 2000, 2013; Rudner, 1999). Confounding variables such as length of treatment, parental involvement, and demographics are often difficult, if not impossible, to control in studies comparing homeschoolers to others. Although researchers would like to establish causal relationships by randomly assigning students to homeschooling, public schooling, and institutional private schooling, this is not feasible. Further, most studies on homeschooling include convenience samples that are likely not representative of the targeted sample. With these methodological limitations in mind, however, at least some of the empirical studies in the review that follows use random selection (Green-Hennessey, 2014; Montes, 2015), key control variables, and student-matching approaches to partially control for possible confounders.

Second, researchers who do future studies on the effect of homeschooling on students and adults should work very hard to gather data on the length or authenticity of the treatment. That is, they should find out for how many years the subjects have been in homeschooling, private schooling, and public schooling. Such precision of data will help in understanding the different effects of schooling approaches.

Next, various scholars have noted that many, if not most, homeschool parents have different objectives and goals for their children than do institutional public and private schools and parents who choose them (e.g., Morrison, 2015). If this is true, then one might wonder why there is so much focus on standard measures of academic achievement, social development, and forms of socialization that are developed and normed with institutional school students and used for holding institutional state schools accountable to the taxpayer. In a similar vein, many homeschool parents are more focused on the spiritual and philosophical education of their children and therefore much of the studies on homeschool students are, as Cizek (1993) posited, "the mismeasure of home schooling effectiveness." Further, some have argued that it is actually inappropriate, based on standards of the testing and measurement industry, to apply standardized testing to homeschoolers (Cizek, 1988).

There are many fascinating aspects of home-based education that will not be reviewed in this article; there is not enough space for them. The fact that the parents in over one million families in the United States – and a rapidly growing number in many other nations – are currently homeschooling their children raises serious issues such as who should be in charge of the education of children? What gave rise to the modern homeschool movement? What services might parents better access via homeschooling rather than public schooling (Cheng, Tuchman, & Wolf, 2016)? What impact will private parent-led home-based education have on institutional schools and society in general? Scholarly works have addressed these questions, but a review of them is outside the scope of this effort.

## Research evidence on the demographic characteristics of homeschoolers

Studies over the past three decades have given a clearer picture of the variety of demographic characteristics of homeschool families. One of the most-cited sources on their traits is from the U.S. Department of Education (Redford et al., 2017). Their 2012 nationwide survey revealed that 62% of homeschool students live in cities and suburban areas, while the others live in towns and rural areas. In terms of ethnicity/race, 32% of the children were minorities (Black/non-Hispanic; Hispanic; Asian or Pacific Islander, non-Hispanic; or other, non-Hispanic) while 68% were White, non-Hispanic. Twenty percent of the students were categorized as "poor" and the other 80% were noted as "nonpoor."

Regarding their parents' highest education level, 32% had a high school diploma or less, while 14% had attended graduate or professional school. Roughly one-fourth of the homeschool students were in each of the following grade-level categories: K-2, 3–5, 6–8, and 9–12 (Redford et al., 2017). For some comparative information, Ray's (2010) nationwide study found homeschool families to be very close to median income compared to married-couple families with minor children living at home nationwide. It also appears that minorities have become an increasing proportion of the homeschool community since 2003 (U.S. Department of Education, 2014).

Research on the religious preferences and political affiliations of homeschool parents is limited. Both U.S. and Canadian nationwide studies (e.g., Ray, 2010; Van Pelt, 2003) and local studies provide evidence that the homeschool community is diverse on both variables. It is clear that parents who identify as liberal, progressive, conservative, and libertarian are all involved in homeschooling. Multiple studies indicate that home education is common among agnostics, atheists, Christians, Jews, Mormons, New Age adherents, and Roman Catholics. Internet searches quickly reveal plenty of homeschool support groups, organizations, and publications that appeal to each of these philosophical, religious, and political groups.

## Research evidence on reasons for homeschooling

Research by the U.S. Department of Education has also become widely cited regarding the reasons that parents choose to homeschool their children, because their surveys are nationwide and engage many statistical controls. Redford et al. (2017) reported the following:

> In 2012, the most commonly selected reason was a concern with other schools' environments, which includes factors such as "safety, drugs, or negative peer pressure" at schools (91 percent). Other commonly reported reasons included, "a desire to provide moral instruction," "a dissatisfaction with academic instruction at other schools," and "a desire to provide religious instruction" (77%, 74%, and 64%, respectively). (p. 11)

Parents were also asked to select the reason their *most* important reason for homeschooling. "Concern about other schools' environments, desire to provide religious instruction, and dissatisfaction with academic standards were cited most frequently as most important" (p. 11).

Montes (2006) also used data from a federal survey and found that, in general, younger and older homeschooled students are educated at home for the same reasons: parents believe they can provide them a better education (47%) and for religious reasons (41%). Montes found, however, that younger homeschooled students are twice as likely as their older counterparts to be educated at home because the parents object to what the institutional school in their area teaches. Younger homeschooled students are three times as likely to be homeschooled as a way to develop character and morality than older homeschoolers.

Some researchers have begun to focus on why African-American parents choose homeschooling. Ray's (2015) quantitative study of black families produced results similar to those already noted. Further, about 40% of the parents gave as a reason that they want to "give the child more instruction on African American/black culture and history" and 20% said another reason they chose homeschooling is that they "desire to avoid racism in public schools."

Along similar lines, Fields-Smith and Kisura (2013) noted "the 'push–pull' factors that motivated black families in the Metro-Atlanta and Metro-DC regions to exit traditional schools in favor of homeschooling their children" (pp. 278–279). The researchers found that these black parents were "able to impart black cultural values to their children while exposing them to a global perspective ..." and the parents reported that "homeschooling also allowed them to 'slow down' their children's exposure to what could be deemed as unsavory elements of school socialization (e.g., racism, violence, drugs, etc.)" (p. 279). There are more studies on minorities' reasons for homeschooling (e.g., Mazama, 2016).

## Research evidence on the academic achievement of the homeschooled

The literature search resulted in 14 peer-reviewed quantitative studies for inclusion for the topic of academic achievement. Most of the studies included, as dependent variables, students' scores on standardized academic achievement tests. A summary of the items and their findings is presented in Table 1.

**Table 1.** Academic achievement of homeschool and institutional school students compared.

| Study (Author/Year) | Design | Subjects' Grade Levels or Ages | Background Variables Controlled? | Findings |
|---|---|---|---|---|
| Aram et al., 2016 | Cross-sectional, explanatory | K | Yes | Literacy skills equal or lower for HS |
| Ray, 2015 | Cross-sectional, explanatory | Grades 4–8 | Yes | Reading, language, & math scores higher for HS by effect sizes 1.13, 0.65, & 0.60 |
| Martin-Chang et al., 2011 | Cross-sectional, explanatory; matched-pair | Ages 5–10 | Yes | Letter-word, comprehension, word attack, science, humanities, & calculation scores higher than Public for structured HS (by 0.06 to 0.15 effect sizes) and lower for unstructured HS |
| Ray, 2010 | Cross-sectional, descriptive | Grades K-12 | No | Reading, language, math, social studies, & science scores higher for HS by effect sizes 0.79, 0.85, 0.85, 0.81, & 0.77 |
| Barwegen, Falciani, Putnam, Reamer, & Stair, 2004 | Cross-sectional, descriptive | High school | Yes, one | No difference in ACT (college admissions test) scores |
| Duvall, Delquadri, & Ward, 2004 | Continuous baseline probe design | Grades 5–6 | Yes | Reading & math scores higher for HS |
| Medlin & Blackmer, 2000 | Cross-sectional, explanatory | Grades 4–8 | Yes | Reading, math, social studies, & science scores higher for HS |
| Ray, 2000 | Cross-sectional, descriptive | Grades K-12 | No | Reading, language, math, social studies, & science scores higher for HS by effect sizes 0.84, 0.90, 0.87, 0.82, & 0.82 |
| Rudner, 1999 | Cross-sectional, descriptive | Grades K-12 | No | Reading, language, math, social studies, & science scores higher for HS by effect size 0.67 |
| Duvall, Ward, Delquadri, & Greenwood, 1997 | Cross-sectional, explanatory, matched-pair | Grades 3–8 | Yes | Language & math scores higher for HS |
| Russell, 1994 | Cross-sectional, explanatory; path analysis | Grades K-12 | Yes | Reading, language, math, & listening scores higher for HS |
| Wartes, 1990 | Cross-sectional, descriptive | Grades K-12 | No | Reading, language, math, & listening scores higher for HS by effect size 0.41 |
| Frost & Morris, 1988 | Cross-sectional, explanatory | Grades 3–6 | Yes | Vocabulary, reading, language skills, work study skills, & mathematics scores higher for HS by effect sizes 0.05 to 0.64 |
| Wartes (1988) | Cross-sectional, descriptive | Grades K-12 | No | Reading, language, math, social studies, & science scores higher for HS, effect size 0.41 |

The research designs terms are largely from Johnson (2001), types of research obtained by crossing research objective and time dimension.
HS = homeschool.
Public = public school.
Private = private school.
Mixed = some findings more positive for homeschool and some more positive for conventional school.
n.r. = not reported or not readily usable/applicable for this type of summary table.

Six of the 14 peer-reviewed studies were cross-sectional, descriptive, seven were cross-sectional, explanatory in nature, and one was a continuous baseline probe design. In nonexperimental explanatory research, investigators try to develop or test a theory about a phenomenon or try to identify the causal factors (Johnson, 2001). In descriptive nonexperimental research, the researchers primarily describe the phenomenon or document the characteristics of the phenomenon (Johnson, 2001). In 11 of the 14 peer-reviewed studies, there was a definite positive effect on achievement for the homeschooled students. One of the 14 studies showed mixed results; that is, some positive and some negative effects were associated with homeschooling. One study revealed no difference between the homeschool and conventional school students, and one study revealed neutral and negative results for homeschooling compared to conventional schooling. Both state-provided data sets showed higher than average academic achievement test scores for the home educated.

Most of the studies did not explicitly use or present effect sizes. Effect sizes could be gleaned, however, from 8 of the 14 studies and both of the state datasets, ranging from 0.05 (small) to 1.13 (very large).

Some brief summaries of a few of the studies provide illustrations. Rudner (1999), in his classic cross-sectional, descriptive study, analyzed the standardized academic achievement test scores of 20,760 K-12 homeschool students from 11,930 families. He summarized his finding this way: "Within each grade level and each skill area, the median scores for home school students fell between the 70th and 80th percentile of students nationwide and between the 60th and 70th percentile of Catholic/Private school students" (pp. 28–29). Rudner was careful to describe the limitations of his study related to generalization and wrote that his "study simply shows that those parents choosing to make a commitment to home schooling are able to provide a very successful academic environment" (p. 29).

Ray's (2015) was the first attempt at a quantitative study assessing the academic achievement of black homeschool children. He collected data from around the country and was able to control for two confounding variables, gender of the student and socioeconomic status of the family. The homeschool students were administered standardized tests by non-family members and their scores were analyzed. The black homeschool children outperformed their black public school peers in the areas of reading, language, math, social studies, and science with large effect sizes of 0.84, 0.90, 0.87, 0.82, and 0.82. Further, the black homeschool children scored the same or higher than all races/ethnicities in the general school-age public.

Two studies found some mixed or negative results related to homeschooling and both involved relatively young students. Aram, Meidan, and Deitcher (2016) studied formal school and homeschool Kindergarten students (matched on age and gender) and found "that there were significant differences between the homeschooling and formal schooling groups in their letter knowledge and name writing, favoring the formal schooling group" (p. 1013). There were, however, no differences between the groups regarding phonological awareness. The authors pointed out that they were studying very young children and outcomes might change as they get older, as the Israeli school system might emphasize things that homeschoolers do not, and that the homeschool families tended to be unschoolers who do not focus on formal instruction.

The second study involved a careful matched-pair design with children of ages 5 to 10 (Martin-Chang, Gould, & Meuse, 2011). The researchers found that children from structured homeschool settings outperformed their conventional school peers, while children from unstructured homeschooling underperformed the institutional school students. The authors also noted the young ages they studied and pondered whether their test performance might change over time, especially in light of research on older homeschool students.

Some observers have also wondered what would be found if achievement test data were available from states where all or most homeschool students are required by law to be tested. Two U.S. state departments of education have made test data relatively easy to access which show that homeschool students' test scores are consistently well above average (Oregon Department of Education, 1999; Washington State Superintendent of Public Instruction, 1985).

## Research evidence on the social development of the home educated

The search for peer-reviewed reports on the social development of home-educated children and adults revealed 15 studies. Thirteen of the 15 showed clearly positive outcomes for the homeschooled compared to those in conventional schools. Two of those studies reported that some of the findings were more positive for homeschool students but some were more positive for institutional school students. Key details of these studies are presented in Table 2.

Most of the studies did not explicitly use or present effect sizes. Effect sizes could be ascertained, however, from five of the 15 studies, ranging from 0.08 (small) to 1.55 (very large).

Only a decade ago, very few large and national databases containing data on homeschool children or youth were available; it appears that this is quickly changing. One example is the study by Thomson and Jang (2016), which utilized data from the National Study of Youth and Religion. They were able to control for several potentially confounding variables, and found "homeschooled adolescents to be less likely to drink alcohol and, if they do, less likely to get drunk than their public and private high school counterparts" (p. 295).

Shyers (1992), in his classic cross-sectional, explanatory, matched-pair study of homeschool and conventional school 8- to 10-year-olds, found

**Table 2.** Social development of homeschool and institutional school students compared.

| Study (Author/Year) | Design | Subjects' grade levels or ages | Background variables controlled? | Findings |
|---|---|---|---|---|
| Guterman and Neuman (2017) | Cross-sectional, explanatory; matched subjects | Ages 6–12 | Yes | Lower depression for HS (0.08 effect), less externalizing problems for HS (0.15 effect); no difference in internalizing problems & attachment security |
| Thomson and Jang (2016) | Cross-sectional, explanatory | Ages 13–17 | Yes | Less underage alcohol drinking by HS |
| Montes (2015) | Cross-sectional, explanatory | Ages 6–17 | Yes | No difference in problem behaviors & social competencies; HS argue less than Conventional; mixed differences on participation in activities |
| Vaughn et al. (2015) | Cross-sectional, explanatory | Ages 12–17 | Yes | Less use/abuse of tobacco, alcohol, & illicit drugs by HS |
| Green-Hennessey (2014) | Cross-sectional, explanatory | Ages 12–17 | Yes | Stronger religious affiliation HS less substance abuse and delinquency than Conventional; weaker religious HS no differences |
| Drenovsky and Cohen (2012) | Cross-sectional, descriptive | College | No | Self-esteem no difference; lower depression for HS; higher GPA & college experience for HS |
| McKinley, Asaro, Bergin, D'Auria, and Gagnon (2007) | Cross-sectional, explanatory | Ages 8–12 | No | Several variables (e.g., cooperation, assertion, self-control, conflict with others); some positive and some negative HS compared to Private; some positive for HS and some neutral HS compared to Public |
| Medlin (2006) | Cross-sectional, descriptive | Grades 3–6 | No | Cooperation, assertiveness, empathy, & self-control higher for HS vs. Public, effect sizes 0.13 to 1.55 |
| McEntire (2005) | | Grades 7–12 | | Several life challenges variables (e.g., tension, sense of upbeatness, drug use; lying, alcohol use), some more positive for HS and some more positive for Conventional |
| Francis and Keith (2004) | Cross-sectional, explanatory; matched-pair | Ages 5–18 | | Social skills higher for HS than Conventional, effect size 0.12; no difference for problem behaviors |
| Sutton and Galloway (2000) | Cross-sectional, explanatory | College | Yes | More positions of leadership for HS |
| Tillman (1995) | Cross-sectional, descriptive | Ages 11–14 | No | Family acceptance, academic competence, peer, & personal security higher for HS, effect size 0.61 |
| Shyers (1992) | Cross-sectional, explanatory; matched-pair | Ages 8–10 | Yes | Fewer problem behaviors (e.g., aggressive/passive) for HS; no difference self-concept |
| Smedley (1992) | Cross-sectional, explanatory | Grades K-12 | No | Social maturity (communication, daily living skills, and the socialization domains) higher for HS, effect size .99 |
| Kelley (1991) | Cross-sectional, descriptive | Grades 2–10 | No | Self-concept higher for HS |

The research designs terms are largely from Johnson (2001), types of research obtained by crossing research objective and time dimension.
HS = homeschool.
Conventional = public or private school.
Public = public school.
Private = private school.
Mixed = some findings more positive for homeschool and some more positive for conventional school.
n.r. = not reported or not readily usable/applicable for this type of summary table.

very few differences on his dependent variables. There were no differences between the two groups on student self-concept or passivity. Upon direct observation of the children's behaviors in play groups by research assistants blinded to the schooling identity of the children, however, they found that homeschool "students received significantly lower problem behavior scores than did their agemates from [a] traditional program" (p. 5).

## Research evidence on the relative success of the homeschooled into college and adulthood

The search for peer-reviewed articles on the relative success of the home-educated who had moved on to adulthood, whether in college or life in general, revealed 16 studies. Eleven of the 16 showed positive outcomes for the homeschooled compared to those in conventional schools. One study found positive outcomes for conventional school students compared to homeschool students. Finally, four of the studies found no significant difference between those from homeschool backgrounds and the others from institutional school backgrounds. Most of the studies did not explicitly use or present effect sizes. In the one study in which an effect size could be ascertained, it was 0.62. Key features of these studies are displayed in Table 3.

It is clear that since the modern homeschool movement is now into its fourth decade, significantly more adults in the U.S. population have been home educated than was the case only a decade ago. Thus, more data are available and more studies on them have been published. Cogan's (2010) was one of the first tightly designed comparative studies. The dependent variables were first-year GPA, fourth-year GPA, retention, and graduation rate and he was able to control for several demographic variables. Multiple regression analysis revealed that the college students who were homeschooled earn higher first-year and fourth-year GPAs when controlling for demographic, pre-college, engagement, and first-term academic factors. Further, there were no differences between homeschooled student's fall-to-fall retention and four-year graduation rates when compared to conventionally educated students.

Cheng (2014), in one of the most methodologically rigorous studies to date comparing college students from homeschool and other backgrounds, investigated their levels of political tolerance. He found that "those with more exposure to homeschooling relative to public schooling tend to be more politically tolerant" (p. 64) and students who attended private schools were at least as tolerant as students who attended public schools. Cheng concluded:

> Both of the results conflict with the belief that a common system of public schools is essential not only for all students but particularly for religiously conservative students to learn political tolerance. Instead of decreasing political tolerance among students who are more conservative in their religious beliefs,

**Table 3.** Relative success in adulthood of homeschool and institutional school students.

| Study (Author/ Year) | Design | Subjects' grade levels or ages | Background variables controlled? | Findings |
|---|---|---|---|---|
| Almasoud and Fowler (2016) | Cross-sectional, explanatory; matched sample | College, ages 17–28 | Yes | College final GPA higher for HS, effect size 0.62 |
| Yu et al. (2016) | Cross-sectional, explanatory, matched sample | College | Yes | No difference first-year GPA & retention |
| Wilkens, Wade, Sonnert, and Sadler (2015) | Cross-sectional, explanatory | College | Yes | Calculus course grade higher for HS |
| Cheng (2014) | Cross-sectional, explanatory | College | Yes | HS more politically tolerant than Public; HS no different from Private |
| Snyder (2013) | Cross-sectional, descriptive | College | No | SAT & ACT scores & GPA higher for HS compared to Public & Catholic school |
| Drenovsky and Cohen (2012) | Cross-sectional, descriptive | College | No | Less depression, more positive college experience, & higher GPA for HS; no difference in self-esteem |
| Cogan (2010) | Cross-sectional, explanatory | College | Yes | Higher first- and fourth-year GPAs for HS; no difference in fall-to-fall retention & four-year graduation rates |
| Jones (2010) | Cross-sectional, descriptive | College | No | No differences in college entrance exam scores, GPA, & activities involvement |
| White, Moore, and Squires (2009) | Cross-sectional, descriptive | College | No | HS more agreeable, conscientious & open than Conventional; no difference in extraversion & neuroticism |
| Uecker (2008) | Cross-sectional, explanatory | Ages 13–17 | Yes | Involvement in religious community & Private religiosity higher for HS |
| Qaqish (2007) | Cross-sectional, explanatory | College-bound | Yes | ACT math scores higher for Conventional |
| White et al. (2007) | Cross-sectional, explanatory | College | Yes | In college adjustment measures, HS less anxious than Conventional; no differences other 8 measures |
| Jones and Gloeckner (2004) | Cross-sectional, explanatory, match-sample | College | Yes | No differences in ACT scores, first-year GPA, retention, & first-year credit earned |
| Ray (2004) | Cross-sectional, descriptive | Ages 16–69 | No | Various variables (e.g., civic involvement, life satisfaction) more positive for HS |
| Sutton and Galloway (2000) | Cross-sectional, explanatory | College | Yes | More positions of leadership for HS; no difference in GPA |
| Oliveira, Watson, and Sutton (1994) | Cross-sectional, descriptive | College | No | No differences in critical thinking skills |

The research designs terms are largely from Johnson (2001), types of research obtained by crossing research objective and time dimension.
HS = homeschool.
Public = public school.
Private = private school.
Mixed = some findings more positive for homeschool and some more positive for conventional school.
n.r. = not reported or not readily usable/applicable for this type of summary table.

> homeschooling is associated with greater political tolerance, and private schooling is not associated with any less tolerance. (p. 64)

While Cogan (2010) found the home educated to be outperforming others, Yu, Sackett, and Kuncel (2016) used a cross-sectional, explanatory, and matched-sample design to explore the first-year GPA and retention rates of college students. They found no difference between the homeschooled and others.

Qaqish (2007), on the other hand, examined the ACT math scores of college-bound students and found, while controlling for background variables, that the conventionally schooled performed slightly better than the home educated. On average, conventionally schooled students performed better than the home educated by about two out of sixty items on the ACT mathematics test. Qaqish conjectured that the result might be due to different teaching/learning media used in teaching each of the two groups, different teacher/student interaction, or to the number of years homeschooled before taking the ACT mathematics test.

## Discussion: thoughts on the future of research on homeschooling and the choice of home education

If this systematic summary of peer-reviewed empirical work on homeschooling had been conducted just one decade ago, about half of the studies in this review would have been missing. With the expansion of the homeschool population has come notably more research on the children and families engaged in it and on adults who were home educated, more support systems to encourage the practice of homeschooling, more media attention, more attention from policymakers, more attention from serious scholarly critics of this educational choice, and the general sense that it is much easier for U.S. parents to make the choice to homeschool than it was only ten years ago. In some ways, homeschooling is a very viable choice for mainstream Americans and a growing variety of Americans who are not in the mainstream.

It is easy to see, even in scholarly literature on the learner outcome effects of homeschooling, a strong current of polemic and contention about what the empirical research does or does not tell academics, policymakers, parents, and the public about homeschooling. Many relatively positive things are associated with homeschooling as compared to institutional public and private schooling. A short half-decade ago, Murphy (2012) presented an insightful survey of scholarship on homeschooling and noted that "we know more than some analysts suggest we do" and "we know a lot less than advocates of homeschooling would have us believe" (p. 140). Since his review of the body of research, several additional empirical studies have emerged. As the present review shows, we now know even more than both the cautious critics of homeschool research and advocates of home education knew back when

Murphy published. The evidence from the studies presented in a new way in this review shed notable light on the generally positive relationship between homeschooling and the three learner outcomes of academic achievement, social development, and relative success in adulthood.

Future researchers should consider a few key questions. Using matched-pair or other carefully controlled nonexperimental designs, how do the academic achievement and useful life skills of adults who were completely home educated compare to that of those who were fully public schooled? What are the differences in attitudes and behaviors regarding learning during adulthood between those completely homeschooled and those completely institutionally public schooled? Is there a difference in the rates of public welfare dependency between adults who were home educated and others? Finally, is there a difference in a sense of personal agency or self-efficacy between adults who were homeschooled and others? While conducting these studies, researchers should always be mindful to gather data on the authenticity and nature of the treatment, such as the number of years homeschooled, institutionally public schooled, and institutionally private schooled and the type of homeschooling and institutional schooling experienced by the student.

It appears that homeschooling is continuing to grow and will do so into the foreseeable future. The reasons why parents and teens homeschool are fundamental and have been durable over the past 30 years. There is some evidence that those who were home educated choose to homeschool their own children at a higher rate than does the general public. With these factors in mind and the positive outcomes that empirical research shows are related to homeschooling, the movement and school choice is likely to continue to expand and the research base on it will continue to flourish.

## References

Almasoud, S., & Fowler, S. R. (2016). The difference in the academic achievements of homeschooled and non-homeschooled students. *Home School Researcher*, *32*(1), 1–4.

Apple, M. W. (2006, December 21). The complexities of black home schooling. From www.TCRecord.org. Retrieved June 22, 2007, from http://cockingasnook.wordpress.com/2007/03/07/michael-apple-expert-on-black-homeschooling-now/

Aram, D., Meidan, I. C., & Deitcher, D. B. (2016). A comparison between homeschooled and formally schooled kindergartners: Children's early literacy, mothers' beliefs, and writing mediation. *Reading Psychology*, *37*(7), 995–1024.

Barwegen, L. M., Falciani, N. K., Putnam, S. J., Reamer, M. B., & Stair, E. E. (2004). Academic achievement of homeschool and public school students and student perception of parent involvement. *School Community Journal*, *14*(1), 39–58.

Cheng, A. (2014). Does homeschooling or private schooling promote political intolerance? Evidence from a Christian university. *Journal of School Choice: International Research and Reform*, *8*(1), 49–68.

Cheng, A., Tuchman, S., & Wolf, P. J. (2016). Homeschool parents and satisfaction with special education services. *Journal of School Choice, 10*(3), 381–398.

Cizek, G. J. (1988). Applying standardized testing to home-based education programs: Reasonable or customary? *Educational Measurement Issues and Practice, 7*(3), 12–19.

Cizek, G. J. (1993). The mismeasure of home schooling effectiveness: A commentary. *Home School Researcher, 9*(3), 1–4.

Cogan, M. F. (2010). Summer). Exploring academic outcomes of homeschooled students. *Journal of College Admission, 208*, 18–25.

Drenovsky, C. K., & Cohen, I. (2012). The impact of homeschooling on the adjustment of college students. *International Social Science Review, 87*(1 & 2), 19–34.

Duvall, S. F., Delquadri, J. C., & Ward, D. L. (2004). A preliminary investigation of the effectiveness of homeschool instructional environments for students with attention-deficit/hyperactivity disorder [ADHD]. *School Psychology Review, 33*(1), 140–158.

Duvall, S. F., Ward, D. L., Delquadri, J. C., & Greenwood, C. R. (1997). An exploratory study of home school instructional environments and their effects on the basic skills of students with learning disabilities. *Education and Treatment of Children, 20*(2), 150–172.

Egalite, A. J., & Wolf, P. J. (2016). A review of the empirical research on private school choice. *Peabody Journal of Education, 91*, 441–454.

Fields-Smith, C., & Kisura, M. W. (2013). Resisting the status quo: The narratives of black homeschoolers in Metro-Atlanta and Metro-DC. *Peabody Journal of Education, 88*(3), 265–283.

Fineman, M. A. (2009). Taking children's interests seriously. In M. A. Fineman, & K. Worthington (Eds.), *What is right for children? The competing paradigms of religion and human rights* (pp. 229–237). Burlington, VT: Ashgate Publishing Company.

Francis, D. J., & Keith, T. Z. (2004). Social skills of home schooled and conventionally schooled children: A comparison study. *Home School Researcher, 16*(1), 15–24.

Frost, E. A., & Morris, R. C. (1988). Does home-schooling work? Some insights for academic success. *Contemporary Education, 59*(4), 223–227.

Goldbeck-Wood, S. (1999). Evidence on peer review—Scientific quality control or smokescreen? *British Medical Journal, 318*, 44–45. Retrieved July 26, 2017, from http://people.ku.edu/~mvitevit/qualitySmoke.pdf

Green-Hennessy, S. (2014). Homeschooled adolescents in the United States: Developmental outcomes. *Journal of Adolescence, 37*, 441–449.

Guterman, O., & Neuman, A. (2017). Schools and emotional and behavioral problems: A comparison of school-going and homeschooled children. *The Journal of Educational Research, 110*(4), 425–432.

Jefferson, T. (2006). Quality and value: Models of quality control for scientific research. *Nature*. Retrieved July 26, 2017, from http://www.nature.com/nature/peerreview/debate/nature05031.html. 10.1038/nature05031

Jennings, C. G. (2006). Quality and value: The true purpose of peer review. *Nature*. Retrieved July 26, 2017, from http://www.nature.com/nature/peerreview/debate/nature05032.html. 10.1038/nature05032

Johnson, B. (2001). Toward a new classification of nonexperimental quantitative research. *Educational Researcher, 30*(2), 3–13.

Jones, E. (2010). Transition from home education to higher education: Academic and social issues. *Home School Researcher, 25*(3), 1–9.

Jones, P., & Gloeckner, G. (2004). First-year college performance: A study of home school graduates and traditional school graduates. *The Journal of College Admission, 183*, 17–20.

Kelley, S. W. (1991). Socialization of home schooled children: A self-concept study. *Home School Researcher, 7*(4), 1–12.

Lines, P. M. (1991). *Estimating the home schooled population* (Working paper OR 91-537). Washington, DC: Office of Educational Research and Improvement, U.S. Department of Education.

Martin-Chang, S., Gould, O. N., & Meuse, R. E. (2011, July). The impact of schooling on academic achievement: Evidence from homeschooled and traditionally schooled students. *Canadian Journal of Behavioural Science/Revue Canadienne Des Sciences Du Comportement, 43*(3), 195–202.

Mazama, A. (2016). African American homeschooling practices: Empirical evidence. *Theory and Research in Education, 14*(1), 26–44.

McEntire, T. W. (2005). Religious outcomes in conventionally schooled and home schooled youth. *Home School Researcher, 16*(2), 13–18.

McKinley, M. J., Asaro, J. N., Bergin, J., D'Auria, N., & Gagnon, K. E. (2007). Social skills and satisfaction with social relationships in home-schooled, private-schooled, and public-schooled children. *Home School Researcher, 17*(3), 1–6.

Medlin, R. G. (2006). Homeschooled children's social skills. *Home School Researcher, 17*(1), 1–8.

Medlin, R. G., & Blackmer, R. E. (2000). Academic intrinsic motivation in homeschooled children. *Home School Researcher, 14*(2), 1–6.

Montes, G. (2006). Do parental reasons to homeschool vary by grade? Evidence from the national household education survey, 2001. *Home School Researcher, 16*(4), 11–17.

Montes, G. (2015). The social and emotional health of homeschooled students in the United States: A population-based comparison with publicly schooled students based on the national survey of children's health, 2007. *Home School Researcher, 31*(1), 1–9.

Morrison, K. (2015). Homeschooling as an act of conscientious objection. *Journal of Thought, Fall-Winter*, 33–56.

Murphy, J. (2012). *Homeschooling in America: Capturing and assessing the movement.* Thousand Oaks, CA: Corwin, a Sage Company.

National Alliance for Public Charter Schools. (2017). Retrieved April 22, 2017, from http://www.publiccharters.org/get-the-facts/

National Catholic Educational Association. (2014). United States Catholic elementary and secondary schools 2013-2014: The annual statistical report on schools, enrollment, and staffing. Retrieved 2/19/15, from http://www.ncea.org/data-information/catholic-school-data

Oliveira, P. C. M., Watson, T. G., & Sutton, J. P. (1994). Differences in critical thinking skills among students educated in public schools, Christian schools, and home schools. *Home School Researcher, 10*(4), 1–8.

Oregon Department of Education [Office of Student Services]. (1999). *1998-1999 home school students registered by county.* Retrieved 3/ 19/03 from http://www.ode.state.or.us/cifs/homesch/1999/county99.pdf; and *Home School Data Collection 1998-99: Test Scores By Percentiles*, retrieved April 22, 2017 from http://www.ode.state.or.us/teachlearn/specialty/home/1999/percen99.pdf

Qaqish, B. (2007). A comparison of home schooled and non-home schooled students on ACT mathematics achievement test. *Home School Researcher, 17*(2), 1–12.

Ray, B. D. (1986). *A comparison of home schooling and conventional schooling: With a focus on learner outcomes.* Corvallis, OR: Oregon State University, Science, Math, and Computer Science Education Department.

Ray, B. D. (1988). Home schools: A synthesis of research on characteristics and learner outcomes. *Education and Urban Society, 21*(1), 16–31.

Ray, B. D. (2000). Home schooling: The ameliorator of negative influences on learning? *Peabody Journal of Education, 75*(1 & 2), 71–106.

Ray, B. D. (2004). Homeschoolers on to college: What research shows us. *Journal of College Admission, 185*, 5–11.

Ray, B. D. (2010, February 3). Academic achievement and demographic traits of homeschool students: A nationwide study. *Academic Leadership Journal, 8*(1). Retrieved April 19, 2017, from http://contentcat.fhsu.edu/cdm/ref/collection/p15732coll4/id/835

Ray, B. D. (2013). Homeschooling associated with beneficial learner and societal outcomes but educators do not promote it. *Peabody Journal of Education, 88*(3), 324–341.

Ray, B. D. (2015). African American homeschool parents' motivations for homeschooling and their Black children's academic achievement. *Journal of School Choice, 9*, 71–96.

Ray, B. D. (2016). Research facts on homeschooling. Retrieved April 6, 2016, http://www.nheri.org/research/research-facts-on-homeschooling.html

Ray, B. D. (2017a). A description and brief history of home schooling in America. In R. A. Fox, & N. K. Buchanan (Eds.), *Handbook of school choice*. Hoboken, NJ: John Wiley and Sons.

Ray, B. D. (2017b). *Home centered learning annotated bibliography*. Salem, OR: National Home Education Research Institute.

Redford, J., Battle, D., & Bielick, S. (2017, April). *Homeschooling in the United States: 2012*. Washington, DC: National Center for Education Statistics, Institute of Education Sciences, U.S. Department of Education. Retrieved August 1, 2017, from. (NCES 2016-096.REV) https://nces.ed.gov/pubsearch/pubsinfo.asp?pubid=2016096rev

Roberts, P. (1999). Scholarly publishing, peer review and the Internet. *First Monday, 4*(4). Retrieved July 28, 2017, from April http://ojphi.org/ojs/index.php/fm/article/view/661/576

Rothermel, P. (Ed.). (2015). *International perspectives on home education: Do we still need schools?* London, United Kingdom: Palgrave Macmillan.

Rudner, L. M. (1999). Scholastic achievement and demographic characteristics of home school students in 1998. *Educational Policy Analysis Archives, 7*(8). Retrieved October 10, 2016, from, http://epaa.asu.edu/ojs/article/viewFile/543/666

Russell, T. (1994). Cross-validation of a multivariate path analysis of predictors of home school student academic achievement. *Home School Researcher, 10*(1), 1–13.

Sampson, C. (2014). What counts as an academic publication? Retrieved July 28, 2017, from https://theconversation.com/what-counts-as-an-academic-publication-34549

Shyers, L. E. (1992). A comparison of social adjustment between home and traditionally schooled students. *Home School Researcher, 8*(3), 1–8.

Sieber, J. E. (2006). Quality and value: How can we research peer review? *Nature*. Retrieved July 26, 2017, from http://www.nature.com/nature/peerreview/debate/nature05006.html. 10.1038/nature05006

Smedley, T. C. (1992). Socialization of home school children. *Home School Researcher, 8*(3), 9–16.

Snyder, M. (2013). An evaluative study of the academic achievement of homeschooled students versus traditionally schooled students attending a Catholic university. *Catholic Education: A Journal of Inquiry and Practice, 16*(2), 288–308.

Sutton, J. P., & Galloway, R. (2000). College success of students from three high school settings. *Journal of Research and Development in Education, 33*(3), 137–146.

Thomson, R. A., Jr., & Jang, S. J. (2016). Homeschool and underage drinking: Is it more protective than public and private schools? *Deviant Behavior, 37*(3), 281–301.

Tillman, V. D. (1995). Home schoolers, self-esteem, and socialization. *Home School Researcher, 11*(3), 1–6.

Uecker, J. E. (2008). Alternative schooling strategies and the religious lives of American adolescents. *Journal for the Scientific Study of Religion, 47*(4), 563–584.

United States Department of Education. (2014, November). *Table 206.10. Number and percentage of homeschooled students ages 5 through 17 with a grade equivalent of kindergarten through 12th grade, by selected child, parent, and household characteristics: 2003, 2007, and 2012*. Retrieved February 9, 2017 from https://nces.ed.gov/programs/digest/d15/tables/dt15_206.10.asp

Van Pelt, D. (2003). *Home education in Canada: A report on the pan-Canadian study on home education 2003*. Medicine Hat, Alberta: Canadian Centre for Home Education.

Vaughn, M. G., Salas-Wright, C. P., Kremer, K. P., Maynard, B. R., Roberts, G., & Vaughn, S. (2015). Are homeschooled adolescents less likely to use alcohol, tobacco, and other drugs? *Drug and Alcohol Dependence, 155*, 97–104.

Wartes, J. (1988). The Washington home school project: Quantitative measures for informing policy decisions. *Education and Urban Society, 21*(1), 42–51.

Wartes, J. (1990). Recent results from the Washington homeschool research project. *Home School Researcher*, *6*(4), 1–7.

Washington State Superintendent of Public Instruction. (1985). *Washington State's experimental programs using the parent as tutor under the supervision of a Washington State certificated teacher 1984-1985*. Olympia, WA: Author.

White, S., Moore, M., & Squires, J. (2009). Examination of previously homeschooled college students with the big five model of personality. *Home School Researcher, 25*(1), 1–7.

White, S., Williford, E., Brower, J., Collins, T., Merry, R., & Washington, M. (2007). Emotional, social and academic adjustment to college: A comparison between Christian home schooled and traditionally schooled college freshmen. *Home School Researcher, 17* (4), 1–7.

Wilkens, C. P., Wade, C. H., Sonnert, G., & Sadler, P. M. (2015). Are homeschoolers prepared for college calculus? *Journal of School Choice: International Research and Reform*, *9*(1), 30–48.

Yu, M. C., Sackett, P. R., & Kuncel, N. R. (2016). Predicting college performance of homeschooled versus traditional students. *Educational Measurement: Issues and Practice, 35*(4), 31–39.

# Can I choose to have grit? Non-cognitive skills, behavior, and school choice

Malachi Nichols

**ABSTRACT**
With the introduction of school choice as a viable option of school reform, researchers have begun to look beyond academic achievement to the effects of choice on alternative outcomes. Recently, non-cognitive skills and behavior stand at the front of those alternative outcomes. From the most up to date relevant literature it appears that school choice has adverse effects on non-cognitive skills but positive effects on behavior. The potential presence of reference group bias highlights the possibility that the negative effects of choice on non-cognitive skills may not be real.

## Introduction

School choice has been proven to be a viable option for reforming schools. Built around the principle that competition should increase performance, educational systems around the world have integrated some form of choice into their policies. Linked to positive effects such as increased likelihood of graduating and academic achievement, evaluators of school choice have measured the most sensible and often easily measurable outcomes associated with a person's cognitive skills (Shakeel, Anderson, & Wolf, 2016).

A student's non-cognitive skills prove as important as their cognitive skills in predicting desirable outcomes (Carneiro, Crawford, & Goodman, 2007). Non-cognitive skills or character skills are a person's traits, social abilities, or characteristics that guide a person through life. They often reference what is not captured by a standardized test. These skills predict academic achievement (Almlund, Duckworth, Heckman, & Kautz, 2011), earnings (Lleras, 2008) and criminal activity as a youth (Heckman, Stixrud, & Urzua, 2006). With the growing knowledge of the effects of school choice on academic outcomes, evaluators now need to look into the effects of school choice on non-cognitive skills (Mills, 2013).

Despite the growing literature on non-cognitive skills within various communities and groups, the attention to their effects in a school choice setting is sparse. Building upon the literature review by Mills (2013), which focuses chiefly on behavior, this article expands on the previous review by elaborating on the promotion of non-cognitive skills alongside student behavior within various school choice settings.

In the first section I present relevant research on the importance of non-cognitive skills, their relationship with behavior, their association with desirable life outcomes, and why we should expect school choice to have an effect. The next section presents the methodology in choosing studies to be included in this review. The following section reviews the current literature on the association between non-cognitive skills, behavior, and school choice. The final two sections present recommendations for further research and conclusions.

## Literature review

### *The importance of non-cognitive skills*

In the search to discover what factors predict success in life, researchers have begun to move beyond IQ, test scores, and other cognitive factors and begun to take an interest in non-cognitive skills such as grit, locus of control, conscientiousness, and self-control. The term non-cognitive skills take on a broad range of titles including: non-cognitive traits, social-emotional learning (SEL), and character skills. Furthermore, the use of each different title presents positives and negatives (Duckworth & Yeager, 2015). Regardless of the name, these skills are generally "independent of cognitive ability, advantageous to the individual, stable yet responsive to intervention, and context dependent" (Duckworth & Yeager, 2015, p. 239). But, overall these various measures predict a plethora of outcomes in the realms of academics, labor market, criminal activity, and health (Almlund et al., 2011).

In the area of education non-cognitive traits are predictive of college persistence, degree attainment, and general educational success (Carneiro et al., 2007; Heckman et al., 2006; Lleras, 2008; Mischel, Shoda, & Peake, 1988). Within the labor market, non-cognitive skills such as a person's social skills, work habits, and directness are associated with employment, wages, and job productivity (Borghans, Ter Weel, & Weinberg, 2008; Farkas, 2003; Heckman et al., 2006; Lleras, 2008). Various character skills are predictive of general health outcomes such as teenage pregnancy (Carneiro et al., 2007; Heckman et al., 2006). For example, Moffitt et al. (2011) followed 1,000 children from birth to age 32, showing that non-cognitive skills, in particular self-control, were associated with general health. Furthermore, the team followed 500 sibling pairs and found that decreases in non-cognitive skills were associated with decreases in school performance and social behavior (Moffitt et al., 2011). These non-cognitive skills such as self-control and grit have helped highlight the importance of the possession and acquisition of character skills in helping achieve short- and long-term goals.

### *The importance of behavioral measures*

Self-reported and observational measures of absences (Gershenson, 2016; Jackson, 2012), crime (Benda, 2005) and participation in risky behavior (Wong et al., 2014) have provided an opportunity to measure underlying non-cognitive skills. These behaviors and others have been shown to be proxies for various non-cognitive skills such as conscientiousness (Jackson, 2012; Segal, 2013; Zamarro, Cheng, Shakeel, & Hitt, 2016). Because non-cognitive skills help govern our behavior, a change in behavior could represent a change in underlying character. Kautz and Zanoni (2014) found participants in the One Goal Program of Chicago, an initiative meant to encourage low-income students to enroll and complete college through the promotion of non-cognitive skills, incurred decreases in absences and arrests. Additionally, participants showed a greater likelihood of college enrollment and persistence.

Undesirable behavior such as stealing and lying are predictive of risky activity later in life including crime (Heckman & Kautz, 2013). Using eighth-grade misbehavior for boys measuring frequent absences, frequent tardiness, class attentiveness, disruptive behavior, and homework completion, Segal (2013) discovered that misbehaver was negatively associated with later life earnings, even after controlling for cognitive ability.

### *School choice, non-cognitive skills, and behavior*

An equally important question is if these non-cognitive measures are fixed or malleable? Despite an acknowledgement by Duckworth and Yeager (2015) that these skills show responsiveness to interventions, the conclusiveness of their malleability is still unsettled (Farrington et al., 2012). Research points toward the inclination that these traits can vary over time and demographic groups and can be responsive to deliberate intervention, pointing toward actual malleability (Carneiro et al., 2007; Cunha & Heckman, 2008; Heckman & Kautz, 2013). If student non-cognitive skills and behavior are malleable, then schools of choice could change them.

Parent considerations go beyond academics when choosing a school (Holmes Erickson, 2017; Hoxby, 2001). Often their considerations include safety, school values, sports, location, school mission, and potential peers, along with a host of other concerns. Because each parental consideration encapsulates multiple factors, theoretically the ability for a parent to choose their child's school allows for a greater likelihood of finding a school that meets those considerations and leads to a greater possibility of desirable results.

Private schools could impact student behavior and non-cognitive skills simply through this mechanism of parent matching of child to school through choice (Coleman, Hoffer, & Kilgore, 1982). Private schools, which usually are religious, also have more distinct policies geared toward diminishing bad behavior by making students aware of the costs of their actions. Those costs include expulsion and a potential reduction of later life income because of crime or reduced educational attainment. Lastly, the potential impact of school choice on non-cognitive outcomes could be from the additional time in class, preventing students from participating in risky activity and learning more character skills (Figlio & Stone, 2000).

The possible mechanisms for change ring similar for charter schools and other forms of choice. Charter schools are not bound by bureaucratic regulatory systems and have flexibility in hiring practices, policy creation, and implementation not afforded to residentially assigned public schools (Gleason, Clark, Tuttle, & Dwoyer, 2010; Abdulkadiroglu et al., 2011). Quite often they have missions geared toward moral and character development, discipline, and school safety (Lake et al., 2012; Weiher & Tedin, 2002). Lastly, charter management organizations (CMOs), which establish and operate charter schools, are more likely to establish school-wide behavioral policies compared to their traditional public school counterparts. Those CMOs with behavioral policies are associated with larger charter school test score impacts than CMOs without such policies (Furgeson et al., 2011). School choice, apparently, can induce change.

In the struggle for school reform, researchers, policymakers, administrators, teachers, and parents have tried alternative methods for producing and evaluating success. Non-cognitive skills and behavior are reliable predictors of later life outcomes and potentially respond to intervention. My review focuses on relevant literature covering the effects of school choice on the direct and proxy measures of non-cognitive skills and behaviors.

## Methodology

This systematic review was conducted in four phases. Phase I consisted of the replication and extension of Mills (2013). All 10 studies from Mills (2013) were coded, gathering the following information: citation, school choice form, purpose of the study, methods, sample, results, and limitations of the study. Once coded, each study was reviewed to determine if it fit the inclusion criteria below. Phase II entailed collaborating with researchers familiar with the school choice and non-cognitive literature to determine if any recent literature had been released or if they knew of any additional relevant literature on the topic. Phase III involved a formal online search of the literature using recognized academic databases with consistent search terms. Each study selected was chosen using consistent inclusion criteria and coded, gathering the same information as in Phase I. Lastly, Phase IV involved combing through the references from chosen articles, school choice literature, and non-cognitive literature to find any possible remaining studies.

### *Phase I: replication and extension of Mills (2013)*

The previous systematic review of the literature relating to school choice, behaviors and non-cognitive skills by Mills (2013) found ten studies, all of which are included in this review. Only two studies included effects of school choice on non-cognitive skills, while the other eight focused on the effects of choice on non-cognitive attitudes. The increased focus of contemporary researchers on non-cognitive behaviors, and the paucity of that research in the previous review, motivated the extension of Mills (2013) to include recent literature pertaining to school choice and non-cognitive skills.

### *Phase II: collaboration with researchers*

Within this phase, I conversed with researchers in the areas of school choice and character skills to see if there were any papers that they knew of in the field. This networked phase of the search process contributed two additional studies by Dills and Hernandez-Julian (2011) and DeAngelis and Wolf (2016), bringing the current review's total to 12.

### *Phase III: formal search*

Inside this phase, I conducted a systematic search of the relevant literature using three academic databases: EBSCO, ProQuest, and the National Bureau of Economic Research (NBER). EBSCO is a general research database that consists of magazines and scholarly articles. ProQuest is a comprehensive database of 30 separate databases that comprises scholarly articles and other types of publications. Finally, NBER is a private nonprofit organization designed to conduct and disseminate economic research. NBER produces a working paper database, allowing individuals to search previous and current working papers. The search terms used across these databases were *school choice, private schools, charter schools, public school choice, open-enrollment districts, intra-district school choice, magnet schools, non-cognitive skills, non-cognitive traits, character skills, character traits, and behavior.*

The search period was from 1992 to the present. This period was chosen because Minnesota passed the first charter school law and Wisconsin launched the first modern private school voucher program both in 1991. From each search, article titles were reviewed for their topical relevance. If titles seemed relevant, the article abstracts were reviewed for relevance. If abstracts were deemed relevant, the methods section was read and, if it described a viable quantitative analysis, the full article was reviewed and coded. Within the full article review, duplicate studies were dropped. Two studies were added from the systematic search, bringing the overall total to 14 articles.

### *Inclusion criteria*

For the initial search, titles were excluded if they did not include any of the search terms or seemed to have no relevance to school choice, non-cognitive skills, or behavior. Abstracts were excluded if they did not suggest that the study included a quantitative analysis or was topical. After reviewing the methods sections, studies were excluded if the results were not based on either experimental or quasi-experimental methods. In program evaluation, experiments are the "gold standard" of research because they allow causal claims about the effects of particular programs. Because experiments are not always practical, quasi-experimental methods are often used to make causal claims. Causal claims are important when reviewing the literature on the effects of school choice on non-cognitive skills and various behaviors because they can present an unbiased effect of a program. Full articles were excluded if they were duplicate studies or only focused on a sub-set of students. Lastly, only studies conducted in the United States were included. Table 1 shows a comprehensive view of the formal search.

### *Phase IV: references and relevant authors*

Authors of the 14 selected articles were searched to discover any additional research that could have been conducted within the scope of this article. From the search, Knechtel et al. (2015) and Mills, Cheng, Hitt, Wolf, and Greene (2016) were discovered but Mills et al. was excluded because of the authors' emphasis that the results, "do not represent reliable estimates of the causal impact" (Mills et al., 2016, p. 1). References from the 14 selected articles to be reviewed and relevant literature in school choice and non-cognitive skills were searched to find any additional literature that would fit within this review. From this process Elder and Jepsen (2014) were found from the references in Mills et al. (2016). Through Phase IV, two additional studies were found, moving the final total of articles reviewed to 16.

**Table 1.** Results from formal search.

| Database | Number of Titles Retrieved | Number of Abstracts Reviewed | Number of Methods Reviewed | Full Articles Reviewed | Selected |
|---|---|---|---|---|---|
| EBSCO | 598 | 18 | 4 | 3 | 0 |
| ProQuest | 1209 | 30 | 10 | 5 | 1 |
| NBER | 86 | 19 | 4 | 3 | 1 |
| *Total* | *1893* | *67* | *18* | *11* | *2* |

## Research on the effects of school choice on non-cognitive skills and behavior

Though the literature on the effects of school choice is deep, the literature on its connection to non-cognitive skills is modest but growing. Since Mills (2013), I have found six additional studies reporting the effects of school choice on personality traits and behavior. These six new studies have focused more attention on measures of student non-cognitive skills often measured by self-reports. The following 16 studies are divided into three subgroups based on type of school choice program: choice of district-run schools, charter schools, and private schools.

### *Choice of district-run schools*

Various policies permit families to choose from among schools operated by local school districts. These policies include Tiebout choice, which is moving to a neighborhood with desirable schools, intra-district choice (a.k.a. open enrollment), and magnet schools. Choice of district-run schools is the least controversial form of school choice. I present four studies on this form of choice (Table 2).

Using lotteries from 19 public high schools of choice in Chicago, Cullen, Jacob, and Levitt (2003) evaluate the effect of district-run school choice on various student outcomes. They find no effect on test scores, attendance, or credits earned. They do find that lottery winners have lower levels of behavior requiring disciplinary actions and lower arrest rates. Additionally, they find no effect on teacher trust and future aspirations. Attended schools of choice were higher in peer achievement, higher in graduation rates, and lower in student poverty. Thus, the witnessed behavioral changes by lottery winners could be context specific and the results might not generalize to wider environments that lack higher quality schools measured by academic standing and student demographics.

Deming (2011) looked at the impact of a winning a lottery to a first-choice public middle or high school in Charlotte-Mecklenburg. In 2002 the

**Table 2.** The literature on intra-district choice and other choice programs.

| | | Results | | |
|---|---|---|---|---|
| Authors | Program or Participants | Non-cognitive | Behavior | Risky-activity |
| Cullen et al. (2003) | 19 public high schools in Chicago | Null | Null | Positive |
| Deming (2011) | Charlotte-Mecklenburg school district: middle and high schools | - | Positive | Positive |
| Dills and Hernandez-Julian (2011) | Eighth-grades from NELS-88 | - | - | Positive |
| Hastings et al. (2012) | Low-income urban district | - | Positive | - |

Notes: (NELS-88) The 1988 National Educational Longitudinal Survey

Charlotte-Mecklenburg school district implemented a district wide open enrollment program. Deming found that winning the lottery is associated with fewer felony arrests, fewer absences, fewer days in jail, and less behavior resulting in suspensions, expulsion, or police involvement. This finding is larger and more significant for the African-American sub-population. Similar to Cullen et al. (2003), Deming found that school choice lottery winners often attended higher quality schools as compared to lottery losers but suggested that school quality accounted for more impact in high school than in middle schools.

Studying the effects of Tiebout choice on various forms of criminal behavior, Dills and Hernandez-Julian (2011) make use of a clever Instrumental Variable (IV). Measuring choice by eighth grade enrollment and the Herfindahl index, which is a measure of market concentration, they counter the endogeneity issue by using the number of rivers and streams as a proven IV. By producing transportation issues, streams and rivers have historically increased the need for additional schools, subsequently producing more school choice. Using data from the eighth graders of the 1988 National Educational Longitudinal Survey (NELS), the succeeding 1992 NELS follow-up survey and the 2004 Uniform Crime Reports, Dills and Hernandez-Julian see that adolescents in metro-areas with more access to choice are less likely to participate in criminal activity. For example, at the student-level an increase in choice is associated with a decrease in the probability of gang affiliation and cocaine use, though the relationship is not statistically significant. At the aggregate-level, a one standard deviation increase in choice is associated with a 25–40% reduction in metro-area juvenile arrest rates.

As acknowledged by the authors, even with the use of a clever IV, the potential of students reporting socially desirable answers in their NELS self-reports introduces potential bias into their estimates. The supplementation of aggregate-level results, independent of self-reported criminal activity, does allude to a potential positive effect of more choice on the reduction of crime. Moreover, these estimates are not measuring the effects of a particular choice policy but just the increase in available schools. Therefore, these results should not be interpreted as the direct effects of school choice policy but the effects of increased schooling options, which could suggest the potential effects of a school choice policy.

Lastly, Hastings, Neilson, and Zimmerman (2012) look at the effects of lottery announcements on behaviors in a low-income urban district, comprised of magnet and charter schools. Driven by the hypothesis that school choice has an affect on intrinsic motivation they study the effects of attendance and behavior in the semester between the lottery announcement and lottery-school enrollment. Using a difference-in-difference (DID)[1] analysis they find that male lottery winners see about a 14-percentage point reduction in truancy rates and females see about a 1-percentage point reduction in truancy rates. In a secondary analysis to determine if the effect is driven by the behavior of winners or losers, they implement a propensity score matching technique. They find that the positive behavior from winners is driving the positive result and not negative behavior from losers. Furthermore, they find winners that subsequently attended charters saw larger increases in test scores than those that attended public magnet schools. The authors conclude that the reduction of truancy rates from choice suggests a change in intrinsic motivation due to the anticipation of enrolling in a school of choice.

From the four studies presented it appears that various forms of district-run school choice have positive effects on student behavior. All three studies that evaluated criminal activity reported a reduction in crime due to choice (Cullen et al., 2003; Deming, 2011; Dills & Hernandez-Julian, 2011). While one of two studies emphasizing attendance saw positive results (Hastings et al., 2012) the other found null results (Cullen et al., 2003). Despite the varying programs studied, the theoretical underpinnings of school choice suggest that choice matters in prompting desirable student behaviors. The changed behaviors hint at possible changes of character within those children. More research is needed to bring greater clarity to the impact of district-run choice programs on character skills and behavior.

### *Charter schools*

Here I present eight studies on the effects of public charter schools on non-cognitive traits and behavior (Table 3). We see more charter studies due to the fact that once charters are at full capacity, lotteries are administered to hopeful enrollees, thus presenting the gold standard of experimental research design for researchers.

After taking advantage of charter lotteries, Gleason and team (2010) evaluated the effectiveness of 35 charter schools in 15 states over the 2004–05 and 2005–06 academic years. They report both the intent-to-treat (ITT)[2] and treatment-on-treated (TOT)[3] and found no effects of charter school enrollment on academic achievement. Secondly, they discovered a null impact of student reported behavior in school, behavior out of school, and suspensions. Lastly, they found null results on the impacts of charters on absences.

It is possible that charter students reported socially desirable activity at higher rates than control group students, thus biasing the estimates. To confront this possibility, Gleason and colleagues estimate the effects of enrollment on parent-reports of student behavior and discover null effects. The possibility of charter parents reporting socially desirable answers is still there, but highly unlikely.

Using start-up and conversion charters in a large urban Southwestern school district, Imberman (2011) analyzes the effects of charter schools on student achievement and behavior. Using students in grades 1 through 12,

**Table 3.** The literature on charter schools.

| Authors | Program or Participants | Results | | |
|---|---|---|---|---|
| | | Non-cognitive | Behavior | Risky-activity |
| Gleason et al. (2010) | 35 charter schools in 15 states | - | Null | - |
| Imberman (2011) | Start-up and conversion charters in a large urban Southwestern school district | - | Positive | - |
| West et al. (2016) | 5 over-subscribed charter schools in Boston | Negative | Positive | - |
| Angrist et al. (2011) | 22 urban and non-urban Massachusetts charter schools | - | Mixed | - |
| Dobbie and Fryer (2011) | Harlem Children's Zone elementary and middle school | - | Positive | - |
| Dobbie and Fryer (2014) | Harlem Children's Zone | Mixed | - | Positive |
| Tuttle et al. (2013) | 41 KIPP middle schools | Null | Negative | Null |
| Knechtel et al. (2015) | Deliberate increase in enrollment of KIPP schools | Null | - | Null |

Imberman takes advantage of a rich 13-year data set, spanning 1994–95 through 2006–07. Conducting an OLS individual fixed effect (FE) analysis[4] Imberman finds that charter enrollment is associated with a decrease in disciplinary infractions and an increase in attendance.

When parceled out, Imberman shows that students attending start-up charters see a decrease of between 0.5 and 0.8 infractions a year and about a 2.3 percentage point increase in school attendance. For conversion charters, Imberman finds null results. Because attendance and discipline are highly correlated the results shown are in the expected direction. Since, unlike conversion charters, start-up charters have the ability to create their own culture, vision, and school emphasis, this autonomy could lead to a greater likelihood of changing student behavior and those non-cognitive skills that are proxied by behavior.

Looking at 8th graders in the spring of 2011 in Boston, West and colleagues (2016) focus on the association between choice and student self-reported non-cognitive skills. The team looks at 22-open enrollment district schools, five over-subscribed charter schools, two test-in exam schools, and three non-oversubscribed charter schools, with the main analysis focusing on the five over-subscribed charter schools.

Using student surveys, West and team measure conscientiousness, self-control, grit, and growth mindset. Looking at all students within the 32 schools, charter students compared to open enrollment students measure higher on test score gains, report higher levels of growth mindsets but report lower levels of conscientiousness, self-control, and grit. These results present the paradox of externally performing well but internally rating your performance low.

Additionally, taking advantage of the lotteries of the five over-subscribed schools, West and colleagues implement a two-stage-least-squares (2SLS)[5] analysis. They find that a year of attendance in a charter school is associated with about a 0.2 standard deviation decrease in self-control, about a 0.1 standard deviation decrease in grit and about a day and a half decrease in days absent; all statistically significant. Furthermore, they find about a 0.15 standard deviation decrease in conscientiousness, a 0.03 standard deviation decrease in growth mindset and an increase in days suspended, all marginally significant.

To better understand the reasoning behind the increase in achievement but decrease in non-cognitive skills West and colleagues (2016) look at the trends for one cohort of students in two over-subscribed Massachusetts charter schools and one open-enrollment district and find similar results. Over the three years analyzed, student's conscientiousness, self-control, and grit declines while growth mindset increases.

These paradoxical results have two hypothetical explanations. The first is that these charter schools did have a negative effect on student non-cognitive skills and the second is the possibility of reference group bias. To address the latter issue, West and team (2016) examine student perceptions of school climate between charter attendees and open-enrollment public school attendees. They find that charter students rate their schools statistically higher in expectations, teacher strictness, and clarity of rules as compared to their open-enrollment counterparts. This finding alludes to the possibility that charter students are comparing themselves to their hardworking peers or to the expectations of their teacher, thus reporting lower levels of non-cognitive behaviors than what they truly are.

Angrist, Pathak, and Walters (2011) reviewed the effects of 22 urban and non-urban Massachusetts charter schools. Exploiting each school's lottery they presented impact-on-treated (IOT)[6] results on the effects of charters on student discipline and absences. Despite null results on non-urban schools Angrist and team found that attendance in an urban charter increased the length of suspensions by 0.88 days in middle school and about one day in high school. In addition they found that urban charter attendance decreased the number of unauthorized absences. Over half of the charters included in the study qualified as "No Excuses" charters. These schools have a low tolerance on misbehavior therefore the increase in suspensions could be caused by a change in discipline policy and not a change in student behavior.

Capitalizing on the lotteries of the Harlem Children's Zone, Dobbie and Fryer (2011) present the first causal results of the program. Using elementary school lotteries from the 2004–05 school year and middle school lotteries from the 2005–06 year, Dobbie and Fryer assess the impacts of academic achievement and absences, presenting IV and 2SLS estimates. In middle school they find that lottery winners see a positive impact in math and ELA achievement. Additionally, they find that winners are absent about 2 fewer days than losers. In elementary school, they find similar results, increases in both math and ELA achievement with about 2.3 fewer absences for lottery winners.

Dobbie and Fryer (2014) extend their experimental analysis of HCZ to determine if the previously found achievement gains in Dobbie and Fryer (2011) translate into other desirable outcomes such as high school graduation, college enrollment and the reduction of drug use, teen pregnancy, and incarceration. Surveying lottery participants of the 2005–06 6th grade cohort, each student filled out a comprehensive survey, which included measures of risky behavior, health, and other self-reported measures of self-esteem, persistence and locus of control.

Dobbie and Fryer find positive impacts of the HCZ on reducing risky behavior but generally negative effects for the other non-cognitive measures. Presented as Local Average Treatment (LATE)[7] effects, they find that HCZ students are about a quarter of a standard deviation less likely to partake in risky behavior, defined as an index of self-reported teen pregnancy, controlled substance use, and crime. Also, they find that HCZ attendance is associated with decreases in self-esteem and grit but increases in locus of control. To confront the issue that students could be underreporting participating in risky behavior, Dobbie and Fryer supplement their analysis with administrative records, finding larger results. Those findings, refuting the likelihood of socially desirable answers biasing their analysis.

Tuttle and team (2013) analyze 41 KIPP middle schools over a 4-year period. Using propensity score matching based on observable characteristics and achievement trajectories they find positive effects on math, reading, science, and social studies achievement. In a secondary analysis they take advantage of 13 school lotteries and determine the effect of winning the lottery on student behavior and characteristics. They find no effect of charters on student reported self-control, academic self-concept, school engagement, persistence, and educational aspirations. Furthermore, they find no effect on behavior measured by self-reported illegal activity and an index of good behavior. KIPP students were found to be more likely to lose their temper, argue, lie, and give their teacher a hard time. Tuttle and colleagues present two possible explanations for the negative impacts on behavior, the first is the reality of true negative effects and the second is the possibility of increased honesty in reporting behavior, often promoted within KIPP schools.

Lastly, Knechtel and team (2015) looked at the effects of a deliberate increase in enrollment of KIPP schools at all three levels; elementary, middle, and high school on non-cognitive outcomes. In 2010, KIPP was awarded an investing in Innovation (i-3) scale-up grant designed to increase the presence and enrollment of KIPP schools across the country. By the 2014–2015 academic year, KIPP had increased its enrollment from 27,000 to 55,000 students (Knechtel et al., 2015). Using student and parent surveys, the team measured their grit, academic confidence and self-control. Overall, using lottery-based and quasi-experimental designs, Knechtel and team found that KIPP had no significant effect on student self-reported measures of grit, academic confidence, or self-control despite showing statistically significant positive effects on student achievement. Furthermore, KIPP showed a null effect on middle school student behavior measures of illegal activity and parent reported disciplinary actions (Knechtel et al., 2015). Despite having positive effects on academic achievement it seems that KIPP hasn't had any effect on non-cognitive skills and student behavior. This could be caused by KIPP's own admission of a greater focus on test scores than on intrinsic values.

Overall, these eight studies suggest that charter schools are associated with null to negative effects on self-reported non-cognitive measures but null to positive results on behavior and risky activity. Six out of eight studies presented effects on behavior, with three showing positive results, and one each for null, mixed, and negative results. School climate could be a possible explanation for the mixed results. Angrist et al. (2011) alluded to a "No Excuses" type policy as a potential reason for an increase in suspensions but a decrease in absences. In Imberman (2011) the variation in school climate between start-up charters and conversion charters could have led to the mixed results. The overwhelming conclusion was null to negative results associated with charters and non-cognitive skills. The potential of biases included reference group bias (West et al., 2016) and students reporting socially desirable answers (Gleason et al., 2010) prevents discerning a strong conclusion. Until these various forms of bias can be accounted for, researchers will not be able to determine if charter schools have positive effects on non-cognitive skills or actually have adverse effects.

### *Private schools*

Four studies have examined the effects of private school choice or private schooling on non-cognitive outcomes (Table 4). Using the Early Longitudinal Survey Kindergarten Class of 1998–99 (ECLS-K), Elder and Jepsen (2014) looked at the effects of Catholic schooling on non-cognitive and cognitive skills measured between kindergarten and 8th grade. Using propensity score matching and OLS they looked at the effects on various outcomes including test scores, days absent, tardiness and self-reported locus of control reported during the students' 5th grade year. They found a consistent negative effect of Catholic schooling on math achievement gains. Additionally, they found no effect on reported locus of control but discovered a statistically significant reduction in absences ranging around one absence, along with a marginally significant increase in tardiness. Overall, these results seem to be mixed, leaving no clear conclusion. Elder and Jepsen attribute the lack of definite conclusion to selection bias, as many private school attendees entered private school with higher math and reading test scores.

Mocan and Tekin (2007) studied the effects of Catholic schools on risky behavior by youths. Using the National Longitudinal Study of Adolescent Health data set, Mocan and Tekin performed a mix of linear probability models and propensity score matching estimators. They find that Catholic schooling reduced risky behavior for females but increased risky behavior for males. For example, female enrollment in private school reduced the probability of sexual activity by 11 to 13 percentage points and the use of cocaine

**Table 4.** The literature on private schools.

| | | Results | | |
|---|---|---|---|---|
| Authors | Program or Participants | Non-cognitive | Behavior | Risky-activity |
| Elder and Jepsen (2014) | Early Longitudinal Survey; Kindergarten Class of 1998–99 | Null | Mixed | - |
| Mocan and Tekin (2007) | Catholic Schools from National Longitudinal Study of Adolescent Health data set | - | - | Mixed |
| Figlio and Ludwig (2012) | Religious private schools from the National Education Longitudinal Study of 1988 | - | - | Mixed |
| DeAngelis and Wolf (2016) | Milwaukee Parental Choice Program (MCP) | - | - | Positive |

by 5 to 6 percentage points. Alternatively, male enrollment increased the probability of cocaine use, marijuana use, and the selling of drugs by 4 to 5, 8 to 11, and 8 to 10 percentage points respectively. To further investigate these mixed effects by gender, Mocan and Tekin evaluate the effect of Catholic enrollment on test scores separately for males and females, using the Add Health Picture Vocabulary Test (AHPVT). They found that Catholic schooling had a positive effect on test scores for students of both genders but the effect on girls was larger. The negative effect of Catholic schooling on risky behavior for boys might be a true effect due to the heterogeneity of experiences in test scores between girls and boys.

Similarly, Figlio and Ludwig (2012) studied the effects of religious private schools on student outcomes using the National Education Longitudinal Study of 1988. Using varying transportation cost as an instrument for private school enrollment, Figlio and Ludwig found positive to null results. Enrollment in Catholic schools was found to decrease involvement in arrest, use of cocaine, and teen pregnancy. For instance, attendance in private school is associated with a 24-percentage point decrease in the likelihood of a student having adolescent sex. Private school attendance was found to have no effect on drinking, smoking, marijuana use, or gang activity. To check for the possibility of students presenting socially desirable answers, Figlio and Ludwig dropped the top 5% of students who had discrepancies between self-reported academic achievement and administrative records, with the hope to relieve the analysis of students who had the greatest potential of reporting socially desirable answers. They found similar results within the secondary analysis. Thus it appears that religious private schools are decreasing severe negative behavior but showing no effect on less severe behavior.

Lastly, DeAngelis and Wolf (2016) look at the effects of the longstanding Milwaukee Parental Choice Program (MPCP) on criminal activity for young adults ages 22–25. Matching voucher students with Milwaukee Public School students on race, grade, neighborhood, gender, ELL, and test scores they study the effects of the MCP on criminal activity, which includes misdemeanors, felonies, drugs, traffic violations, and theft. Reporting Local Average Treatment Effects (LATE), full exposure to the program was associated with a 12-percentage point and a 7-percentage point decrease in the likelihood of being accused of a crime and being convicted of a misdemeanor, respectively. Both estimates were statistically significant. The lack of variation in the dependent variable posed trouble in some samples but did not prevent the team from identifying a reduction in misdemeanors, felonies, and thefts (DeAngelis & Wolf, 2016). This study shows that the MPCP could have had a positive effect on character development, shown through the reduction of crime.

From these four studies it seems that private schools have mixed results on non-cognitive outcomes, with no effect on non-cognitive skills and mixed results on behaviors. Three of the four studies concentrated on risky behavior, with two (Mocan and Tekin, 2007; Figlio & Ludwig, 2012) presenting mixed results and one (DeAngelis & Wolf, 2016) showing positive results. The null effect for drinking, smoking, and gang activity alongside with the decreases in arrests, hard drug use, and teen pregnancy found by Figlio and Ludwig alludes to the variation of the potential impacts of private schools on behaviors. More research is needed on the association between private schools, non-cognitive skills and behavior.

### *Need for further research*

Even with the emergence of recent literature focusing on the impacts of school choice on non-cognitive skills and behavior, more research is needed. To enhance the current survey of the literature there are four areas of emphasis that would bring depth to this shallow field. The first emphasis would be fixing the reference group bias problem. The second would be to increase the use and validation of behavioral measures. The third would be to emphasize a greater understanding of what factors do non-cognitive skills and behavior measure. The last improvement would be to continue to use randomization often associated with lotteries to generate valid causal findings.

Most researchers measure non-cognitive skills with self-reported measures. The subsequent reference group bias calls for the further development of methods that can be used to control this form of bias. One relevant method includes the use of anchoring vignettes. Designed to correct for varying frames of reference, these vignettes have been found to increase the reliability of conscientiousness and openness measures within various student populations (Primi, Zanon, Santos, De Fruit, & John, 2016; Vonkova, Zamarro, & DeBerg, 2015). If similar methods can be designed to account for this type of bias, it could help control and prevent additional paradoxical findings (West et al., 2016).

Secondly, there is a need for the further use and validation of alternative behavioral measures. Researchers have begun to validate external behaviors such as absences (Jackson, 2012) and underlying behaviors such as careless-answering and item non-response (Zamarro et al., 2016) as proxy measures for non-cognitive skills, but more work is needed. These proxies could prove to be practical, economical, and reliable methods of measuring non-cognitive skills.

Thirdly, because there is a range of non-cognitive skills measured throughout the literature, researchers should bring a greater emphasis to acknowledging what factors are responsive to varying fields and outcomes. Within labor economics the two-factor framework consisting of a cognitive factor and a non-cognitive factor, (i.e. locus of control) leads the way, but within education economics, behavioral measures (i.e. absences and risky activity) act as proxy measures of non-cognitive skills, while general non-cognitive skills measured through questionnaires (i.e. the Big Five) represent the main measurement tool within psychology and behavioral economics. This discrepancy in consistent measures despite the implementation and overlap across fields could lead to the miss interpretation of findings. Humphries and Kosse (2016) show that non-cognitive measures from psychology and behavioral economics are greater predictors of educational outcomes than measures from labor and education economics. Self-reported behavioral measures could capture underlying traits with the same power as non-cognitive constructs. Acknowledging the source of the non-cognitive construct used within a program evaluation could lead to a greater interpretation of findings.

Lastly, researchers should continue to make use of randomization often found in lotteries. Using randomization would help with the self-selection often seen in school choice settings. It would also provide more identifications of causal effects of choice on non-cognitive skills, thus further helping shed light into the black box of choice.

## *Conclusion*

Continuing the work of Mills (2013) who found 10 studies showing generally positive results on the effects of school choice on behavior and non-cognitive skills, this article presented six additional relevant pieces of literature on the promotion of non-cognitive measures and behavior in various school choice settings. The four studies covering intra-district choice and other choice programs appeared to have relatively positive results. The eight studies covering charter schools found null to negative effects on student character and generally positive results on behavior. Lastly, from the four studies covering the effects of private schools, there seems to be no effect on non-cognitive skills, mixed results on short-term behavior, but positive effects on long-term behavior.

The literature suggests that school choice has a negative effect on non-cognitive skills but positive effects on student behavior. A common occurrence within the literature was the potential presences of reference group bias and reporting socially desirable answers. Thus, further research should begin to develop new methods for controlling different frames of reference and continuing to create behavioral measures which proxy for non-cognitive skills.

## Notes

1. The DID analysis measures the difference between the average outcomes for the treatment and control groups assuming they have the same trends in the absence of the intervention.
2. The ITT estimates report the effects of winning the charter lottery compared to not winning the lottery.

3. The TOT estimates report the effects of attending a charter school compared to attending another school.
4. The FE analysis works to remove selection and omitted variable bias by measuring change within an individual by using the individuals past as the counterfactual.
5. The 2SLS analysis uses the prediction of charter attendance based on being offered admission to estimate an unbiased effect of charter attendance on various outcomes.
6. The IOT analysis uses lottery results as an instrument of charter attendance to estimate the impact of charter attendance on various outcomes.
7. The LATE effects measure the average effect of attending HCZ by way of winning the lottery.

## References

Abdulkadiroglu, A., Angrist, J. D., Dynarski, S. M., Kane, T. J., & Pathak, P. A. (2011). Accountability and flexibility in public schools: Evidence from Boston's charters and pilots. *The Quarterly Journal of Economics, 126*, 699–748. doi:10.1093/qje/qjr017

Almlund, M., Duckworth, A. L., Heckman, J. J., & Kautz, T. D. (2011). Personality psychology and economics. In E. A. Hanushek, S. Machin, & L. Woessmann (Eds.), *Handbook of the economics of education* (Vol. 4, pp. 1–181). Amsterdam, The Netherlands: Elsevier.

Angrist, J. D., Pathak, P. A., & Walters, C. R. (2011). *Explaining charter school effectiveness (Working Paper No. 17332).* Cambridge, MA: National Bureau of Economic Research.

Benda, B. B. (2005). The robustness of self-control in relation to form of delinquency. *Youth & Society, 36*(4), 418–444. doi:10.1177/0044118X04268071

Borghans, L., Ter Weel, B., & Weinberg, B. A. (2008). Interpersonal styles and labor market outcomes. *Journal of Human Resources, 43*(4), 815–858.

Carneiro, P., Crawford, C., & Goodman, A. (2007). The impact of early cognitive and non-cognitive skills on later outcomes. CEE DP 92. *Centre For The Economics Of Education.*

Coleman, J., Hoffer, T., & Kilgore, S. (1982). Cognitive outcomes in public and private schools. *Sociology of Education, 55*, 65–76.

Cullen, J. B., Jacob, B. A., & Levitt, S. (2003). *The effect of school choice on student outcomes: Evidence from randomized lotteries (Working Paper No. 10113).* Cambridge, MA: National Bureau of Economic Research.

Cunha, F., & Heckman, J. J. (2008). Formulating, identifying and estimating the technology of cognitive and noncognitive skill formation. *Journal of Human Resources, 43*(4), 738–782.

DeAngelis, C., & Wolf, P. (2016, March). *The school choice voucher: A 'Get Out of Jail' Card?* SSRN Working Paper 2016-03, University of Arkansas, Fayetteville, AR.

Deming, D. (2011). Better schools, less crime? *The Quarterly Journal of Economics, 126*(4), 2063–2115.

Dills, A., & Hernandez-Julian, R. (2011). More choice, less crime. *Education Finance and Policy, 6*(2), 246–266.

Dobbie, W., & Fryer, R. G. (2011). Are high-quality schools enough to increase achievement among the poor? Evidence from the Harlem Children's Zone. *American Economic Journal: Applied Economics, 3*(3), 158–187.

Dobbie, W., & Fryer, R. G., Jr. (2014). *The medium- term impacts of high-achieving charter schools on non-test score outcomes.* (NBER Working Paper No. 19581) Cambridge, MA: National Bureau of Economic Research.

Duckworth, A., & Yeager, D. (2015). Measurement matters assessing personal qualities other than cognitive ability for educational purposes. *Educational Researcher, 44*(4), 237–251.

Elder, T., & Jepsen, C. (2014). Are Catholic primary schools more effective than public primary schools?. *Journal of Urban Economics, 80,* 28–38.

Farkas, G. (2003). Cognitive skills and noncognitive traits and behaviors in stratification processes. *Annual Review of Sociology, 29,* 541–568.

Farrington, C., Roderick, M., Allensworth, E., Nagaoka, J., Keyes, T. S., Johnson, D., & Beechum, N. O. (2012). *Teaching adolescents to become learners: The role of noncognitive factors in shaping school performance.* Chicago, IL: University of Chicago Consortium on Chicago School Research.

Figlio, D., & Ludwig, J. (2012). Sex, drugs, and Catholic schools: Private schooling and non-market adolescent behaviors. *German Economic Review, 13*(4), 385–415.

Figlio, D. N., & Stone, J. A. (2000). Are private schools really better? *Research in Labor Economics, 18,* 115–140.

Furgeson, J., Gill, B., Haimson, J., Killewald, A., McCollough, M., Nichols-Barrer, I., & Lake, R. (2011). *Charter-school management organizations: Diverse strategies and diverse student impacts.* Washington, DC: Mathematica Policy Research.

Gershenson, S. (2016). Linking teacher quality, student attendance, and student achievement. *Education Finance and Policy, 11*(2), 125–149.

Gleason, P., Clark, M., Tuttle, C. C., & Dwoyer, E. (2010). *The evaluation of charter school impacts: Final report.* Washington, DC: National Center for Education Evaluation and Regional Assistance, Institute for Education Sciences, U.S. Department of Education.

Hastings, J. S., Neilson, C. A., & Zimmerman, S. D. (2012). The effect of school choice on intrinsic motivation and academic outcomes (Working Paper No. 18324). Cambridge, MA: National Bureau of Economic Research.

Heckman, J. J., & Kautz, T. (2013). Fostering and measuring skills: Interventions that improve character and cognition. In J. J. Heckman, J. E. Humphries, & T. Kautz (Eds.), *The myth of achievement tests: The GED and the role of character in American life* (pp. 341–430). Chicago, IL: University of Chicago Press.

Heckman, J. J., Stixrud, J., & Urzua, S. (2006). The effects of cognitive and noncognitive abilities on labor market outcomes and social behavior. *Journal of Labor Economics, 24*(3), 411–482.

Holmes Erickson, H. (2017). How do parents choose schools, and what schools do they choose? A literature review of private school choice programs in the United States. *Journal of School Choice.* doi:10.1080/15582159.2017.1395618

Hoxby, C. (2001). If families matter most, where do schools come in? In T. M. Moe (Eds.), *A primer on America's schools* (pp. 89–126). Stanford, CA: Hoover Institution Press.

Humphries, J. E., & Kosse, F. (2016). *On the interpretation of non-cognitive skills: What is being measured and why it matters,* IZA Discussion Papers 10397, Institute for the Study of Labor (IZA).

Imberman, S. A. (2011). Achievement and behavior in charter schools: Drawing a more complete picture. *The Review of Economics and Statistics, 93*(2), 416–435.

Jackson, C. K. (2012). *Non-cognitive ability, test scores, and teacher quality: Evidence from 9th grade teachers in North Carolina* (NBER Working Paper No. 18624). Retrieved from http://www.nber.org/papers/w18624.

Kautz, T., & Zanoni, W. (2014). Measuring and fostering non-cognitive skills in adolescents: Evidence from Chicago public schools and the onegoal program. Unpublished manuscript, University of Chicago, Department of Economics.

Knechtel, V., Anderson, M. A., Burnett, A., Coen, T., Sullivan, M., Tuttle, C. C., & Gleason,, P. (2015). *Understanding the Effect of KIPP as It Scales, Vol. 2: Leadership Practices at KIPP.* Princeton, NJ: Mathematica Policy Research.

Lake, R., Bowen, M., Demeritt, A., McCullough, M., Haimson, J., & Gill, B. (2012). *Learning from char- ter school management organizations: Strategies for student behavior and teacher coaching*. Washington, DC: Center on Reinventing Public Education and Mathematica Policy Research.

Lleras, C. (2008). Do skills and behaviors in high school matter? The contribution of noncognitive factors in explaining differences in educational attainment and earnings. *Social Science Research, 37*(3), 888–902.

Mills, J., Cheng, A., Hitt, C., Wolf, P., & Greene, J., (2016). Measures of student non-cognitive skills and political tolerance after two years of the louisiana scholarship program. Available at SSRN: https://ssrn.com/abstract=2738782

Mills, J. N. (2013). Behaviors, noncognitive skills, and school choice. *Journal of School Choice, 7*(3), 372–388.

Mischel, W., Shoda, Y., & Peake, P. K. (1988). The nature of adolescent competencies predicted by preschool delay of gratification. *Journal of Personality and Social Psychology, 54*(4), 687–696.

Mocan, H. N., & Tekin, E. (2007). *Catholic schools and bad behavior: A propensity score matching analysis* (Working Paper No. 9172). Cambridge, MA: National Bureau of Economic Research.

Moffitt, T. E., Arseneault, L., Belsky, D., Dickson, N., Hancox, R. J., Harrington, H. L., … Caspi, A. (2011). A gradient of childhood self-control predicts health, wealth, and public safety. *Proceedings of the National Academy of Sciences, 108*(7), 2693–2698.

Primi, R., Zanon, C., Santos, D., De Fruit, F., & John, O. P. (2016). Can they make adolescent self-reports of social-emotional skills more reliable, discriminant, and criterion-valid? *European Journal of Psychological Assessment, 32*, 39–51.

Segal, C. (2013). Misbehavior, education, and labor market outcomes. *Journal of European Economics Association, 11*, 743–799.

Shakeel, D., Anderson, K., & Wolf, P. (2016, May) *The participant effects of private school vouchers across the Globe: A meta-analytic and systematic review*. SSRN Working Paper 2016-07, University of Arkansas, Fayetteville, AR.

Tuttle, C. C., Gill, B., Gleason, P., Knechtel, V., Nichols-Barrer, I., & Resch, A. (2013). *KIPP middle schools: Impacts on achievement and other outcomes, final report*. Washington, DC: Mathematica Policy Research.

Vonkova, H., Zamarro, G., & DeBerg, V. (2015). *Comparisons of student perceptions of teacher's performance in the classroom: Using parametric anchoring vignette methods for improving comparability*. AEFP 40th annual conference—paper. Retrieved from http://aefpweb.org/conferences/aefp40-download

Weiher, G. R., & Tedin, K. L. (2002). Does choice lead to racially distinctive schools? Charter schools and household preferences. *Journal of Policy Analysis and Management, 21*, 79–92.

West, M. R., Kraft, M. K., Finn, A. S., Martin, R., Duckworth, A. L., Gabrieli, C. F. O., & Gabrieli, J. D. E. (2016). Promise and paradox: Measuring students' non-cognitive skills and the impact of schooling. *Educational Evaluation and Policy Analysis, 38*(1), 148–170.

Wong, M. D., Coller, K. M., Dudovitz, R. N., Kennedy, D. P., Buddin, R., Shapiro, M. F., … Chung, P. J. (2014). Successful schools and risky behaviors among low-income adolescents. *Pediatrics, 134*(2), e389–e396.

Zamarro, G., Cheng, A., Shakeel, M., & Hitt, C. (2016) *Comparing and validating measures of character skills: Findings from a nationally representative sample*. EDRE Working Paper No 2016-08. Retrieved from http://dx.doi.org/10.2139/ssrn.2777635

# Educational attainment effects of public and private school choice

Leesa M. Foreman

**ABSTRACT**
The two fastest growing school choice options are charter schools and private school choice programs, which include vouchers, tax credit scholarships, and education savings accounts. Most research assessing the effects of these programs focuses on student achievement. I review the literature to determine the impact public and private school choice programs have on high school completion, college enrollment, and college persistence which, ultimately, may be different and of greater consequence than test scores. Of the limited research available, it appears that both type of school choice programs have a positive effect on educational attainment overall, however, more research is needed.

Over the past 25 years, dissatisfaction with the public education system in the United States has led to an increase in school choice policies. Of the choice options available, the two fastest growing are charter schools and private school voucher programs, which include vouchers, tax credit scholarships, and education savings accounts (ESAs). Most of the research assessing the effects of these programs focuses on student achievement based on annual assessment scores. The empirical studies have primarily used either experimental randomized control trials, taking advantage of over-subscription, or quasi-experimental matching methods.

A meta-analysis of the literature on the effects of charter schools on student achievement by Betts and Tang (2014) indicates that the average effect of charter schooling in general is modest. Overall, charter schools are performing better in math than traditional public schools in most grades, with middle schools producing the largest gains. The impact of charter school enrollment on reading achievement appears to be positive but statistically insignificant on average, though the large confidence interval around the positive estimate seems to be driven by a few studies with large negative estimated effect sizes. Impacts in the charter sector vary considerably, in particular across geographic areas, with larger and more consistent positive achievement benefits for urban charters, especially with disadvantaged populations of students (see Gleason, 2017 in this volume).

A recent review of the empirical research on private school choice programs by Egalite and Wolf (2016) found effects similar to the studies on charter schools. Overall, the results of voucher programs are mixed, with null to moderate positive effects on math and reading achievement, and more consistent benefits for African-American students. However, impacts also vary greatly based on geographic area and program design.

While measuring the effects of choice programs on test scores is important, it may not capture the full scope of the impact these programs have on students. Non-test score outcomes such as high school graduation, college enrollment, and persistence may be different and of greater significance than test scores. Furthermore, test scores may not be a good way to compare public and private schools with different curriculum alignment, differing stakes attached to assessments, and varied experience with test administration. Additionally, research has shown that individuals with more education have greater employment opportunities and earn more income, both annually and over their lifetime (Becker, 1993; Day & Newburger, 2002; Griliches & Mason, 1972; Heckman, Lochner, & Todd, 2008). More educated individuals are healthier, have greater longevity, contribute more in tax revenues, and are less likely to commit crime (Belfield & Levin, 2007; Deming, 2011; Levin, Belfield, Muennig, & Rouse, 2006). Researchers have begun to evaluate educational attainment outcomes for district-wide choice in Charlotte–Mecklenburg (Deming, Hastings, Kane, & Staiger, 2014), groups of students in charter schools in Texas (Dobbie & Fryer, 2016), Florida (Booker, Gill, Sass, & Zimmer, 2014; Sass, Zimmer, Gill, & Booker, 2016), Chicago (Booker et al., 2014; Davis & Heller, 2015), Boston (Angrist et al., 2016), and for voucher programs in Florida (Chingos & Kuehn, 2017), New York City (Chingos & Peterson, 2015, 2012), Milwaukee (Cowen, Fleming, Witte, Wolf, & Kisida, 2013; Warren, 2011), and Washington, D.C. (Wolf et al., 2013).[1]

This review examines the impact public and private school choice programs have on high school completion, college enrollment, and college persistence. These programs might have a different effect on attainment than on achievement because they are providing students with skills, knowledge, work habits, motivation, and values that are important for long-term success but are not fully captured by test scores. Additionally, impacts on attainment may further affect earnings and other life outcomes. After two decades, it is important to begin to assess the long-term impact these choice programs are having on students. Through this review, I contribute more information to the discussion, and to policymakers, on the effects and effectiveness of these programs.

## Review of literature

The literature on the attainment effects of public and private school choice programs is sparse. Few studies examine high school graduation, college enrollment, or college persistence as the focus of the research. In many cases, attainment is an additional outcome included in achievement studies. Searching the literature for studies related to educational attainment, high school graduation, college enrollment, or college persistence, and school choice, charter schools, or school vouchers, 13 papers were included in this review. Previous versions of studies and prior literature reviews were not included to reduce redundancy. Two recent papers begin to look at the long-term impacts of charter programs on earnings. As yet, there are no studies of voucher programs which look at earnings. In sum, I found one study of a public school choice program, seven studies of charter school programs, and five studies of voucher programs which included attainment.

The analytic approaches used in the studies presented have different trade-offs. While experimental evaluations are likely to obtain unbiased estimates by taking advantage of over-subscribed admissions lotteries, such studies tell us little about programs without over-subscription. The effects of over-subscribed programs are not likely to be representative of the effects of similar choice schools across a district or state. Furthermore, while quasi-experimental matching studies allow for the inclusion of students in schools with and without admissions lotteries, they introduce the possibility of selection bias, leading to biased estimates of effects, as certain types of students may select into choice programs. While experimental studies are preferred, there are shortcomings to both types of design.

## Public school choice

Charlotte–Mecklenburg Schools implemented an open enrollment public school choice program in fall 2002 in which all high school students were allowed to choose and rank up to three schools in the district (Deming et al., 2014). As with other choice programs, seats to over-subscribed schools were assigned by random lottery. As this is the only open enrollment school choice program with research on attainment effects, it is included here as more evidence of the impact of public school choice (Table 1). The authors find small, statistically significant increases in the rates of 5-year high school graduation, college attendance, and degree completion for students who win the lottery to their first choice school, with greater gains for girls. Girls were 14 percentage points more likely to complete a 4-year degree if they won the public school choice lottery. There were no statistically significant estimated impacts for boys.

**Table 1.** Educational attainment of *Public School Choice Programs.*

| Author(s) | Year | Location | Evaluation Method | HS Graduation | College-Enrollment | College Persistence | Subgroups |
|---|---|---|---|---|---|---|---|
| **Public School Choice (Open-enrollment District)** | | | | | | | |
| **Deming et al.** | 2014 | Charlotte-Mecklenburg | RCT | Small, sig. increases in HS graduation (within 5 yrs), postsecondary attendance, and degree completion for students who win lottery to first choice school. | 4 ppt increase in enrolling in "very competitive" colleges (Baron's). | 60% increase in degree completion (from the mean). | Girls are 14 ppts more likely to complete a 4-yr degree. |
| **Charter School Choice** | | | | | | | |
| **Angrist et al.** | 2016 | Boston | RCT | No clear effect. Reduces 4 yr grad rate by 14.5 ppts but effect falls to a one percentage point reduction with 5 yr graduation. | Modest effects (insig) with shift from 2-yr (decreases by 11 ppts) to 4-yr institutions (increases by 13 ppts). Nearly half enroll in college in the fall after graduation, 60% within 18 months. | Increases the likelihood of persisting for three semesters at 4-yr schools by 12 ppts. | Larger effects for at-risk groups, including boys, special ed, and those who enter HS with low achievement. |
| **Booker et al.** | 2014 | Chicago & Florida | Matching | 7-15 ppts more likely to graduate within 5 yrs (increases FL by 13%, CHI by 9%). | 8-10 ppts more likely to enroll in any postsecondary institution within 6 yrs of starting high school (increases FL by 17%, CHI by 9%). | Increases 2-yr persistence for FL by 13 ppts (36%), CHI by 7 ppts (14%) (insig). | |
| **Davis & Heller** | 2015 | Chicago | RCT | | 7-9 yrs after lottery, winners are 10 ppts more likely to attend college and more likely to enroll immediately after graduating. | Winners are 9.5 ppts more likely to stay enrolled at least four semesters. (Small, insig. effect on degree completion of 0.7 ppts.) | |
| **Dobbie & Fryer** | 2016 | Texas | Matching | At the mean, charters are no more effective. Graduation increases by 1.2 ppts. (No Excuses increase by 2.5 ppts; regular charters by 0.4 ppts). | No Excuses schools increase 4-yr college enrollment; other charter schools decrease enrollment. | No Excuses schools increase persistence in 2-yr and 4-yr colleges. | No Excuses schools are particularly effective with minority students - more likely to graduate HS, enroll in 2-yr or 4-yr college. |
| **Dobbie & Fryer** | 2013 | New York City | RCT (Survey) | Regents exams for graduation - lottery winners pass one additional exam, score higher, and are more than twice as likely to take and pass more advanced exams. | 14.1 ppts more likely to enroll in college in the fall after graduation; 21.3 ppts more likely to enroll in 4-yr college, 7.2 ppts less likely to enroll in 2-yr college. | | |
| **Furgeson et al.** | 2012 | U.S. | Matching | 6 CMOs - on average, increase probability of graduating by 7 ppts (but insig.) | 4 CMOs - on average positive impact on enrollment of 13 ppts (but insig.) | | |

☐ Positive effects ☐ Mixed effects ☐ Null effects ☐ Negative effects

*Table Key:* ☐ Positive effects ☐ Mixed effects ☐ Null effects ☐ Negative effects
All high school graduation results are based on administrative records.

## Charter school choice

Charter schools are public schools of choice which means they are open to all children, are tuition-free, and most do not have entrance requirements. If they are over-subscribed, meaning they have more applications than seats available, they must hold lotteries for admission. Some schools are part of charter management organizations (CMOs) while others are "mom and pop"-type independent charter schools. The first charter school law was passed in Minnesota in 1991. Currently there are more than 6,700 charter schools in 42 states and the District of Columbia (NAPCS, 2016).

Of the seven studies assessing the attainment effects of charter schools in Table 1, three use experimental methods and four use quasi-experimental matching methods. The experimental studies examine charter schools in Boston (Angrist et al., 2016), Chicago (Davis & Heller, 2015), and New York City (Dobbie & Fryer, 2013). The matching studies look at charter programs in Texas (Dobbie & Fryer, 2016), Chicago and Florida (Booker et al., 2014; Sass et al., 2016),[2] and CMOs nationwide (Furgeson et al., 2012). Five of six studies include impacts on high school graduation, all six include effects on college enrollment, and four include impacts on college persistence. Two studies look at longer-term impacts on earnings and one presents information on risky behaviors and health outcomes.

### *High school graduation*

The effect of attending a charter school appears to be null to positive on the likelihood of high school graduation. Three studies found positive while two found null effects. In the matching study of Chicago and Florida, charter students were 7–15 percentage points more likely to graduate high school (within 5 years) than their counterparts (Booker et al., 2014; Sass et al., 2016), and the CMO study found a 7-percentage point average increase in the probability of graduating, though not statistically significant (Furgeson et al., 2012). Both the Boston experiment (Angrist et al., 2016) and the Texas matching study (Dobbie & Fryer, 2016) found no clear effect of charters on graduation rates.

### *College enrollment*

Estimated effects of charters on college enrollment also appear to be positive. Charter school students are more likely than traditional public school peers to enroll in college (Angrist et al., 2016; Booker et al., 2014; Davis & Heller, 2015; Dobbie & Fryer, 2013; Furgeson et al., 2012; Sass et al., 2016), enroll immediately after graduating (Angrist et al., 2016; Davis & Heller, 2015; Dobbie & Fryer, 2013), and attend a 4-year rather than 2-year institution

(Angrist et al., 2016; Dobbie & Fryer, 2016, 2013). The Boston study found larger estimated effects for special needs students, lower achieving students at baseline, and boys (Angrist et al., 2016). The Texas study saw greater impacts for "No Excuses"-type charter schools (Dobbie & Fryer, 2016).

### *College persistence*

The evidence on college persistence for charter students appears positive as well. The four studies that examine this all found that charter students were more likely to stay enrolled in college at least three semesters after graduation (Angrist et al., 2016; Booker et al., 2014; Davis & Heller, 2015; Dobbie & Fryer, 2013; Sass et al., 2016). One study looked at college matriculation but found no clear effect on degree completion (Davis & Heller, 2015).

### *Earnings and other future life outcomes*

Two of the seven studies also examined charter school outcomes on earnings and one explored the impacts on risky behaviors and health outcomes. Findings for all of these outcomes, presented in Table 2, are mixed. The Texas study found no measurable benefit to earnings or employment for students who attended a charter school (Dobbie & Fryer, 2016). In fact, "all

**Table 2.** Other long-term outcomes of *Public School Choice Programs.*

| Author(s) | Year | Location | Evaluation Method | Other Long-term Outcomes |
|---|---|---|---|---|
| **Charter School Choice** | | | | |
| **Dobbie & Fryer** | 2016 | Texas | Matching | Schools that decrease test scores or college enrollment also decrease earnings and employment; those that increase them demonstrate no measurable benefit. Positive correlation with HS graduation and labor market effects. All charter students appear to be in lower paying industries. |
| **Dobbie & Fryer** | 2013 | New York City | RCT (Survey) | Females 12.1 ppts less likely to be pregnant as teens, males 4.3 ppts less likely to be incarcerated. Similar drug, alcohol use and criminal behavior as lottery losers. Little impact on self-reported health - asthma, obesity, mental health. |
| **Sass et al.** | 2016 | Florida | Matching | Maximum annual earnings up to 12 years from initial enrollment in grade 8 (accounts for initial employment in temp jobs, early unemployment, or employment outside one's long-term profession) increases by $4,400; 11-yrs increases earnings by $2,200. Charter students have earnings advantage not explained by college attendance alone. Charter HS students have higher earnings even if they do not attend college. |

☐ Positive effects ☐ Mixed effects ☐ Null effects ☐ Negative effects

*Table Key*: ☐ Positive effects ☐ Mixed effects ☐ Null effects ☐ Negative effects
Sass et al. (2016) is an updated version of Booker et al. (2014); however, the Sass et al. paper focuses on earnings for the Florida sample so is included additionally.

charter students appear to be in lower paying industries" (p. 23) compared to earnings in other industries (at the 25th, 50th, and 75th percentiles). Contrary to this, the Florida study found that charter students had an earnings advantage, even among students who went to college; college attendance alone cannot explain the earning difference (Sass et al., 2016). Charter high school students had higher earnings than public school peers even if they did not attend college. It should be noted that these two matching studies used different models and samples which may account for the differing results.[3]

Turning to the behavior and health outcomes, the New York City study found that girls who attended a charter school were less likely to become pregnant in their teens and boys were less likely to go to jail (Dobbie & Fryer, 2013). There was little difference in drug and alcohol use or criminal behavior between lottery winners and losers, or much of an impact on self-reported health.

Overall, charter school attendance appears to have positive effects on high school graduation, college enrollment, enrollment in 4-year institutions, and college persistence for at least three consecutive semesters. Impacts on earnings, and behavior and health outcomes are mixed. While most studies evaluated programs in urban settings, there is some variation in findings between geographic regions.

## Private school choice

Private school choice programs have historically been implemented in urban areas, with more recent growth in statewide programs, in particular as part of ESAs. School vouchers are state-funded or privately funded scholarships that pay for students to attend private school rather than public school (NCSL, 2016). Most programs are means-tested, which means they are targeted to low-income students. These voucher programs tend to enroll students who otherwise would attend chronically low-performing or failing public schools. The first modern voucher program was created in 1990 in Milwaukee, Wisconsin (Witte & Wolf, 2017). Twenty-three states and the District of Columbia had school voucher programs as of 2015[4] (Egalite & Wolf, 2016; Frendeway et al., 2015).

Only five studies assess educational attainment effects of private school voucher programs – one in Florida, the Florida tax credit scholarship (Chingos & Kuehn, 2017); one in New York City, the New York School Choice Scholarships Foundation Program (Chingos & Peterson, 2015, 2012); two in Milwaukee, the Milwaukee Parental Choice Program (Cowen et al., 2013; Warren, 2011); and one in Washington, D.C., the District of Columbia Opportunity Scholarship Program (Wolf et al., 2013). The studies on New York City and Washington, D.C., use experimental methods, while the Florida and Milwaukee studies use matching and observational methods. All but the New York City and Florida studies include effects on high school graduation, and three studies address college enrollment or persistence. No studies were found that examined earnings or other life outcomes.

### High school graduation

With the limited evidence presented in Table 3, there appears to be a positive impact on high school graduation rates for voucher students. Voucher students in Milwaukee were about four percentage points more likely to graduate in 4 years than their traditional public school counterparts (Cowen et al., 2013), and the impact of using a voucher in Washington, D.C., increased the likelihood of graduating by 21 percentage points (Wolf et al., 2013). These studies found greater impacts for female students and an increased probability of graduating for students from "Schools in Need of Improvement" who used the scholarship in the D.C. study (Cowen et al., 2013; Wolf et al., 2013).

### College enrollment

Effects on college enrollment are mixed, with only three studies to reference. Both the Florida and Milwaukee studies found positive impacts on college enrollment for voucher students while the New York City study found no effect (Chingos & Kuehn, 2017; Chingos & Peterson, 2015, 2012; Cowen et al., 2013). The Florida matching study found a statistically significant increase of 6 percentage points in college enrollment due to the voucher program, with effects concentrated on community college enrollment and larger effects for students who participated in the program for more than four years (Chingos & Kuehn, 2017). Conversely, the matching study in Milwaukee found a greater likelihood for voucher students of attending a 4-year institution rather than a 2-year or technical college (Cowen et al., 2013).

### College persistence

The voucher evidence on college persistence is also mixed using the same three studies for Florida, Milwaukee, and New York City. Again, the Florida and Milwaukee studies saw positive impacts on college persistence for voucher students while the New York City study found no effect (Chingos & Kuehn, 2017; Chingos & Peterson, 2015, 2012; Cowen et al., 2013). The Florida study found a 0.5 percentage point increase in associate degree attainment for those voucher students enrolled in the program prior to high school, but no impact on bachelor's degree attainment (Chingos & Kuehn, 2017). The Milwaukee study found voucher students had a greater

**Table 3.** Educational attainment of *Private School Choice Programs*.

| Author(s) | Year | Location | Evaluation Method | HS Graduation | College-Enrollment | College Persistence | Subgroups |
|---|---|---|---|---|---|---|---|
| **Chingos & Kuehn** | 2017 | Florida | Matching | | Increases college enrollment rates by 6 ppts (15%) within 2 yrs of expected HS graduation. Larger effect if in program longer- up to 18 pppts (43%) for those in program 4+ years. Almost all of the effect is for 2-yr colleges. | Small increase of 0.5 ppts (8%) in associate degree attainment for those in program before HS. No impact on bachelor's degree attainment. | Greater benefit for children born outside U.S.; Catholic and non-Christian religious schools have higher impact on college enrollment than non-Catholic Christian schools and nonreligious private schools. |
| **Chingos & Peterson** | 2015 | New York City | RCT | | No significant effects on enrollment within 5 yrs of expected HS graduation (1.4 ppts, not sig). | No significant effects. | Large, marginally sig. impacts for minority students (African American, Hispanic); large, sig. impacts for children of U.S.-born women. |
| **Cowen et al.** | 2013 | Milwaukee | Matching | Voucher student graduation rate higher (74-76%) than TPS (69-72%) and more likely to graduate in 4 yrs, TPS in 5 yrs. | Less likely to attend 2-yr or technical college. | 5 ppts more likely to attend or persist in 4-yr institution 4-5 years later. | African Americans considerably less likely to enroll or persist in college than non-African-Americans; female students more likely. |
| **Warren** | 2011 | Milwaukee | Observational | Higher graduation rate in 6-7 years; 12 ppts higher than state-wide graduation rate (82% compared to 70%, 2008-09). | | | Low-income school choice students 18% more likely to graduate from HS than students from across economic spectrum in TPS. |
| **Wolf et al.** | 2013 | Washington DC | RCT | Positive impact on HS graduation rates; voucher use raised probability of graduating by 21 ppts. | | | Students from "Schools in Need of Improvement" increased probability of graduating by 13 ppts if offered voucher, 20 points if used; students with higher levels of performance, increased probability by 14 ppts; for females, increased probability by 20 ppts. |

☐ Positive effects ☐ Mixed effects ☐ Null effects ☐ Negative effects

*Table Key:* ☐ Positive effects ☐ Mixed effects ☐ Null effects ☐ Negative effects

High school graduation results for Cowen et al. (2013) are based on administrative records and parent self-reports; Warren (2011) is based on administrative records; Wolf et al. (2013) are based on parent self-reports.

likelihood (5 percentage points) of persisting in a 4-year institution 4–5 years later (Cowen et al., 2013).

Overall, findings for private school choice attainment appear similar to those of charter schools. However, effects on high school graduation, college enrollment, and college persistence are inconclusive at this stage, as there is not enough research to determine the impacts of vouchers. In sum, from the 13 studies presented it appears that school choice programs are having a positive effect on educational attainment overall. Evidence suggests similar results for both charter and private school choice programs, however, there are more studies examining attainment effects for charter schools than for school voucher programs. In general, more research is needed in this area overall.

## Conclusion

School choice programs have been around for more than 25 years. Most research has focused on achievement effects. There is a dearth of literature on the educational attainment effects of school choice, particularly related to private school choice. While a couple of recent studies have begun to look at the long-term impacts of charter schools, very little attention has been paid to voucher programs. Quite simply, more research is needed. There are a number of mature choice programs nationwide that have the long-term data needed to perform such evaluations. If we believe that students are learning skills, work habits, or values that do not translate into test scores but that might be more important for long-term success, we need to begin assessing whether that is the case (Greene, 2016). Thus far, the limited evidence suggests that school choice has positive effects on attainment outcomes. Researchers need to examine longer-term attainment effects of choice which include impacts on high school graduation, college enrollment, and college persistence, but also college degree attainment and earnings. There is too little research at present to draw firm conclusions on the effects of school choice on educational attainment.

## Notes

1. The research on educational attainment and long-term outcomes of education interventions and programs is limited. There is an older, mostly observational literature which generally found larger effects on attainment than on achievement. Studies examining the benefits from Catholic schooling found small benefits in achievement for students in general with more substantial impacts for minority and disadvantaged students (Chingos & Peterson, 2012; Jencks, 1985), and larger positive effects on the probability of high school completion and college enrollment, especially for urban minority students (Altonji, Elder, & Taber, 2005; Chingos & Peterson, 2012; Evans & Schwab, 1995; Neal, 1997). Studies examining longer-term impacts have evaluated the Perry Preschool and Abecedarian programs (Almond & Curry, 2010; Chingos & Peterson, 2012; Heckman & Krueger, 2002), Job Corps

(Burghardt et al., 2001; Chingos & Peterson, 2012), and a class size reduction intervention in Tennessee for grades K-3 (Chingos & Peterson, 2012; Dynarski, Hyman, & Schanzenbach, 2011).

2. Sass et al. (2016) is an updated version of Booker et al. (2014); however, the Sass et al. article focuses on earnings for the Florida sample so is also included.
3. Sass et al. (2016) restrict the sample to students who attended a charter middle school in eighth grade and then compare traditional public high school attendees with charter high school attendees. In contrast, Dobbie and Fryer (2016) match on third grade school/race/gender and include all students, whether or not they ever attend a charter school.
4. While there are voucher programs in Maine and Vermont, they were established for students in towns that lacked public schools for their grade level, not to provide additional schooling options and thus are not included (Egalite & Wolf, 2016).

## References


Almond, D., Jr., & Currie, J. (2010). Human capital development before age five. *SSRN Working Paper No. 15827*. Retrieved from http://papers.ssrn.com/sol3/papers.cfm?abstract_id=1574646

Altonji, J. G., Elder, T. E., & Taber, C. R. (2005). Selection on observed and unobserved variables: Assessing the effectiveness of catholic schools. *Journal of Political Economy, 113* (1), 151–184.

Angrist, J. D., Cohodes, S. R., Dynarski, S. M., Pathak, P. A., & Walters, C. R. (2016). Stand and deliver: Effects of Boston's charter high schools on college preparation, entry, and choice. *Journal of Labor Economics, 34*(2), 275–318.

Becker, G. S. (1993). *Human capital: A theoretical and empirical analysis, with special reference to education* (3rd ed.). Chicago, IL: University of Chicago Press.

Belfield, C. R., & Levin, H. M. (Eds.). (2007). *The price we pay: Economic and social consequences of inadequate education*. Washington, D.C.: Brookings Institution Press.

Betts, J., & Tang, Y. (2014). A meta-analysis of the literature on the effect of charter schools on student achievement. *Center on Reinventing Public Education, Working paper*.

Booker, K., Gill, B., Sass, T., & Zimmer, R. (2014). Charter high schools' effects on long-term attainment and earnings, *Mathematica policy research, Working paper*.

Burghardt, J., Schochet, P. Z., McConnell, S., Johnson, T., Gritz, R. M., Glazerman, S., … Jackson, R. (2001). *Does job corps work? Summary of the national job corps study*. Princeton, NJ: Mathematic Policy Research.

Chingos, M. M., & Kuehn, D. (2017). *The effects of statewide private school choice on college enrollment and graduation: Evidence from the Florida tax credit scholarship program*. Washington, DC, USA and Cambridge, MA, USA: Urban Institute.

Chingos, M. M., & Peterson, P. E. (2012). *The effects of school vouchers on college enrollment: Experimental evidence from New York City*. Washington, DC: Brown center on education policy at Brookings and Harvard Kennedy school.

Chingos, M. M., & Peterson, P. E. (2015). Experimentally estimated impacts of school vouchers on college enrollment and degree attainment. *Journal of Public Economics, 122*, 1–12.

Cowen, J. M., Fleming, D. J., Witte, J. F., Wolf, P. J., & Kisida, B. (2013). School vouchers and student attainment: Evidence from a state-mandated study of Milwaukee's parental choice program. *The Policy Studies Journal, 41*(1), 147–168.

Davis, M., & Heller, H. (2015). "No Excuses" charter schools and college enrollment: New evidence from a high school network in Chicago. Retrieved from SSRN 2606059.

Day, J. C., & Newburger, E. C. (2002). The big payoff: Educational attainment and synthetic estimates of work-life earnings. Special studies. Current population reports. *U.S. Census Bureau.*

Deming, D. J. (2011). Better schools, less crime? *The Quarterly Journal of Economics, 126,* 2063–2115.

Deming, D. J., Hastings, J. S., Kane, T. J., & Staiger, D. O. (2014). School choice, school quality and postsecondary attainment. *American Economics Review, 104*(3), 991–1013.

Dobbie, W. S., & Fryer, R. G. (2013). The medium-term impacts of high-achieving charter schools on non-test score outcomes, *NBER Working Paper Series 19581.*

Dobbie, W. S., & Fryer, R. G. (2016). Charter schools and labor market outcomes, *NBER Working Paper Series 22502.*

Dynarski, S., Hyman, J., & Schanzenbach, D. W. (2011). Experimental evidence on the effect of childhood investment on postsecondary attainment and degree completion. *NBER Working Paper No. 17533.*

Egalite, A. J., & Wolf, P. J. (2016). A review of the empirical research on private school choice. *Peabody Journal of Education, 91*(4), 441–454.

Evans, W. N., & Schwab, R. M. (1995). Finishing high school and starting college: Do catholic schools make a difference? *Quarterly Journal of Economics, 110*(4), 941–974.

Frendeway, M., Sawatka, K., Marcavage, W., Carney, K., Martinez, K., & Dauphin, P. (2015). *School choice yearbook 2014–15: Breaking down barriers to school choice.* Washington, DC: Alliance for School Choice.

Furgeson, J., Gill, B., Haimson, J., Killewald, A., McCullough, M., Nichols-Barrer, I., ... Verbitsky-Savitz, N. (2012). *Charter-school management organizations: Diverse strategies and diverse student impacts, the national study of charter management organization (CMO) effectiveness.* Princeton, NJ, USA: Mathematica Policy Research, January 2012 Updated Edition.

Gleason, P. M. (2017). What's the secret ingredient? Searching for policies and practices that make charter schools successful. *Journal of School Choice, 11,* 4.

Greene, J. P. (2016). The weak predictive power of test scores, *Education Next,* 05/ 02/2016.

Griliches, Z., & Mason, W. M. (1972). Education, income, and ability. *Journal of Political Economy, 80*(3), S74–S103.

Heckman, J. J., & Krueger, A. B. (2002). *Inequality in America: What role for human capital policies?* In B. M. Friedman (Eds.). Cambridge, MA: MIT Press.

Heckman, J. J., Lochner, L. J., & Todd, P. E. (2008). Earnings functions and rates of return. *Handbook of the Economics of Education, 1,* 307–458.

Jencks, C. (1985). How much do high school students learn? *Sociology of Education, 58* (April), 128–135.

Levin, H., Belfield, C., Muennig, P., & Rouse, C. (2006). *The costs and benefits of an excellent education for all of America's children.* New York: Center for benefit-cost studies of education at teachers college, Teachers College, Columbia University October 2006.

National Alliance for Public Charter Schools (NAPCS). (2016). About charter schools. Retrieved from: http://www.publiccharters.org/get-the-facts/public-charter-schools/

National Conference of State Legislatures (NCSL). (2016). School vouchers. Retrieved from: http://www.ncsl.org/research/education/school-choice-vouchers.aspx

Neal, D. (1997). The effect of Catholic secondary schooling on educational achievement. *Journal of Labor Economics, 15*(1), 98–123.

Sass, T. R., Zimmer, R. W., Gill, B. P., & Booker, T. K. (2016). Charter high schools' effects on long-term attainment and earnings. *Journal of Policy Analysis and Management, 35*(3), 683–706.

Warren, J. R. (2011). *Graduation rates for choice and public school students in Milwaukee, 2003–2009.* Milwaukee, WI, USA: School choice Wisconsin, January 2011.

Witte, J. F., & Wolf, P. J. (2017). The Wisconsin role in the school choice movement. *EDRE Working Paper No. 2017-12. Social Science Research Network.* Retrieved from https://papers.ssrn.com/sol3/papers.cfm?abstract_id=2978094.

Wolf, P. J., Kisida, B., Gutmann, B., Puma, M., Eissa, N., & Rizzo, L. (2013). School vouchers and student outcomes: Experimental evidence from Washington, DC. *Journal of Policy Analysis and Management, 32*(2), 246–270.

# Index